British socialists and the politics of popular culture

For Pam and Ted, my parents

CHRIS WATERS

British Socialists
and the Politics of Popular Culture,
1884–1914

Stanford University Press
Stanford, California   1990

Stanford University Press
Stanford, California
© 1990 Chris Waters
Originating publisher: Manchester University Press
  Manchester
First published in the U.S.A. by
  Stanford University Press, 1990
Printed in Great Britain
ISBN 0–8047–1758–3
LC 89–62182

CONTENTS

ILLUSTRATIONS

The illustrations are to be found between Chapters 3 and 4, pp. 96–97

Grateful acknowledgement is made to the Documentary Photography Archive, Manchester, to publish illustrations 3, 4, 6, 7, 15, 16, 17, 18 and 21. Grateful acknowledgement is also made to the London History Workshop Centre to publish illustrations 10, 11 and 20.

PREFACE

In May 1981, when a Labour administration took control of County Hall in London, the Arts and Recreation Committee of the Greater London Council (GLC) was determined to re-draw the map of cultural politics in the metropolis. Five years later, in its pamphlet *Campaign for a Popular Culture* the committee concluded that despite many set-backs the achievements of the GLC had been numerous and had been accompanied by a growing interest in popular culture on the left. During its tenure at County Hall, the Labour Party had helped to spark that interest by questioning the efficacy of a left cultural policy which merely emphasised bringing 'the best that had been thought and said' to the 'masses'. Instead of pursuing a policy of financial support for the great cultural institutions of the nation – a policy that had dominated Labour Party thinking throughout the twentieth century – the GLC embarked upon a bold new programme, sponsoring street festivals, supporting the community art movement and encouraging members of subordinate groups in British society to develop their own forms of cultural expression.

Living in London while these experiments were in progress, I set out to discover what the left had to say about popular culture almost a century ago. While recent discussions of the subject have often been fuelled by the advent of new communication technologies, new forms of recreational activity in the 1880s also gave rise to debates about the significance of changes occurring in the cultural arena. Characterised by the 'football mania' and the growth of music-hall entertainment and Bank Holiday excursions, late Victorian popular culture generated widespread fears about the links being forged between 'business and pastime'. Not only did socialists share these fears but they also attempted to establish alternatives to the recreations they disliked. In this they were not unlike many of the activists on the GLC in the 1980s. But their aspirations and policies differed radically from those encountered in the recent past and thus need to be dissected. In this study I want to relate socialist cultural thought and practice to the wider political and cultural structures of late Victorian society. In so doing, I hope to shed some light both on the history of popular culture and cultural criticism in Britain and on the dilemmas faced by a socialist movement which tried – often in vain – to compete with an emerging leisure industry for the allegiance of the working class.

I have become indebted to many individuals during the course of writing this study. First, I would like to thank John Bohstedt, Molly Nolan, Andy Rosen, Ann Swidler and Bill Weber, teachers who introduced me to ways of thinking that have influenced my work over the course of the last decade. I would also like to express my gratitude to Peter Bailey. Eager to identify with my own cultural anomie as an Englishman transplanted to North America, Peter has also shared his wit and wisdom with me. In the process my own thinking has been clarified.

As I began to conceive of writing a complete study of the late Victorian socialist movement and the politics of popular culture, I benefited enormously from the advice of John Clive. By encouraging me in my work, he gave me the confidence to venture forth and share my interests with others. Moreover, when

PREFACE

the time came to sit down and put all my ideas together, his editorial supervision made the task of writing a less formidable one.

A number of friends and colleagues have also taken time from their own busy schedules to suggest new avenues of research, or to offer much-appreciated comments on early drafts of my work. For their help I would like to thank Henry Abelove, Florence Boos, John Brewer, Anna Davin, Cyril Ehrlich, Steve Epstein, Helen Jones, Neville Kirk, Seth Koven, Jan Lambertz, Jill Liddington, John Lowerson, Peter Mandler, Susan Pennybacker, Mike Pickering, Doug Reid, Aron Rodrigue, Raph Samuel, Debra Satz (who lived with me while I wrote this study on two separate occasions), Miles Taylor, Wray Vamplew and Eileen Yeo. Finally, Hugh Cunningham, Gail Malmgreen, Duncan Tanner and Stephen Yeo all read an earlier version of this manuscript in its entirety. I greatly appreciate their suggestions, many of which have forced me either to modify or to defend with greater vigour a number of my arguments.

I also want to acknowledge the financial support I have received during the past few years, support which has made the monetary worries of a novice historian less burdensome than they otherwise might have been. Harvard University awarded me a Frank Knox Memorial Fellowship, which allowed me to undertake much of the research for this study. In addition, the Center for European Studies at Harvard not only provided me with a congenial and intellectually stimulating environment in which to work but also awarded me a summer research grant and a Krupp Foundation Fellowship. Under the auspices of an Andrew W. Mellon Postdoctoral Fellowship in the Humanities at Stanford University I have, more recently, been able to complete the revisions of this study. At Stanford I enjoyed the encouragement of Peter Stansky – whose many kindnesses are too numerous to mention – and the good advice and assistance of Norris Pope at Stanford University Press. Moreover, the task of revision was made a pleasant one by the support of my editor at Manchester University Press, John Banks.

Finally, I am indebted beyond words to Mike Whewell. While sharing many of my hopes and frustrations as I sought to make sense of the connections between British socialists and working-class leisure patterns in the late nineteenth century, Mike also convinced me of the need to develop new forms of cultural politics in the less-optimistic climate of Margaret Thatcher's Britain. In the process I was made aware both of the limitations of late Victorian cultural criticism and of my own shortcomings as an 'academic' historian merely writing about politics.

Chris Waters
Williamstown, Massachusetts

INTRODUCTION

The three decades prior to World War I are of crucial importance to the social historian of leisure in Britain. In these years the commercial provision of entertainment acquired a significance it has maintained to this day. This is not to say that changes in the social and economic organisation of leisure led to the appearance of 'mass culture' – for that the country would have to wait until the 1950s. None the less, rising real wages for many skilled workers, accompanied by a decline in working hours and a new entrepreneurial spirit in an emerging leisure industry, worked together to establish the preconditions for the development of that culture. As early as the 1890s, for example, some fourteen million visits were paid each year to thirty-five of London's music halls, while, by the end of that decade, 50,000 spectators attended the annual Football Association cup finals.[1]

The advent of this new world of commercial recreation was accompanied by significant changes in the debates that took place about the relationship between popular culture and social reform. While the question of 'improving' working-class uses of leisure had been central to discussions of social well-being throughout the nineteenth century, it was only towards the end of the century that such discussions acquired a new urgency – and a greater complexity. This is a study of those discussions, and of their relationship to the larger political, economic and cultural structures of British society. In particular, it is a study of the part played by socialists in debates about popular culture. Not that socialists always had the most interesting things to say about the subject; but what they did say affords us an opportunity to examine the initial attempts made on the left to formulate a theory of popular culture and social change in Britain.

At one time or another individuals in various socialist organisations expressed their concern about the changes occurring in late Victorian popular culture. Much has been written about these organisations, although the starting point for this study was my belief that despite the formal differences between them, the Social Democratic Federation (SDF), the Socialist League (SL), the Independent Labour Party (ILP), the Fabian Society and Robert Blatchford's 'Clarionettes' shared many assumptions which ultimately informed both their critique of popular culture and their suggestions for the creation of alternative cultural forms. On the one hand, Fabians stressed the importance of the

1

municipal provision of leisure, believing that popular culture could be provided by the community as easily as could gas and water. On the other hand, 'ethical' socialists believed that the reform of popular culture was of crucial importance in so far as it might allow workers to see what leisure could be like in a new, socialist society, thereby fuelling their desire to bring that society about. Beneath the activities of both groups, however, was the belief that popular culture was important – too important, in fact, to be left to the purveyors of commercial entertainment. This work will attempt to unravel the beliefs which fuelled socialist activity in the cultural arena and to examine their significance in the political battles socialists fought.

Studies of socialist cultural thought have rarely been anchored in an analysis of the late Victorian transformation of working-class leisure patterns. Moreover, in some recent histories of cultural policy in Britain there has been a tendency to attack the left for its failure to advance any new ideas that could have informed the creation of a viable, alternative popular culture. As Geoff Mulgan and Ken Worpole have suggested, the history of Labour Party policy in cultural matters is 'littered with missed opportunities'.[2] While this study will suggest that such has indeed been the case, we need to understand why those opportunities were missed. And that requires an assessment of socialist thought within the context both of the development of a commercial leisure industry and of the debates which surrounded that development.

While some historians have been eager to dismiss the cultural initiatives of British socialists, they have, by contrast, admired the work of the Social Democratic Party (SPD) in pre-World War I Germany. The SPD developed a vast network of recreational clubs and a rich associational life that contributed to the flowering of an alternative culture, which, even at the time, was the envy of British socialists.[3] In Germany, over 100,000 workers were active in the socialist choral movement, while in Britain Robert and Montague Blatchford were lucky if they could draw 2,000–3,000 individuals to meetings of their own socialist Clarion Vocal Union. As Martin Pugh has noted, the entire paid membership of the Independent Labour Party in 1900 numbered a mere 6,000 – roughly the same as the Bolton branch of the Primrose League, the Conservative organisation that dealt with the social and recreational side of working-class life.[4]

Reasons for the failure of British socialists to develop an extensive alternative culture are as numerous as they are complex. But in one of the most convincing arguments to be made about the dilemmas faced by late

Victorian socialists, Ross McKibbin has suggested that, unlike its German counterpart, the left in Britain was faced by a working class already embedded in a complex system of associational ties and cultural rituals which were difficult to penetrate. Moreover, the commercialisation of leisure in Britain gave workers 'an opportunity to choose between alternative activities not available to any other European workforce', activities with which the socialist movement was forced to compete.[5] In addition, not only did socialists encounter a working class increasingly dependent on commercial forms of recreation but they were plagued by problems in their own attempt to make sense of these new aspects of working-class culture.

When socialists discussed the commercialisation of leisure, they often deployed the terminology which had accompanied the early and mid-Victorian call for 'rational recreation'. While the working class had enjoyed its own leisure activities in the 1830s and 1840s – street football, popular blood sports, penny theatres and the like – the middle class hoped to eradicate or improve these forms of amusement by offering 'rational' alternatives. From temperance cafés to mechanics' institutes, from public lectures to the factory outings sponsored by industrialists, all were examples of rational recreation, of attempts to inculcate a series of values in the working class that were important to the middle class in its own uses of leisure. The belief that 'rational recreation' could bring about desirable social change was widespread in Victorian society; indeed, it was central to the discourse through which individuals of various political persuasions discussed popular culture. As we shall see, socialists were not immune from the rhetoric of rational recreation in their own attempts to understand popular culture in the 1880s and 1890s.

Some of the schemes which grew out of the demand for 'rational recreation' were successful. Most were not, and there existed no coherent ideology to unite these various piecemeal attempts at recreational reform. Moreover, the fears that had prompted their development in the first place diminished in the 1860s and 1870s. Chartism had become a fading memory, and the Reform Act of 1867 proved just how respectable the respectable artisan could be. More important, a whole new world of commercial recreation developed, which, according to Hugh Cunningham, imposed its own controls on leisure, lessening its potential to be used in morally or politically subversive ways. If leisure could not be reformed by the custodians of rational recreation, it could be contained in a commercial sphere in which it could do no harm.[6]

The story, however, does not end in the 1880s with a complacent middle class congratulating itself on the appearance of an equally complacent working class enjoying its pleasures in the pit of a music hall. Leisure was still a contested arena, while the growth of commercial recreation gave rise to new fears – and led to the rejuvenation of many old ones as well. Although socialists were alarmed by these changes, they often called simply for a hefty dose of 'rational recreation' as a cure-all for the cultural ills of society. I want to argue in this study that it was because so many socialists shared the widely held nineteenth-century belief that 'culture' could exert a desirable 'civilising' influence that they could not fully understand the realities of actually existing working-class culture. This, in turn, I would suggest, was in part responsible for the inability of the British socialist movement to obtain the same levels of mass support garnered by the SPD in Germany. While the failure of British socialism has been attributed to a variety of causes, it might well be that dominant cultural discourses in Victorian Britain were strong enough either to deflect or to co-opt many socialist aspirations. In other words, I would like to suggest that there are important cultural, as well as political, reasons that account for the difficulties faced by British socialists in their attempt to transform late Victorian society.

The ideas about the reform of popular culture put forward by Robert Blatchford encapsulate many of the themes that will be central to this study. No major theorist, Blatchford was still one of the most popular socialists of the 1890s. He wrote extensively about leisure in the newspaper he established in 1891, the *Clarion*, and in his best-selling book, *Merrie England*, he offered a vision of a socialist society in which 'we shall have plenty of leisure'. But Blatchford's image of a society in which leisure would be abundant was as threatening as it was enticing. Of this leisure which workers would acquire, he asked, 'What are we to do with it?'[7] This was a question that was debated endlessly by socialists, uneasy about the fact that even in their own society a decrease in working hours did not appear to be accompanied by a desire to devote leisure to edifying pursuits. Moreover, it is a question that offers a natural introduction to the hopes and fears nurtured by British socialists when they wrote about the relationship between class, leisure and politics.

One answer to the problem Blatchford posed had already been put forward by the French socialist Paul Lafargue. Following the collapse of the Paris Commune, Lafargue settled in London, where he wrote one of his most widely read works, *La Droit à la Paresse: réfutation du Droit au Travail de 1848*. Originally written for the French radical journal,

L'Egalité, the work was translated by James Blackwell as 'The Right to Leisure', appearing in *Justice*, the organ of the SDF, in 1886. In 1893 the Labour Literature Society in Glasgow printed Blackwell's translation as a pamphlet, while Keir Hardie's *Labour Leader* serialised a condensed version of the work in its April and May issues of that year.[8]

The argument put forward by Lafargue was a simple one. While the French proletariat had, in 1848, demanded the right to work, Lafargue believed that they should have demanded the right *not* to work. Indeed, the more they worked, he claimed, the more goods they produced for the consumption of the capitalist. A crisis of over-production had left workers exhausted in mind and body and had necessitated the development of colonies for the disposal of surplus products. Through the advent of a shorter working day, Lafargue argued, levels of production would fall, thereby eliminating dependence on colonial trade. Moreover, a shorter working day would allow workers the time in which to consume a greater share of the products of their own labour. Capitalism, wrote Lafargue, needs 'to discover consumers, to excite their appetites and create in them fictitious needs'.[9]

Had Blatchford been familiar with Lafargue's apparent call for an increase in working-class consumption, he would have been appalled: he had hoped that an abundance of leisure would be used by workers for 'the acquirement of knowledge'. Moreover, Blatchford's fear of an emerging culture of consumption was widely shared on the left in Britain. Herbert Burrows, the prominent secularist and member of the executive of the SDF, for example, claimed that Lafargue's call for the development of 'sublime, gluttonish stomachs' would prevent the emergence of the 'unselfishness, enthusiasm, self-sacrifice and zeal' which was necessary in the struggle for socialism.[10]

James Blackwell responded to these concerns, arguing that Lafargue had written a satire and that Burrows had missed its point.[11] Lafargue had indeed intended his work to be taken with a grain of salt, for he too put forward ideas that many British socialists would have agreed with, had they understood his argument. Leisure, claimed Lafargue, was responsible for 'all that makes life beautiful and worth living' and it was also the 'mother of the arts and noble virtues'.[12] In short, Lafargue believed that leisure was a double-edged sword that offered both emancipation and new forms of slavery. On the one hand, more leisure meant more time for learning and political activity – not to mention freedom from the drudgery of work. But what if that time were to be squandered in frivolous amusement, or devoted to an emulation of the foibles of the rich? It was this particular fear that so worried socialists in Britain. For them, Lafargue's scenario of a world of leisure devoted to hedonistic consumption was frightening. Thus, when Blackwell, in defending Lafargue, also called for the right to leisure, he insisted that it should be used correctly: 'We consider work, however necessary it may be, an evil to be avoided if possible, and we consider pleasure – *true rational pleasure that is* – the end and aim of existence.'[13]

In their response to Lafargue, some socialists, like Blackwell, borrowed from earlier discourses of 'rational recreation' and demanded that an increase in leisure be used for the pursuit of 'true rational pleasure'. Others suggested that workers were still denied adequate leisure and should thus engage in Lafargue's demand for the 'right to be lazy'. H. Halliday Sparling, William Morris's son-in-law and ally in the work of the Socialist League, argued that in his own society there was an unequal division of leisure between the rich and the poor, 'the one satiated by idleness from which all pleasure has been taken . . .; the other degraded and brutalised by never-ending toil, unenlightened by leisure, unrefreshed by rest'. Likewise, Ethel Carnie discussed the extent to which the domestic drudgery that was the lot of working women prevented them, too, from being able to savour the delights of leisure. For both writers the answer, as Sparling wrote, was to revolt against the class which had usurped the leisure that belonged to the entire community.[14]

Despite the dismal picture of the life of the British worker painted by Sparling and Carnie, the late nineteenth century witnessed a gradual shortening of working hours and a rise in real wages – although the benefits brought about by these changes were often bestowed only on male workers in regular and skilled employment. While the Ten Hours Act of 1847 was heralded as a landmark in the reduction of working hours, its immediate effects were confined to the textile industry; it was only in the 1870s that trade unions secured substantial reductions in working hours for a large number of male workers. By 1875 a working week of fifty-four to fifty-seven hours was common and the ten-hour day had in many trades given way to the nine-hour day. The general economic boom that preceded the depression of 1873 was responsible for this rapid decrease in working hours, although widespread granting of the Saturday half-holiday was a result of changes that came later in the decade. In the 1880s, the persistence of economic depression and the lack of unionisation amongst the unskilled combined to put a brake on the progress of the previous decade. By the 1890s and early 1900s, however, the unskilled began to gain some of the advantages the skilled had acquired earlier.[15]

The demand for shorter working hours was accompanied by the demand for higher wages. In fact, the period between 1870 and 1905 witnessed the growth of working-class preference for income over leisure, substantiating Edward Thompson's claim that while the first generation of factory workers was taught the importance of time, and the second formed 'short-time' committees, the third struck for overtime.[16] In families where income was sufficient to pay for the necessities of daily existence, any surplus was often devoted to entertainment. One study has shown that 80 per cent of those workers regularly employed in semi-skilled or skilled trades purchased books and newspapers. Moreover, as a group they spent an average of 3·5 per cent of their annual income on amusement of one kind or another and their preference seemed to be for leisure activities outside of the home.[17]

By comparison with the situation of skilled, male workers, that of working-class women and virtually all unskilled workers was bleak. H. W. Hobart discussed the limitations still faced by such individuals in their pursuit of leisure in the 1890s. Hobart was active in the Salford branch of the SDF, standing as a socialist for Salford South in 1895. He wrote extensively about leisure for *Justice*, where he claimed that of the 168 hours in a week, the average worker spent fifty-six in bed, sixty in work and most of the rest travelling to and from work and consuming meals. Sundays were usually devoted to attending church, walking or reading the papers. What few hours remained, according to Hobart, were spent by the 'average British workman' in a pub or a club, or perhaps in a music hall. Hobart believed that the general reduction of working hours was gradually providing some workers with greater opportunities for leisure. But he then asked, much as Blatchford had, 'what do [the workers] do in the direction of rationally enjoying life? Or what do they do towards improving and amending society?' Hobart concluded, albeit with some hesitation, 'In the great majority of cases the British workman makes very bad use of his leisure; but because we know there are a few who use it well, we are anxious to see more leisure for the workers.'[18]

Hobart's article is important in so far as it prevents us from exaggerating the claims made about the reduction of working hours in late Victorian society. While there was little dramatic change in the length of the working week, however, the changes that did occur were accompanied by intense debates about the relationship between work, leisure and social well-being: a small increase in the amount of leisure available to some workers was accompanied by a disproportionate amount of writing about how that leisure should be used. Moreover, in arguing for a reduction of working hours, socialists were responsible for raising new questions pertaining to the uses of leisure. As one observer wrote, 'One thing . . . the Labour Movement has brought into prominence is the Leisure Problem.'[19]

While leisure rarely seemed a problem for workers – they merely demanded more of it – it was indeed a problem for socialists. In addition, and as the later chapters of this study will suggest, it became an even greater problem in the decade prior to World War I. But in the 1890s, socialists, especially those who campaigned for the eight-hour day, still hoped that an increase in the amount of leisure available to workers would be used constructively in one or more of three ways: it would be dedicated to education and self-improvement; it would be devoted to acquiring knowledge of the cultural heritage of the nation; and, finally, it would be used constructively in the struggle for socialism.

The desire expressed by socialists for leisure to be dedicated to rational and educational pursuits should be obvious by now. It was central to the thinking of Robert Blatchford, as it was to many members of John Trevor's Labour Church.[20] Other socialists were less didactic in their demand for a shorter working day, and on behalf of the Fabian Society Sidney Webb and Harold Cox argued that 'the real force which gives vitality to the Eight Hours' Movement is the spontaneous longing for a brighter, fuller life'. But even for Webb, that 'brighter and fuller' life would be one in which workers would finally acquire the 'benefits of civilisation'.[21] The belief that more leisure meant more time for 'cultured' pursuits was widespread and was perhaps most succinctly put by Philip Snowden, who wrote that shorter hours and better wages would finally allow workers to 'share in the intellectual heritage of the race'.[22] We shall be returning to this theme at several points in the study, for the emphasis placed on the need for workers to demand access to the cultural heritage of the nation often sat uncomfortably with more radical demands for the uses of leisure.

Suggestions that leisure should be devoted to the struggle for socialism were put forward by Tom Mann and H. M. Hyndman. Both men believed that additional free time was required so that workers could study the system that oppressed them and then use their knowledge in the struggle to overthrow that system.[23] The most articulate statement of this position came from James Leatham, the Aberdeen socialist and journalist. While Leatham also complained that many workers seemed to be devoting their leisure to 'dangling about the gallery of a theatre or the bar of a public house', he believed there were some who read and thought. A shorter working day would allow these workers to develop 'the mental alertness necessary to an understanding of their position, and the courage, hope, and initiative to set about improving it'.[24]

So far we have outlined some of the general arguments socialists made about the uses of leisure in late Victorian society. But in this preliminary investigation we have been using a series of terms that need to be defined with greater precision. What did socialists mean when they spoke of 'leisure', 'play', 'amusement' and 'recreation'? And how was their use of these terms shaped by contemporary definitions of them? Just as it has been necessary to introduce some of the various positions that emerged in late Victorian discussions of leisure, it is also necessary to introduce the terminology of the debate itself.

The term 'popular culture' was seldom used before the 1870s. Raymond Williams has suggested that it has traditionally referred either to cultural products judged to be inferior by the standards of 'high culture', or to works consciously created in order to become popular with the masses.[25] More recently, 'popular culture' has also referred to the culture made by subordinate groups in society. In the late nineteenth century, however, the term, when used at all, often had a different meaning. Especially for members of the middle class, 'popular culture' referred to components of their own culture made available for working-class consumption. Thus, in 1876, John Morley suggested that the working class needed to learn how to amuse and refresh itself through an appreciation of popularised forms of culture most cherished by Morley and his own class. In a similar vein, T. H. S. Escott, in an essay, 'Popular Culture in the Crucible', claimed that people's palaces, university settlements and working men's clubs were all important because they served to popularise those cultural values that were a central part of middle-class life.[26]

The most significant challenge to this use of the term came from Thomas Wright, the 'journeyman engineer'. In his essay, 'On a Possible Popular Culture', Wright differentiated between the cultural require-ments of middle-class and working-class life. Condemning social critics who viewed working-class neighbourhoods as devoid of culture, Wright believed that workers enjoyed a rich cultural existence of their own, although he feared that new forms of light reading and commercialised amusement had 'usurped the place of the only reading by which . . . the foundations of a cultured taste could be laid, and the means to the end of a new happiness created.'[27] But Wright never suggested – as Morley and Escott did – that workers should imbibe the cultural values of the middle class. Even when he argued that workers needed to familiarise themselves with ideas and cultural practices commonly encountered in middle-class life, Wright always viewed such phenomena as strengthening the 'shrewd common-sense' that was a central part of working-class culture itself.

Wright's article anticipated the more recent definition of popular culture as a culture made by 'the people'. Such thinking emerged from Wright's own observation that cultural forms which appeared distant from the realities and requirements of working-class life would be rejected. But while he thought it impossible for workers to adopt the cultural life of the middle class, he advocated – as did socialists a decade later – the dissemination of many aspects of that way of life in working-class circles. For Wright, and for many socialists, an ideal popular culture was not to be a watered-down version of middle-class culture, but a culture that grew from the social situation of the working class, incorporating certain middle-class values which could be of benefit to workers in their own social and political struggles. In short, the question Wright grappled with was this: whose culture was popular culture? Socialists also had some difficulty answering this question, for, like earlier middle-class reformers, they often wanted to impose their own cultural standards on the working class. They, too, were engaged in an attempt to redefine the politics of popular culture.

If the term 'popular culture' was only beginning to enter cultural discourse in the late nineteenth century, other terms had enjoyed a long history. Hugh Cunningham has suggested that earlier in the century 'sports', 'pastimes' and 'diversions' were used in the discussion of what we would refer to as the leisure activities of the working class. By the middle of the century, however, these were being replaced by an emphasis on 'amusement' and 'recreation', the complex meanings of which were derived from a series of values pertaining to their social utility.[28] 'Recreation' was defined by one critic in 1883 as 'the cessation of the regular work of our lives, and the active occupation, whether of body or mind or both, in something different in which we find pleasure'. But, he continued, in order to be truly recreative, such activities had to offer 'renewed fitness in our regular work'.[29] By contrast, 'amusements', while often a begrudgingly acknowledged necessity, were usually viewed with disdain. The novelist Walter Besant claimed that while genuine recreations were of an improving nature, mere amusement was usually purposeless.[30]

'Leisure' also underwent significant changes in its meaning in the nineteenth century. Before the 1880s it simply referred to free, non-obligated time: amusement and recreation consisted of the activities that one engaged in during one's leisure. Self-taught artisans who reached maturity in the first third of the century all adhered to this definition: Joseph Gutteridge, for example, declared that his 'leisure was not now given up to promiscuous rambling'.[31] By the late nineteenth century, however, there was a shift away from a narrow sense of leisure as free time to a more complicated belief in leisure as a state of mind: 'We speak of *leisure time*', wrote one observer, 'but what we really mean thereby is *time in which we feel at leisure*.'[32] The shift is an important one. No longer did reformers view leisure as empty time, merely to be filled with rational recreation. Leisure had instead become a special frame of mind in which particular identities could be developed.

This new belief held that the essential character of an individual could be deciphered from that individual's leisure activities, and it led to the development of a body of literature which attempted to study leisure 'scientifically'. If leisure was so important in character-building, the reasoning went, then it should be studied with greater precision than it had been in the past. Thus the appearance of the first detailed surveys of the uses of leisure time. In 1885, a Committee to Inquire into the Conditions of the Poor in Bristol established a subcommittee on recreations. While general studies of urban life had often commented on popular culture, rarely before had such comments resulted from the extensive findings of specially appointed subcommittees. In order to understand how the uses of leisure differentiated various groups within the working class, the investigators collecting material for this report were encouraged to ask numerous questions, such as: 'Among the lowest classes of the poor, as distinguished from the artizan [*sic*] class, where do the men of your district spend their evenings and unoccupied leisure?' (the same question was then to be asked of women and children).[33]

Studies such as these were informed by the belief that play was a necessity of human existence and that if improving recreations were not provided, idle amusements might be sought instead. This belief was not a new one, for it had its roots in utilitarian notions of human nature. None the less, the utilitarian emphasis on the tendency of all individuals to seek pleasure and avoid pain seldom gave rise to detailed studies of the effects of particular recreational pleasures on individual consciousness and social well-being. It took a generation or more after the advent of utilitarianism before any detailed taxonomies of pleasure were developed. At times they appeared ludicrous. But they are illustrative of the growing need felt by social reformers to understand exactly how recreational reform might bring about desirable changes in personal behaviour. Attempting to establish 'the science of . . . developing and training the manifold forms of pleasure which Nature has given us, [and] to cultivate them into rational happiness', William Haig Miller, who wrote extensively for the Religious Tract Society, developed his own arguments about pleasure from biological metaphors:

> The Pleasure Plant, though not to be found in the great botanical work of Linnaeus, is one which grows in every country inhabited by man. . . . The Pleasure Plant naturally grows wild, and often but little attention is paid to its culture. When its fruit is taken in excess, it is followed by many unpleasant symptoms – such as nausea, depression, insanity, and even death. When cultivated, however, and used moderately, the Pleasure Plant yields the finest exhilarant that nature has given us.[34]

Biological metaphors abounded in the 'scientific' study of leisure, as did those derived from physiology. In Switzerland the noted physiologist Karl Groos developed the 'instinct-practice theory' of play in two seminal works, *The Play of Animals* and *The Play of Man*. Groos believed that the origins of play were instinctive and that through play children began to imitate the behaviour of adults, thus learning the various roles that would be required of them in their own adulthood. Most important was his suggestion that during play children were socialised into the established order: play, he wrote, 'affords good preliminary practice of the art of ruling, just as it is the first school for voluntary subordination to social law'.[35]

These ideas enjoyed widespread support in England. Samuel Barnett, the settlement house champion, praised the work of Groos. So did A. M. Thompson, a founder of the *Clarion*.[36] They also believed that through play children could be taught to appreciate values important in their own lives. As early as the 1840s and 1850s, the Band of Hope anticipated the theories of Groos when it developed its recreational activities for children, offering them an environment in which they might learn the importance of temperance. Such activities became even more important in the work of the settlements. Moreover – and the point was not lost on socialists – if play could be used to bolster the social order, it could also be used to challenge it. Hence the importance of the socialist

Sunday schools and Cinderella clubs, which provided education and entertainment for working-class children. Praising the work of the Cinderella clubs, along with that of the settlement-related Guilds of Play, one writer in Blatchford's *Women Folk* wrote that 'Our duty is to meet the awakening instincts with tactful sympathy', because 'to get hold of the children . . . and organise them for sweet, wholesome play is a work of immeasurable value.'[37]

By the turn of the century, the discussion of popular culture in Britain differed radically from discussions that had taken place a generation earlier. As the *Socialist Review* claimed, the 'anatomy of amusement' had become an important issue which had to be studied in more detail than it had been in the past if socialists were to intervene successfully in the nation's cultural affairs.[38] It was no longer enough merely to offer rational recreation in direct competition with less-rational amusements in the hope that the masses would be able to differentiate the good from the bad. Differentiation required guidance, and guidance could not be offered unless an understanding of the relationship between pleasure, individual identity and the mechanisms of socialisation had first been developed.

It has been necessary to touch upon the contours of these late Victorian debates about popular culture because they were important in providing socialists with the conceptual framework through which they understood the subject. Socialists were particularly interested in the 'anatomy of amusement' because, as we shall see, many of them desired to establish the basis for the emergence of a socialist identity in workers' uses of leisure. Little attention has been paid to this aspect of socialist thought and practice, although Stephen Yeo has offered important suggestions for the study of the social aspects of the socialist movement in these years. Arguing that the period from the mid-1880s to the mid-1890s was no mere backwater in the history of socialism, Yeo claimed the period had 'its own special dynamic'.[39] Socialism was not just an abstract system of ideas nor a series of political programmes, but rather a whole way of life. As William Morris once wrote: 'Socialism is an all-embracing theory of life, and . . . it has an ethic and a religion of its own.'[40] It was, moreover, a religion with its own gospel of play.

The 'religion of socialism' was a term seldom used between the time it appeared as the title of a number of pamphlets in the 1880s and 1890s and the time it was reconsidered by Stephen Yeo. But it characterised an important period when the socialist movement attempted to

13

develop a politics of everyday life – and a politics of popular culture. Philip Wicksteed, the Unitarian minister who helped John Trevor establish the Labour Church, was one of many socialists who recognised that socialism needed to be more than a narrow, political movement: '. . . the great danger of the Labour Movement lies in the belief that all the evils of life may be removed by the readjustment of social and industrial machinery'.[41] One important aspect of the religion of socialism, then, was its emphasis on the lived experience of the working class and on the importance of individual transformation rather than – or hopefully along with – political and economic change. As Edward Carpenter claimed: 'All the problems of society depend ultimately on the problem of the individual's own life.'[42] Tom Maguire, the trade unionist and socialist in Leeds, was even more adamant about the need for socialism to cultivate 'the whole of a man's desires and aspirations – physical, mental, social and moral'.[43] While the religion of socialism has been studied in general terms, a large part of this work is dedicated to a specific examination of what it meant to cultivate those desires and how the process entailed a radical transformation of popular culture.

The religion of socialism entailed a way of thinking which united members of various socialist organisations. Even H. M. Hyndman, the austere leader of the SDF, shared with other adherents of the faith a belief in the importance of individual, as well as social, transformation.[44] Such beliefs permeated one organisation after another and often migrated with individuals between them. James Leatham, for example, began his radical career as a member of the Aberdeen Socialist Society, abandoned it for the SDF and went on to establish branches of the ILP in the North while lecturing for the Labour Church. Likewise, Robert Blatchford, known for his cavalier independence, had in the early 1890s been affiliated with the ILP, the SDF and the Fabian Society.[45] Even the Fabian Society cannot be studied in isolation from the religion of socialism. The growing 'consciousness of sin' that makes for such compelling reading in Beatrice Webb's autobiography led to a moral critique of society that was characteristic of a broader movement from which Fabianism never completely separated itself.[46]

In their desire to transform everyday life, socialists insisted that leisure activities should be carefully studied and reformed because it was in their leisure that workers could be reached by the message of socialism. While advocating these ideas, however, they became increasingly alarmed at the growing importance of new forms of commercial entertainment in the lives of many workers. But it was precisely because the emerging leisure industry had not yet come to dominate working-class uses of leisure that socialists could still believe, at least in the 1880s and 1890s, that other identities – not merely that of the passive and politically quiescent worker in an emerging system of consumer capitalism – might yet be generated. Leisure was a contested territory, but there was still space available in which socialists could attempt to construct alternative and even oppositional forms that might themselves become the basis of a genuinely popular, socialist culture. If the massiveness of the leisure industry in the twentieth century has tended to obscure these possibilities, we should not turn a blind eye to the existence of 'alternative clusters of potential'[47] in the past, especially when socialists were themselves often optimistic about the possibility of change.

This study, then, offers an analysis of the attempt made by socialists to understand and to transform late Victorian popular culture. More important, it offers an analysis of the increasingly restricted space available to them for their reforms and of the conflicts that existed between individuals with differing visions as to what should be inserted into that space. It is a study in which the vast majority of workers will remain silent, often forced to be the object of socialist reforms rather than fully-fledged participants in them.[48] Popular culture underwent enormous changes in the late nineteenth century and socialists, if not workers themselves, wanted to see it develop in other directions. As Stuart Hall has recently written: 'One of the main difficulties standing in the way of a proper periodisation of popular culture is the profound transformation in the culture of the popular classes between the 1880s and 1920s. There are whole histories yet to be written about this period.'[49] It is my hope that this study might contribute to the writing of that history.

CHAPTER ONE

Capitalism
and the control of leisure

To the student of popular culture in Britain, the late nineteenth century poses a dilemma. On the one hand, historians are now aware of the role played by an emerging leisure industry in the transformation of popular culture which took place in those years. On the other hand, individuals living through that transformation seemed perplexed, unable to make sense of it. Moreover, in discussing popular culture, they often remained attached to particular cultural discourses that had been formulated much earlier in the century and which seemed to have little bearing on the new world of commercial entertainment. Stated baldly, this resulted in a widening gulf between what was going on and the perception of what was going on. This chapter is concerned with those perceptions and, hence, with the nature of the discourse through which an emerging world of commercial recreation was judged and often found wanting.

Perhaps only historical hindsight can allow us to understand fully the dimensions of cultural change in the final third of the nineteenth century. As Patrick Joyce has written:

> Developments such as the success of the mass circulation popular press, the rise of Blackpool, and the organisation of football and rugby league, worked together with changes in public and private transport to shatter the social mould of ritual life upon which the communities of work and sect had deeply drawn for sustenance. The old order had flowered in a culture marked by the concrete particular, the local view, and personal participation. . . . [T]he expansion of leisure competed with and finally triumphed over the hold on people's social life which political and denominational organisation and work had exercised for so long.[1]

Late Victorian social critics were aware that the old order, described by Joyce, was breaking down and they searched for words through which they could attempt to make sense of the changes. At best those changes were perceived as baffling; at worst as totally incomprehensible. Take,

17

for example, an article that appeared in 1895 in *Chambers's Journal*. Entitled 'Pastime and Business', it opened with the observation that posterity would 'select as one of the most remarkable features of the social history of the nineteenth century – indeed, of the latter half only of the nineteenth century – the extraordinary alliance that was brought about between pastime and business.'[2] Many individuals were aware of the existence of this new alliance, but most of them remained uncertain about how to discuss it. The author of this particular article claimed that fifty years earlier 'pastime' and 'business' were believed to be distinct fields of activity. But now, in an age in which speculators were profiting by exploiting the need for leisure, these distinctions were breaking apart. This was 'certainly not as it should be', remarked the author, afraid lest the marketing of amusement should somehow undermine both public morality and the business aptitude of the nation. Despite the uneasiness, however, this particular author's fears remained vague and unfocused.

When social reformers discussed leisure in the middle of the nineteenth century, they seemed able to express their concerns more clearly. Moreover, they seldom mentioned business. Instead, they concentrated their efforts on combating the pernicious social influences of those amusements they considered were not healthy, moral, or uplifting. They demanded rational recreation, and they measured all leisure pursuits in terms of their social utility, opposing those that encouraged personal dissipation or those that threatened social stability. It mattered very little to them whether the activities they disliked stemmed from proto-commercial places of entertainment, such as penny gaffs and gin palaces, from the cultural initiatives of Chartists and other radicals, or from particular communities eager to preserve the importance of fairs and blood sports in the fabric of local life. It was the activity itself, not the means by which it was provided, that came under attack.

The rapid growth of a commercial leisure industry changed all of this. Old certainties began to wane, while new suspicions were only vaguely formulated. Indeed, the muddled thought which characterised the argument developed by the author of 'Pastime and Business' seemed to be less the exception than the rule. Unable to understand the dynamic appeal of an emerging leisure industry – unable, even, to develop an adequate terminology through which to discuss that industry – many critics felt profoundly uncomfortable amidst a new world of commercial entertainment for which they neither cared nor understood. Confusion was pervasive, and socialists, when they discussed the new union of 'pastime and business', were as prone to that confusion as settlement house workers, philanthropists, temperance advocates and all those other advocates of the reform of popular culture towards the end of the century.

The business of pleasure

The process by which dominant ways of organising leisure become profit-oriented and market-controlled has been termed the 'commercialisation of leisure'. As a way of describing the important changes in the social and economic production of leisure that took place in the late nineteenth century, the term itself was widely used by 1914. Moreover, its significance for this particular study arises from the fact that its use often denoted a new interest in the mechanisms that accounted for the existence of particular types of recreation and amusement. For those who wrote about the commercialisation of leisure, the critique of specific leisure activities could no longer be separated from an analysis of how those activities were actually produced.

It has been only in the past few decades that historians and sociologists have begun to discuss the leisure industry in depth. The origins of that industry are hard to uncover, although more than twenty years ago Leo Lowenthal claimed that if 'one takes the term "mass" media to mean marketable cultural goods produced for a substantial buying public, the eighteenth century in England is the first period in history where it can be meaningfully applied'.[3] By the mid-1800s the existence of a leisure industry was readily apparent: a middle-class public devoured a growing number of books and periodicals produced by that industry, while resort towns, spas, assembly rooms, theatres, lending libraries and public subscription concerts – all commercially operated – gradually assumed a larger role in filling up the leisure time of the urban bourgeoisie. As J. H. Plumb has suggested, changes in the production of leisure in the eighteenth century were significant enough to warrant their discussion in terms of a process of commercialisation.[4]

It was not, however, until the nineteenth century that the leisure industry began to cater significantly for the demands of workers. Even here the problem of periodisation has been a difficult one, although recent scholarship has stressed the importance of the 1840s and 1850s. The Ten Hours' Act of 1847 'drew attention to the fact of leisure as a desirable thing in itself'[5] and it contributed to the demarcation of a special sphere for leisure which led to the establishment of a large number of concert rooms, penny theatres and dancing saloons. In

19

addition, the railway 'speeded up the recreational revolution', especially after the advent of the excursion train.[6] Publicans also contributed to this revolution, sponsoring outdoor sports and itinerant musicians, and initiating amateur theatrical and choral productions. Hugh Cunningham has suggested that this period witnessed a commercialisation of leisure for the working class as extensive as that for the middle class in the eighteenth century.[7]

Observers were very much aware that important changes were taking place as early as the 1860s. Thomas Wright claimed that 'amusements are a speculation upon the part of the "enterprising lessee" who provides them', while Edmund Yates wrote that 'the Business of Pleasure is carried on in the most methodical manner, is of enormous extent, employs countless "hands", and avails itself of . . . the counting-house clerk, day-book and ledger system.'[8] There is general agreement, however, that the 'take-off' occurred only after the Bank Holiday Act of 1871. John Lowerson, John Myerscough and Stephen Yeo all opt for the 1880s as the crucial decade. And while Asa Briggs sees the 1880s as pivotal, like Gareth Stedman Jones and Michael Marrus he stresses the importance of the 1890s, both in consolidating earlier trends and in developing new forms of leisure such as the cinema.[9]

T. H. S. Escott, writing in the 1880s about the enormous transformation he felt had taken place, claimed that it '. . . would be impossible to form a better idea of the advance made by Englishmen of all classes . . . in the art of "popular amusement" than from a comparison of the advertisements relating to sports, pastimes and recreation in a newspaper of today with those which made their appearance less than half a century ago.'[10] Where this advance was most noticeable was in the music hall and related forms of variety entertainment. In 1892, Philip Rutland, solicitor to the Proprietors of Entertainments Association, claimed that English towns boasted some 1,300 places of entertainment, backed by a capital of £6 million, and offering direct employment to 350,000 workers. Fifteen years later, Samuel Barnett estimated that there were 1,250,000 weekly attendances in London music halls alone.[11]

Despite the prevalence of such claims, the penetration of capitalist enterprise into the domain of leisure was uneven. Moreover, our knowledge of specific rates of growth in different localities remains sketchy at best. In Bristol, patterns of popular culture seemed to be much the same in the 1890s as they had been in 1870. In smaller towns in the North, like Rochdale, the commercial challenge to the local pub and chapel as centres of communal recreation had scarcely begun. And in villages of

East Anglia there was little formal leisure provision, despite the fact that the larger coastal resorts of Yarmouth and Lowestoft were beginning to cater extensively for new recreational tastes.[12] In short, amateurism was still important and regional diversity still great in smaller towns, and where commercial variety entertainment did exist it seldom put an end to the dialogue between performer and audience that had characterised pub-based entertainment earlier in the century. Outside London, most music halls remained firmly rooted in the community and cannot be viewed simply as precursors of the modern entertainment empires of Rank and Mecca. Even cinemas, in their early days, were seldom owned by large conglomerates and thus remained important as small-scale neighbourhood forms of entertainment.[13]

The Halifax Royal Skating Rink Company is a good example of a typical form of commercial entertainment found outside London for which records still exist. Established in the late 1870s, its prospectus claimed that with 'great confidence' the Board of Directors 'recommended the . . . company to the public as a sound commercial investment': £7,500 was to be raised in £5 shares, and several textile manufacturers purchased upwards of fifty shares each. This suggests that leisure was now seen as a good investment for those engaged in more traditional trades. Moreover, as the manufacturers who purchased shares operated in the vicinity of Halifax, it also suggests that the control of entertainment often remained in the hands of local entrepreneurs who, in this particular case, seemed to act out of motives of civic pride, business acumen and the desire to retain at least some control over the amusements enjoyed by their workers. Despite the presence of a handful of large shareholders, there were sizeable numbers of shopkeepers, clerks and various professionals in Halifax who also bought shares in the company, indicative of prevailing patterns of local and small-scale control.[14]

Thus the commercialisation of leisure, even by the end of the century, was a process that had scarcely touched many communities, or at least had left untouched other ways of organising leisure. No ruthless exploiter of the masses – despite what the critics would say – the recreational entrepreneur was sometimes less a captain of industry than a small-time businessman, well known in the community in which he operated. And yet, taken together, these local capitalists began to have a profound effect on working-class uses of leisure. While individuals who demanded rational recreation earlier in the century had called for moral restraint, a necessary correlative of economic scarcity, the new recreational entrepreneur encouraged workers to abandon restraint and

21

succumb to their desires for the new leisure pursuits on offer. As part of a new world of consumer capitalism, the leisure industry thus gave rise to a growing fear about social change in general and to an attack on working-class behaviour in particular.

The persistence of rational recreation

What concerns us here is less the history of the late Victorian leisure industry than the response to that industry. Ways of thinking developed by the Frankfurt School in the 1920s or by American 'mass culture' theorists in the 1950s were obviously not available to individuals writing about popular culture in late Victorian Britain. Such individuals often tried to make sense of cultural change through the evaluative criteria which accompanied the earlier call for rational recreation. Just as the language of eighteenth-century political radicalism offered the only vocabulary through which Chartists could express their own social and economic grievances, so the language of rational recreation offered a way of talking about popular culture which remained in force long after the fears that had fuelled its development had declined. Rational recreation thus consisted of both a series of activities that the middle class urged workers to adopt and a way of talking about leisure, a codification of middle-class experience and values constituted as an entire discourse. William Sewell has discussed the importance of – and the difficulties involved in – reconstituting the history of such discourses:

> the coherence of the thought lies not in particular texts or in the work of particular authors, but in the entire ideological discourse constituted by a large number of individually fragmentary and incomplete statements, gestures, images and actions. The key problem thus becomes not the delineation of the thought of a series of authors but the reconstruction of discourse out of fragmentary sources.[15]

One self-taught artisan captured the essence of rational recreation, both of its evaluative terminology and its preferred activities, in the 1840s: 'Rational amusements . . . we define as those particular pursuits which, while they are administrative of the highest and purest pleasure, are perfectly accordant with the dictates of soundest reason. We entirely exclude from our estimate any provision for frivolity or unmeaning mirth.'[16] So many reformers desired rational recreation that it is easy to believe that the activities they sponsored, and the terms they used to differentiate rational from irrational recreation – 'purest pleasure', 'soundest reason' – constituted various aspects of a uniform movement.

But recreational activities considered rational were numerous and varied, demanded by individuals with different motives for desiring them. Behind the rhetoric which gave a certain coherence to their demands there often existed a specific rationale for the encouragement of certain activities and the repudiation of others. Anthony Trollope, for example, ranked various recreational activities according to his assessment of their 'dignity'. Such classifications were common among educated Victorians of the period, suggestive of the complex value systems that underlay class-specific descriptions of popular recreation.[17]

Other writers who emphasised the need for rational recreation arranged them in ways different from Trollope. In 1849 the 'Committee for Conducting the Saturday Evening Concerts, Established for the Purpose of Providing Rational and Elevating Amusements for the Working Classes of Liverpool' published three essays written by local artisans on the importance of recreational reform. All three railed against concert rooms, of which Liverpool seemed to possess a large number, and they praised the effects of elevating and rational music. None the less, these three authors – a journeyman printer, a watchmaker and a toolmaker – seemed to emphasise private intellectual development to a far greater degree than did those middle-class reformers who feared their own inability to supervise private uses of leisure and who, thus, became much more enamoured of public recreational pursuits.[18] Despite such differences, however, artisans and middle-class reformers who demanded rational recreation all contributed to a taxonomy of pleasure that judged entertainment along a broad spectrum, from the orderly and rational at one end to the dissipating and thus irrational at the other.

The moral critique of popular culture which informed the call for rational recreation did not give way to something different as soon as entrepreneurs began to exploit the new market for mass entertainment. Indeed, so far did the old moral arguments permeate a developing critique of commercial recreation that, until the early 1900s, one cannot speak of the emergence of a new discourse through which changes in popular culture were filtered. Moreover, the language developed earlier by middle-class reformers, and occasionally by working-class autodidacts in their own assault on disreputable pastimes, became so universal that entrepreneurs were compelled to appropriate it when arguing for the respectability of their own offerings. In the 1840s and 1850s, for example, opposition to the metropolitan fairs in part diminished only when the showmen who performed at them strove to overcome public hostility, often by adopting the moral vocabulary of the reformer as a means of advertising their own virtues.[19]

By the 1890s, entrepreneurs were particularly adept at describing their products within a discursive framework pioneered by the advocates of rational recreation. This can be seen in the wording of the advertisements placed in Keir Hardie's *Labour Leader* by businessmen eager to sell their recreational wares. The Glasgow People's Palace was advertised in the *Leader* in ways that would give little cause for alarm:

> The comfort and convenience of patrons [in the Palace] is studied in a manner that is not even attempted in higher price halls. Seats are guaranteed or money returned. No crowding allowed. ... Family night every Friday, when Sweethearts and Wives are admitted Free. Special stair reserved for ladies and children. Lavatories on every floor, and a host of other advantages. ... Such enterprise does not go unrewarded. The working class – that is, the independent, respectable working class – know who are their best friends. ... HENCE THE SUCCESS OF THE PEOPLE'S PALACE. We should have a dozen such Palaces. With a proper amount of demand the working class can confidently look for a supply.[20]

In a similar vein, E. J. Riley Ltd, billiard table makers in Accrington, believed that their own commercial brand of rational recreation would be of direct benefit to the socialist movement: ' "All propaganda and no recreation" is not sufficiently interesting to the man on the street to induce him to join the Labour Club', they wrote. 'Provide him with pleasant recreation, and he will soon take an interest in the more serious work.'[21]

The idea that moral improvement – a central demand of rational recreation – could coexist with *laissez-faire* principles in the provision of entertainment was seized upon by numerous entrepreneurs, eager to gain the support of those who would readily condemn all forms of commercial recreation. By carefully studying, and then deploying, the language of the enemy, entrepreneurs hoped to disarm many of their critics. Like those critics, they stressed the importance of separating the 'respectable' from the 'rough' in working-class audiences. Also like their critics, they suggested that women might play an important role in preventing male rowdiness in places of entertainment. Some even went so far as to suggest that because 'wholesome, rational amusement is a factor in national well-being', and that because entrepreneurs were developing a 'gigantic industry' devoted to national well-being, all restrictions placed on them should be removed as being 'inimical to the best interests of the public'.[22]

Certainly by the 1890s, business leaders had adopted the moral rhetoric of rational recreation in order to placate their would-be critics. But in so doing, as we can see in the self-promotional claims made by the Glasgow People's Palace, they also attempted to flatter the would-be consumer. Entrepreneurs conceived of the consumer not as the self-disciplined citizen, eager for the benefits of rational recreation, but as the discerning customer, choosing judiciously between alternative commodities in a marketplace where 'comfort and convenience' was merely one of many criteria of value. This promotional language of consumer rights was quite new, although it borrowed heavily from the language of rational recreation. By situating their products within the moral discourses through which Victorian critics made sense of popular culture, entrepreneurs thus attempted to appeal not only to middle-class reformers but also to skilled workers concerned with issues of respectability in their own leisure choices.

In this way the marketing strategies of recreational entrepreneurs took some of the bite out of the opposition to the commercialisation of leisure. But they did not convince everybody; there remained those who doubted that commerce could provide truly *rational* recreation – and who doubted that consumers could make the careful choices of which entrepreneurs believed they were capable. As early as the 1850s the Liverpudlian journalist Hugh Shimmin, saw through the new entrepreneurial version of rational recreation. Visiting a fairground, he was handed a small scrap of paper that read: 'To the lovers of rational mirth this place is open nightly for scientific and instructive entertainment.' That evening Shimmin discovered that the 'rational mirth' consisted of large doses of nitrous oxide being administered to members of a paying audience, resulting in their exhibition of 'bilious' temperament, 'maniacal fury' and 'shamefully indecent and obscene language'.[23] Shimmin exposed not only what he considered to be the immorality of the amusements he witnessed but also the advertising practices of the entrepreneurs who promoted them.

Reconstituting cultural criticism

Shimmin's suspicion that business was unable to offer truly rational pastimes was shared by a large number of critics who faced a much more formidable leisure industry a generation or two later. Initially their criticism was vague and it was rarely articulated without reference to the moral hierarchies associated with rational recreation. Slowly, however,

25

they began to take note of the entrepreneurial system responsible for the activities they disliked and to break free – at least to a limited extent – from the ways of seeing conditioned by the call for rational recreation. Often their thoughts were muddled, and one cannot speak of an entirely new cultural discourse emerging in these years. By studying the general attitudes to the commercial provision of leisure in the late nineteenth century, however, we may be able to assess the extent to which critics transcended certain aspects of the rhetoric of rational recreation, even while remaining limited by it.

Unlike their earlier counterparts, many individuals who attacked late Victorian popular culture argued that commercially provided leisure activities were often produced by workers who were exploited by the industry that employed them. This was, of course, an argument largely derived from the belief that capitalism exploited all workers. But it was a new argument when directed against the leisure industry, for it had found no place in the vocabulary of rational recreation. Ernest Ensor was one of many critics of football who condemned professional sport for creating wage-slaves out of amateur players. Central to his discussion of sport was his belief that, while appearing to be independent and prosperous, football players were 'treated like chattels'.[24] The socialist press made similar points about other forms of entertainment. An article in the first issue of *Justice*, for example, claimed that individuals who were hired to assist in the staging of various theatrical spectaculars were also exploited. Helpless and degraded, under the autocratic authority of the stage-manager, they were 'so down-trodden that they became obedient machines for the smallest possible wage'. *Justice* also joined in the outcry against the exploitation of child labour in pantomimes: 'We object to the enterprising theatrical manager – just as we object to the factory owner – getting cheap labour at the expense of . . . [the children's] health and general well-being.'[25]

Such arguments, particularly when advanced by socialists, often linked a specific attack on the employment practices of the commercial leisure industry with a more general indictment of capitalism as a whole. Moreover, critics not only reprimanded the leisure industry for its treatment of workers, but also for swamping the countryside and small towns with its standardised products, threatening both regional diversity in the provision of entertainment and the livelihood of local performers. As we have seen, one can exaggerate the extent to which leisure became standardised in these years. Nevertheless, travelling showmen felt particularly challenged by new ways of organising entertainment and they condemned those commercially backed troupes which tended to steal their business. Just as the handloom weavers of the 1830s faced a direct threat to their livelihood from new forms of industrial production, so did these showmen obstinately cling 'to the ownership of the means of production without the capital to expand to meet the new conditions'.[26]

These performers railed against proto-commercial forms of entertainment because they felt their own livelihood to be threatened. But they also sensed that newer, more highly capitalised ventures were gradually undermining regional patterns of recreation and culture that were important in their own right. Socialists tended to agree with them. They claimed that small, co-operative companies were losing their custom to the commercial venues that had little regard for anything beyond their own immediate profits. The *Clarion*, for example, joined in the crusade to protect regional dramatic circuits from competition with newer ways of organising leisure. That paper's drama critic, A. M. Thompson, once complained that London theatres monopolised dramatic initiative, forcing provincial managers to accept those productions that had first been a commercial success in London.[27]

Radicals who had been active in the 1830s and 1840s were especially vociferous in opposing those pursuits which threatened older ways of organising leisure time. In his nostalgia for Chartist culture, Thomas Cooper came to associate the decline of Chartism with an increase in organised betting and gambling. He deplored the new uses of leisure and was of the opinion that the working class had 'gone back, intellectually and morally'.[28] While Ross McKibbin has argued persuasively that gambling never played quite the debilitating role Cooper attributed to it[29] what is important is that the demise of a radical culture, which itself had often spoken the language of rational recreation, was seen by one of its foremost defenders as somehow related to the commercial exploitation of new demands for leisure. Such beliefs were pervasive, outliving many Chartists and finding their way into the ranks of the socialist movement. In 1889, for example, Edward Carpenter mourned the death of Joseph Sharpe, a Chartist and a harpist whose music was central to his politics. According to Carpenter, the advent of the Bank Holiday and the railway excursion diminished Sharpe's audience, which reduced him to poverty and made vulnerable the radical culture to which he had devoted his life. 'People began to save their cash and their holidays for trips to the seaside and day excursions to London', wrote Carpenter, 'and the money dribbled away from the old channels.'[30]

While Chartists often linked the decline of their culture with the rise of commercial entertainment, socialists shared a different fear: that the entertainment industry was growing so large it would prevent workers from ever developing such a culture in the first place. Ernest Belfort Bax, the most important intellectual spokesperson for the SDF, was vociferous in his own condemnation of an industry which, he believed, was suppressing the hopes of would-be socialists. For Bax, leisure, not religion, was the new opiate of the masses: 'A well-conducted English workman, "thrifty and industrious", is no doubt kept in a state of dogged contentment by never knowing what leisure intelligently occu-pied means, by his tastes being carefully kept under, and by his weekly holiday being "empty, swept, and garnished" of all relaxation.'[31] While Bax's beliefs about the ideal uses of leisure were coloured by aspirations firmly anchored in the world of rational recreation, he also believed that the capitalist organisation of leisure made it more difficult to realise those aspirations.

In the battle that ensued over the uses of leisure, critics in the 1880s and 1890s contrasted the pervasive influence of business ethics on present-day pleasure with what they considered to be the healthier pastimes of an earlier age. 'In "the fine old days of leisure", which George Eliot laments', claimed one writer, 'there was nothing like the same industry in pursuing recreation as there is in these days of perennial shop and unceasing work.'[32] While socialists feared that the new pursuit of pleasure might restrict the growth of socialism, they, too, believed that many new activities were unhealthy in their own right. Hence the importance of William Morris's demand for 'rest', a demand that must be understood against the backdrop of this perceived intensification of the search for excitement encouraged by the new industry. Under capi-talism, wrote Morris, workers were susceptible to new, 'make-shift' amusements which offered superficial jollity but no time for real thought and dreaming. In looking to the future, Morris demanded that workers' leisure 'must be ample enough to allow them full rest of mind and body'.[33] While Morris did not always conceive of 'rest' as a space for the development of an alternative culture, he did oppose an industry that was encroaching on what he believed to be hitherto sacrosanct territory, limiting all kinds of uses to which leisure might be devoted.

Finally, socialists argued that while the excitement found in music halls, at football matches and on Bank Holidays was not at all truly recreative, the proprietors of those amusements tried to claim that it was. Here socialists seemed to be disputing the very definition of leisure put forward by the new industry. Their argument was never well developed, although it is implicit in many of the positions outlined above. Socialists suggested that by claiming to offer rational recreation, the leisure industry was gradually coming to monopolise socially valid definitions of leisure. Such ideas were hinted at by James Leatham, the Aberdeen socialist. Manchester, he wrote, had once been home to a number of political rallies and street spectacles that were no longer perceived as recreational because a narrower definition of leisure as a purchasable commodity was usurping one that still had space for the culture of daily street life. For Leatham the change was not a pleasant one.[34]

Despite the fact that critics of late Victorian popular culture tried to make sense of the new world of commercial entertainment, their ideas were often unfocused. While some of them cloaked their arguments in the rhetoric of rational recreation, others attempted to transcend the boundaries of a discourse which, in retrospect, seems singularly inappropriate as a vehicle for comprehending the mechanisms of the late Victorian leisure industry. While critics attacked that industry, many did so simply because they believed it was unable to offer rational recreation. Gradually, though, a number of individuals, socialists among them, put forward new arguments about the commercial provision of leisure: the leisure industry, they claimed, exploited workers who provided entertainment for the masses; it directly threatened the livelihood of those who produced leisure activities in less-commercial ways; it encouraged homogeneity; it threatened older, radical ways of organising leisure; it fostered a dependence on its products, thereby blocking the development of socialist cultural alternatives; and, finally, it began to redefine recreation as a mere purchasable commodity. These arguments were seldom elaborated. But, in a hesitating manner, the individuals who made them began to shift attention away from the morality of particular pursuits to the industry responsible for them.

Socialism and the leisure industry

That socialists actively disliked the transformation of late Victorian popular culture should be obvious by now. Thus, when Willie Stewart, president of the Scottish ILP, objected to commercial entertainment he expressed a belief that was widely shared in socialist circles:

> Production for profit, which is the basis of modern industrialism, is also the basis of modern amusement, as indeed it is also of nearly every form of modern art, to the degradation alike of industrialism, amusement and art. Commercialism controls the theatre, the music hall, and the football field:

29

the providing of healthy amusement and recreation is of secondary consideration.[35]

This suspicion was voiced again and again. But when socialists actually turned their attention to specific forms of 'commercialism' in the cultural arena their arguments were often complex and their tone less strident. A detailed examination of socialist attitudes towards the capitalist organisation of music halls, the drink trade, Association Football and Bank Holiday excursions can further illuminate the relationship between socialists and the emerging leisure industry.

The music hall was not only the most visible manifestation of the new leisure industry: it was also one of the more acceptable. While critics in the 1880s and 1890s often lamented the general passivity of music-hall audiences, and while they still attacked the quality of entertainment offered by small, backstreet venues, they usually accepted the self-promotional language of edifying recreation and wholesome amusement offered by music-hall proprietors. *The New Age*, for which a number of socialists wrote at the turn of the century, praised the efforts made by the larger halls to improve the quality of music-hall entertainment; while Matthew Hanly, a lithographic printer, told the Commons Select Committee on Theatres and Places of Entertainment that music-hall entertainment had improved in quality, suggesting that the government should not attempt to interfere with its provision.[36]

More important (because drink, in the moral hierarchies of pleasure that accompanied the demand for rational recreation, was considered to be one of the greatest of evils) music halls – when and where they could draw workers away from drink – were praised. T. H. S. Escott believed that the halls were 'not without their mischievous influence upon ... moral currency', but he also suggested that when properly conducted they were at least 'antidotes to the popular curse of drunkenness'.[37] When, however, variety entertainment became so popular that it threatened other ways of organising leisure, voices were raised against it. As Charles Russell and Lilian Rigby claimed in their 1908 survey of working lads' clubs, many adolescents attended the halls three or four times a week and thus did not make use of the clubs that Russell and Rigby were eager to promote. 'The danger of the ... music hall is not the occasional or even the weekly visit', they wrote. 'It lies in the gradual growth of a liking for this form of entertainment to the exclusion of all else.'[38]

When socialists discussed the halls they often remained sceptical, and yet, like Russell and Rigby, they believed that in small doses music-hall entertainment seldom threatened alternative ways of organising leisure. Perhaps J. A. Hobson, the prominent social democratic theorist, offered some of the most thought-provoking comments on the halls when he suggested that the spirit of jingoism they fostered was 'inimical to rational politics and radical social and democratic reform'.[39] Unlike Hobson, however, most socialists did not attempt to explore the ideological content of music-hall songs and the beliefs they fostered. Instead, they judged the halls according to their own preconceived notions of order and rationality. The main question facing them was not – as it has been for recent historians – whether or not dominant ideologies were disseminated through music-hall songs but whether or not respectability and decorum were encouraged in the halls themselves. Once again we see a critique informed by the priorities of rational recreation. Will Thorne, for example, General Secretary of the Gas Workers' Union and member of the SDF, implied that music halls in Birmingham were acceptable because they were well conducted, encouraging respectability through the enforcement of a strict dress code.[40]

Socialists attacked music halls, then, only when they believed that the desire for profit might be inimical to the provision of rational recreation – only when they remained unconvinced by the advertising strategy of music-hall proprietors. John Burns believed that '. . . the best interests of the profession are subordinated to dividends', and that the quality of entertainment offered by the halls had declined because more and more of them were now operated by major syndicates. Burns, as a borough councillor for Battersea, member of the London County Council and self-proclaimed socialist, was noted for his opposition to various forms of popular culture. Thus, it is not surprising to find him suggesting that the music halls were not what they ought to be, namely 'places of education and instruction with amusement and delight'.[41] Nevertheless, the ideas espoused by Burns were not widely shared, while the increasing appearance of respectability, consciously manufactured by music-hall proprietors, convinced most socialists that the halls should be tolerated.

The extent to which socialists accepted the halls can be seen if we turn our attention to Bradford, where, by 1900, variety entertainment had become a respectable part of the cultural fabric of that city. The halls had mastered the language of rational recreation and in so doing had disarmed their critics. This had not always been the case. In the 1870s, one study condemned music-hall proprietors for pandering to the lowest levels of public taste.[42] By the end of the century, however, comments such as these were rare, at least in socialist circles. The *Bradford Labour Echo* carried a regular column on 'Amusements', a perusal of which suggests that socialists had become convinced that the halls could offer elevating amusement. When the New Empire Theatre opened its doors in 1899, the local labour paper did complain that it was owned by a large syndicate – the Liverpool, Leeds, Hull and Bradford Empire Palaces Ltd. But it also argued that because the theatre would offer wholesome entertainment on a grand scale, it was a desirable acquisition.[43]

The *Bradford Labour Echo* implied that if capitalism could provide rational recreation, then its intrusion into the cultural arena could be tolerated. This point of view was more forcefully expressed in the debates carried in the *Clarion* about the Manchester Palace of Varieties. One of the largest music halls in the country, boasting a seating capacity of over 3,000, the Palace offered its customers entertainment on a grand scale. It was opened in 1891 at a cost of over £40,000. One might expect that, as one of the more expensive ventures of its kind, the Palace would have drawn the wrath of those opposed to commercial entertainment. When the proprietors applied for a licence to sell alcoholic beverages there was indeed opposition, but it emanated not from socialists but from local temperance reformers, who succeeded in preventing the Palace from acquiring such a licence.

The managers of the Palace tried desperately to ingratiate themselves with the magistrates who considered their application to sell alcohol. They also attempted to convince their critics that they offered wholesome amusement. When, in 1913, they decided to raze the Palace of Varieties to make way for the Palace Theatre, they suggested that the old Palace had indeed lived up to the claims put forward on its behalf:

> Its opening marked a new era in the domain of public entertainment, for up to that time the old-time music hall – with its ill construction, bad accommodation, and, in many respects, objectionable pabulum – held sway in these counties. . . . The Palace proved the triumph of good, clean, wholesome vaudeville entertainment, over the piffle that previously had been ladled out to music hall patrons.[44]

Behind this rhetoric, however, were a series of business intrigues which sharply differed from the image of order and respectability which the Palace tried to cultivate, an image which certainly appealed to socialists.[45]

Robert Blatchford led the *Clarion*'s drive to muster support for the Palace. While not an ardent admirer of music-hall entertainment, he adopted a pragmatic position in regard to the Palace: 'As the people will have music halls', he wrote, 'it is well they should have the best that can be provided.' Blatchford praised the Palace because he felt that it would add to the 'moral and intellectual' evolution of the community by drawing workers away from more sordid places of entertainment. When the debate over the drink licence intensified, Blatchford visited several other halls in Manchester in order to compare them with the new Palace. In most of them he considered the music coarse, the ventilation inadequate and the drinking excessive. In none of them did he discover any evidence of wholesome amusement. The survey forced him to conclude that the Palace of Varieties was the cleanest, best-conducted music hall in the city.[46] Blatchford and his colleagues thus came to accept the validity of the capitalist provision of certain forms of entertainment – providing the entertainment offered was acceptable in terms of their own moral hierarchies of pleasure.

It is ironic that socialists should throw their support behind the Palace, and, hence, by implication behind an industry that was in the process of re-making working-class culture and reducing the space available for autonomous forms of working-class expression. Blatchford often spoke out against 'commercial tyranny', although because he rejected the teetotal Puritanism of individuals like John Burns he came to accept the arguments put forward by music-hall proprietors in Manchester. The Palace may have been a capitalist venture, but it was one that treated workers as respectable consumers, capable of differentiating wholesome from disreputable pastimes. The kind of worker the directors claimed visited the Palace was the kind Blatchford wanted for his own movement. Rather than pose a threat to the moral fabric of society, the Palace – and in time the whole industry it represented – managed to convince some of the most ardent critics of capitalism of its own worthiness.

Although some socialists supported the Palace's appeal for a drink licence, seldom did they approve of drinking in general. And yet here, too, opposition was more concerned with the morality of drink than with the commercial organisation of the drink trade. Despite the fact that he later joined a Liberal Cabinet, John Burns often spoke for labour teetotalers in his suggestion that drink led to industrial bondage, personal debasement and domestic misery: only through total abstinence, he claimed, could workers hope to improve their position in society. When he was attacked for being a Puritan, opposed to all forms of amusement, Burns responded that he supported 'good' amusement, but that amusement could never be good when subordinated to the sale of drink.[47]

Socialist attacks on drink were most evident in the opposition to the sale of alcohol in labour clubs. In 1896 John Bruce Glasier wrote in his diary that his wife, Katharine, 'publicly rebukes members for allowing drink selling in Club – thus hurting the growth of the movement. Many members express gratitude to her.' Glasier was as adamant as his wife in opposing alcohol: in 1910, after speaking at an ILP club in Oxford, he claimed that he would not have made an appearance had he known that drink was sold there.[48] Likewise when John Trevor, founder of the Labour Church, opened up the pages of the *Labour Prophet* to a debate about whether drink should be sold in labour clubs, most letters expressed views similar to Glasier's. W. H. Drew, vice-president of the Bradford Trades Council, was one of the few correspondents who claimed that drunkenness was not the result of the moral failings of the individual, but instead was induced by an unhealthy environment brought about by a system of capitalist exploitation. Drew was virtually alone amongst those who took part in the debate in the *Prophet*: most respondents were content to indict those who drank, not the industry that profited from the sale of drink.[49]

Elsewhere in the ranks of the socialist movement, however, Drew's beliefs enjoyed a wider currency. Like Drew, Charles Muse suggested, in 1895, that 'wretched social conditions' were responsible for drunkenness, although even Muse remained unclear about whether poverty was the cause, or the result, of drink.[50] And as early as 1884, H. M. Hyndman wrote that 'the temperance cry ... serves the purpose of the capitalist class to divert attention away from the real causes of the whole social depression which engenders the drunkenness, the misery, the pauperism that they so hypocritically deplore.'[51] Hyndman also suggested that publicans were coming under greater pressure to sell more drink and were thus less likely to provide the recreational facilities that had figured so prominently in public houses earlier in the century. In a similar vein, Edward Carpenter also lamented that the increasing importance of the tied house forced publicans to sell more drink at the expense of 'sociable converse'. Carpenter hoped that pubs might once again be provided with games, papers and 'similar recreations', although he argued that this could occur only after they had been liberated from 'the clutch of the Brewers'.[52]

Liberating the pub from the 'clutch' of the brewers was, as we shall see, a demand which fuelled socialist calls for the municipalisation of the drink trade. But the prevalence of teetotalers in the socialist movement made it difficult for the movement as a whole to advance new lines of thinking about that trade. Socialists certainly began to conceive of the 'drink problem' in a broader social context than hitherto had been the case. And they adopted the idea, first put forward by various Chartists, that the causes of drinking could be alleviated by a reform of the environment. But, on the whole, a large number of them still blamed the individual worker for the massive problem of drunkenness in late Victorian society.[53]

The new links being forged between business and sport, particularly football, were also attacked in late nineteenth-century Britain. Two arguments against the commercialisation of sport dominated critical thinking. First, opponents held that the development of a national market for football players reduced the importance of regional loyalties in recreation:

> Enterprising speculators will hire a team of professionals, paying wages which will secure the best of talent, so as to attract large crowds of spectators, and bring in profitable returns by way of gate-money. There will be eager competition among rival troupes in snapping up promising players ... and the link which now exists between the player and the locality which he nominally represents will be broken.[54]

Second, they argued that Association Football encouraged passivity, robbing spectators of any desire to make their own amusements. John Burns wrote in 1902 that the poor, 'over-specialised in their work, over-athleticised in their play ... were rearing up a race of people who could and did applaud sport in which they could not indulge, as did the Greeks and Romans in the days of their degradation'.[55] What bothered socialists about this trend was that as workers became passive spectators they were rendered immune from the appeal of socialism, made 'mentally incapable of understanding their own needs and rights', reduced, according to Carpenter, from the lofty levels of self-expression to a state of 'passive absorption'.[56] This idea was stated most eloquently in 1908 by Matt Simm, chair of the North East Federation of the ILP and editor of Newcastle-upon-Tyne's *Northern Democrat*:

> I do not suggest there is anything wrong with football, but there does seem something wrong with the majority of people who habitually attend football matches and fill their minds with things that don't matter. ... Difficult though the task may be to push football out of heads and push Socialism in, the task must be undertaken, for just as surely as football doesn't matter, Socialism matters a very great deal.[57]

Once again, it was the moral failings of those who habitually attended football matches that was the problem, not the sport industry that encouraged them to do so.

Occasionally socialists broke free of this kind of rhetoric, suggesting that professional sport tainted all recreation through the competitive spirit it fostered. By turning talent into a commodity sold to the highest bidder, it reduced the opportunity for talent to be shared communally. As Robert Blatchford suggested in 1908, in an ideal social gathering those with particular talents would provide entertainment for those without, under no illusion that this entitled them to economic compensation.[58] The increasingly competitive nature of recreation meant that such altruism in an important arena of social life was being undermined by calculated greed, resulting in the contamination of valuable social relationships by the cash nexus.

This is not to suggest that socialists simply called for a return to amateurism because they were opposed to the commercialisation of sport. Some, such as 'Olympian' (Sam Hobson), who wrote the 'Athletics' column in the *Labour Leader*, did indeed urge ILP clubs to form amateur football teams in order to counter the effects of professionalism.[59] But amateurism was itself suspect because it smacked of the elitism associated with the 'gentleman player'. One writer for the socialist *Sheffield Guardian* argued in 1909 that professional football, like any other industry, took control away from those involved in the production of commodities (in this case entertainment), and in the process proletarianised them. But, he continued, individuals most opposed to professional sport – those who championed amateurism – were usually the captains of industry who upheld other aspects of the industrial system. The answer was not to return to amateurism but to strengthen players' unions so that professional footballers could bargain over conditions of employment like other workers.[60]

The socialist attack on professionalism in sport was thus two-pronged. As an activity spectator sport encouraged passivity, making it difficult for workers to choose rational recreations which might assist in the development of an alternative culture. Moreover, as an industry it made a fetish of competition, reducing the importance of the valuable social relationships that had been central to sport in earlier times. H. Stratton, a writer for *Justice*, was adamant in his own denunciation of professional sport because for him capitalism had robbed it of this important function. 'The truth is', he claimed, 'that sport, like every other thing, is demoralised and damned by capitalism.' Only after the 'collective ownership of all the means of producing the . . . pleasures of life' had been brought about, he continued, could sport once again serve the important social functions it once had.[61]

The working-class excursions and seaside holidays which prolifer-ated following the passage of the 1871 Bank Holiday Act alarmed critics as much as did the development of professional sports. John Lubbock, who sponsored the Act in Parliament, claimed that any increase in leisure should be devoted to cultivating friendships, acquiring a love of books, music and poetry, and reading – his list was endless, but it had no place for holiday excursions, or indeed for any form of commercial recrea-tion.[62] Georgia Pearce, the music critic for the *Clarion*, agreed: 'A holiday should be a pause time, a breaking off to think.'[63] Despite such hopes, the 1870s and 1880s witnessed a rapid expansion of commercial entertainment at seaside resorts as entrepreneurs stepped in to meet the growing demand for leisure and channel it in particular directions. By the 1890s, Blackpool in particular was a attracting a large number of working-class holiday-makers and the entertainments offered there 'embodied a programme of ideological and cultural re-formation'[64] that threatened the values individuals like Lubbock and Pearce cherished.

When workers appeared to be enjoying their seaside holidays in rational ways, socialists were seldom alarmed. Moreover, given that only the 'top people' as Robert Roberts called them could afford even the excursion fare to Blackpool, it might be expected that the resort could boast a large number of holiday-makers who eschewed frivolity and spent their savings carefully. Entrepreneurs tried to cultivate a picture of recreational rationality in Blackpool and there was enough evidence to convince some socialists that Blackpool posed little threat to other ways of organising leisure. Blatchford once wrote to a colleague, claiming that excursion trains poured 'the best of the rank and fashion of Lancashire and Yorkshire' into the streets of Blackpool and the pier and promenade were populated by a 'highbred' – rather than 'hybrid' – crowd, engaged in the orderly pursuit of pleasure.[65]

When such crowds were 'highbred', exhibiting the traits of leisure rationally used, all was well. When they were not, however, Blatchford's praise soured: 'The crowd lack initiative and are not blessed with much imagination. . . . Ruled by the instinct of the herd they flock in dense masses upon excursion trains . . ., packed like cattle, to the towns of their choice, where they sit for hours huddled like sheep in a pen and gaze blankly at the sea.'[66] Admittedly, Blatchford offered this observation between the wars, long after his faith in the working class had dimi-nished. But other socialists writing in the 1890s and early 1900s were also apt to describe Blackpool in similar terms. One writer in the *Labour*

Leader invoked the image of a 'scarred mass of people', while Katharine Bruce Glasier described Blackpool as particularly 'hideous', full of 'unrest and fevered energy'.[67] For such individuals, the democratisation of leisure appeared to erase social distinctions as the undifferentiated masses all eagerly worshipped at the altar of the new mammon, commercialised entertainment. If Blackpool represented an embryonic form of mass culture, then in statements such as these we can uncover an attempt to develop a new language through which to make sense of it. Images of 'dense crowds', of 'scarred masses' and of 'herd instinct' had seldom before been invoked by critics of popular culture. Now they were, and the picture socialists drew with them was hardly comforting.

One writer for Bradford's socialist *Forward*, David West, tried in 1906 to make sense of the 'fevered energy' which he believed characterised the activity of working-class excursionists. In the process he moved away from a discussion of the moral attributes of those who failed to use their leisure rationally. West was less interested in individual uses of leisure than he was in the connection between the nature of work and the pressures that led workers to desire 'a kind of a "burst" ', an exploitable 'burst' from the point of view of recreational entrepreneurs. Keenly aware that a discussion of the uses of leisure in late Victorian society could not be undertaken without first discussing capitalism and the working conditions it fostered, West wrote:

> It is not that we have to alter the method of spending our leisure time, or our holidays . . . these things are the result of something which goes far deeper. They are the result of the conditions of life, and these are determined and must always be largely determined, by the conditions under which the nation does its work and the ideas which it places before itself in doing that work.[68]

The problem for West, then, was not simply the failure of workers to pursue rational pleasures but the extent to which the nature of their work allowed them to be duped into becoming slaves to commercialised pleasures. It was only at this point, when they stepped back from the platitudes of rational recreation and focused on leisure in a broader context, that socialists could begin to develop a critique of the leisure industry related to their critique of industrial capitalism as a whole. In so doing, they began to realise the extent to which the capitalist organisation of leisure had already deeply penetrated working-class life. As a critic in the *Labour Leader* wrote, coming close to a Gramscian analysis of the situation: 'Capitalism is not altogether an enemy outside of us, but a foe in our own household with whom we have to grapple in a deadly grip.'[69]

38

Socialism and the culture of consumption

By 1900 the exploitative labour practices of producer capitalism were solidly coupled with a new world of consumer capitalism in which the masses – or the 'herd', to use Blatchford's term – were flattered by the new entrepreneurs of pleasure. Socialists were beginning to recognise the significance of these developments and to address them in ways that increasingly owed little to earlier discourses of rational recreation. Although Philip Snowden, for example, continued to be enamoured of rational recreation, he also suggested that the enemy was not so much the individual worker who failed its test but an entire system of consumer capitalism that was gradually coming to redefine the relationship between work and leisure. With grave consequences, Snowden suggested, respectable workers were now encouraged to abandon the world of thrift for a new world of instant gratification. On the eve of World War I he wrote:

> New expenses have come into the category of necessaries. The develop-ment of tramways, the coming of the halfpenny newspaper, the cheap but better-class music hall and the picture palace, the cheap periodicals and books, the very municipal enterprise which was intended to provide free libraries, free parks, free concerts, has added to the expenditure of the working classes, who cannot take advantage of these boons without incur-ring some little expense in sundries. ... People cannot ... see others taking a holiday into the country or to the seaside without desiring to do the same. These additional items of expenditure, coming out of wages that are stationary, make the struggle to live more intense, and compel a lessening of expenditure on absolute necessaries.[70]

Snowden was implicitly concerned with a process first dissected a decade earlier by the American sociologist Thorstein Veblen. For Veblen, individuals in the USA attempted to emulate the life-style of those higher on the status hierarchy through a process of conspicuous consumption, an outward display of the leisure pursuits and material attributes of those in more comfortable positions.[71] For Snowden, the same process was at work in England, even amongst workers. The most influential British critic to develop these ideas was J. A. Hobson. In a lengthy review of Veblen's work, he was quick to note the extent to which the very existence of a 'predatory' upper class of 'unproductive' individuals was leading to the establishment of a replica of itself in working-class circles. In the process leisure was becoming the site of status emulation. The public house, for example, had become 'the stage on which even the common working man might assume upon occasion, in his awkward way, some of the carousing, combative, sporting habits of the real gentleman'.[72]

The most detailed analysis of working-class consumption – and a particularly valuable one for the connections it made between consumer capitalism and radical politics – was put forward by James Ramsay Mac-Donald, the future prime minister, who had known Hobson in the 1890s when they were both active in the progressive Rainbow Circle. In an article on gambling which appeared in 1905, MacDonald attacked a new elite, which had made its fortune in various imperialist ventures, for encouraging working-class gambling through the example of its own profligacy. Like Hobson, MacDonald stressed the importance of the 'law of imitation' in this process: 'In a subtle way', he wrote, 'the grossness at the top percolates through to the bottom.'[73] MacDonald was vague about how this process of 'percolation' worked. He was less vague, however, in exposing its dangers. Not only would the working class become impoverished in attempting to increase its command of leisure, but the façade of classlessness in the pursuit of pleasure encouraged by the entertainment industry would undermine working-class solidarity. A year before the Labour Representation Committee became the twentieth-century Labour Party, MacDonald already feared the possible effects of a classless, mass culture on the success of that party, anticipating the 'embourgeoisement' theories put forward by British sociologists in the 1950s.

The arguments developed by Hobson, MacDonald and others share more with recent critiques of mass culture and society than they do with the rhetoric of rational recreation. MacDonald, for example, was less interested in 'the moral breakdown of isolated individuals' than in 'a serious failure on the part of society'.[74] Thus the importance of the first decade of this century in the history of cultural criticism in Britain, a decade which finally witnessed a rupture in particular discursive formations through which leisure had been understood and discussed at least since the 1830s. But one should not overestimate the significance of these changes. Even MacDonald, notwithstanding his attempts to link the study of leisure to broader social and economic phenomena, still called for municipal control of the public house as 'the first step . . . towards the provision of that rational amusement which is to protect our industrial population from vicious allurements'.[75]

With few exceptions, then, socialists' statements about the commercialisation of leisure were informed by the discursive structure of rational recreation. When socialists claimed, for example, that commercial entertainment overwhelmed both an earlier radical culture and more recent attempts to develop an alternative culture, they blamed workers for succumbing to the blandishments of recreational entrepreneurs, reminding them of the importance of personal responsibility in the uses of leisure. That emphasis on moral sobriety had also been central to the demands of middle-class reformers in the 1840s. Likewise, socialist attacks on the leisure industry for its provision of frivolous pastimes, while new in that it was a specific assault on capitalism, developed from an ordering of amusements as useful or useless that would have found many supporters amongst those who had desired rational recreation in an earlier generation. In short, much of the late Victorian attack on popular culture consisted merely of the old arguments of rational recreation, slightly modified to fit the new, commercial circumstances. Blatchford's praise of the 'highbred' crowd he saw at Blackpool was a direct manifestation of this demand for older virtues of moral sobriety in the uses of leisure in the face of a perceived massive challenge to them.

Critics around the turn of the century may not have understood the precise nature of the change, but they were at least aware that a change was taking place. Even when they seemed to desire nothing more than the improving recreations advocated by an earlier generation, this should not obscure the fact that they often believed that the capitalist organisation of leisure made such desires more difficult to realise – hence the intensity of the their outrage. Charles Charrington once claimed in a lecture he delivered to the Fabian Society in 1900 that recreation should be organised by the community because 'every attempt to supply public recreation by private enterprise has been ... invariably cheap, tawdry and demoralising.'[76] In a longer version of his talk, Charrington exposed the tremendous profits made by those exploiting the demand for leisure on Bank Holidays, concluding bitterly: 'One of the first discoveries that one makes in studying recreation ... is that whereas individual enterprise often muddles industry, it almost always muddles recreation.'[77]

Whether or not capitalism 'muddled' recreation did not matter to millions of workers who relished the opportunity to enjoy a temporary respite from the drudgery of work. But the more workers attended football matches and music halls, and the more they read the tabloid press and went to working-class resorts, the more socialists feared they would be lost to their own cause. Clearly alarmed by these developments, they complained bitterly about working-class leisure preferences. On the eve of World War I, the London socialist weekly, *The Willesden Call*, cautioned them, arguing that attacks on workers' pastimes damaged workers' self-image and suggesting that the socialist movement ought to take a greater interest in what interested workers.[78] But most socialists seemed unable to focus in depth on the actual mechanics of the leisure industry as part of a shifting ensemble of capitalist social relations and they merely invoked the old moral discourse of rational recreation. Against an array of commercial leisure activities, however, its dictates worked less – even though they appeared to socialists to be needed more.

It is no use suggesting that late Victorian socialists should have read their Frankfurt School reader before the advent of the Frankfurt School – or, better still, that they should have understood their Gramsci before Gramsci began to offer his own thoughts on popular culture. But it is necessary to point out that because socialists couched their analysis in a moral discourse about the individual, their attack on the leisure industry could seldom transcend the 'problem' of the individual and focus instead on the entire apparatus of commercial entertainment. This, as we shall see, had far-reaching repercussions: few workers were willing to stomach once again the same kind of attack on their own leisure preferences that they had encountered before in the work of middle-class do-gooders.

Had they not, in the end, lost faith in the 'people' for being unable to share their vision of rational recreation, socialists might have been able to develop some of the interesting ideas put forward after 1900. In so doing they might have advanced a new critique of the entertainment industry which would not have alienated a large number of workers. As it was, however, whenever socialists attempted to dissect that industry itself it was not long before they gave up, finding it much easier to attack workers for succumbing to its allurements. In an article entitled 'Pleasure', published in 1894, H. W. Hobart tried to make his readers aware of the enormous power exercised over them in the new order of things: 'Those who have a monopoly of pleasure are your enemies. Do not trust them anyhow. Under no conditions put them in that position of domination which means a bridle on your pleasure.' But then he faltered, his imagination failed, and by way of suggesting a solution to the dilemma he had made explicit, Hobart lapsed into the rhetoric of rational recreation: 'Educate yourselves for the enjoyment of rational pleasure, agitate for the opportunities of taking pleasure, and organise yourselves for its final realisation.'[79]

CHAPTER TWO

Utopia
and the education of desire

The 'Leisure Problem' grew in direct proportion to the shortening of working hours and the expansion of the entertainment industry in late Victorian Britain. As we have seen, individuals of varying ideological persuasions responded to that problem by stressing the benefits of rational recreation. This was to be an answer – perhaps the only conceivable answer – to the 'crisis' of working-class culture. Not surprisingly, however, the enthusiasm that the advocates of rational recreation hoped to generate was not forthcoming, largely because their movement failed to develop any appealing scenarios of a transformed popular culture: the 'visionary indulgence' of rational recreation remained 'limited to the occasional invocation of a bowdlerised Merrie England'.[1]

Despite the fact that rational recreation failed in its stated goals, individuals who supported recreational reform continued to search for new weapons which might assist them in their struggle. By the 1880s, most of them realised that they would never succeed if they offered merely recreational alternatives to commercial pursuits: workers themselves had to desire the higher pleasures which accompanied the rational recreations on offer. In their attempt to discover strategies through which that desire could be encouraged, reformers thus began to study the relationship between the social construction of pleasure and the anatomy of desire as a crucial component of individual psychology. This chapter examines the discussion of pleasure and desire in the utopian fiction written by socialists and their enemies prior to World War I. On the one hand, socialists conceived of a total reordering of pleasure in a socialist society; on the other, they hoped that by reading about the pleasures of utopian life workers would begin to desire more pleasure in their own lives. Once awakened, that desire was supposed to lead them to struggle for a society in which genuine pleasure would be abundant.

Advocates of rational recreation claimed that in their own society

43

most workers viewed pleasure as the antithesis of that which was not so pleasurable, namely work. But the activities pursued as an escape from work, they suggested, could hardly be edifying. Many socialists agreed with these claims and in their utopian fiction they attempted to bridge the divide between work and leisure, suggesting that genuine pleasure should be experienced in all aspects of daily life. Moreover, utopian writing was an ideal genre in which they could explore these themes because, as one of its students has claimed, utopian thought offers an image of a world in which work would be pleasurable and the need to escape its demands virtually non-existent.[2]

The ideas of William Morris were central to socialist discussions of pleasure. Reflecting on the commodities available to workers in his own society, Morris claimed that these were mere encumbrances to 'real' work, thought and pleasure,[3] an idea he elaborated in many lectures and in his novel, *News from Nowhere*. But while for Morris a socialist society would avoid the 'Leisure Problem' by making work itself pleasurable, other socialists believed that a reduction of working hours would result in a vast amount of 'empty' time that would need to be filled – often with rational recreation. This concern was expressed in *A Prospectus of Socialism, or, a Glimpse of the Millennium* by William Thompson, in *The Sorcery Shop* by Robert Blatchford and in *The Coming Day: Some Scenes from Life Under Socialism* by Philip Frankford.[4]

In all of these novels socialists explored the connection between work and leisure and discussed the nature of pleasure in a socialist society. Their work also gave rise to a number of anti-utopian novels, such as Edward Herbert's *Newaera: A Socialist Romance* and Ernest Bramah's *The Secret of the League*, which questioned socialist conceptions of pleasure and expressed doubts about the ability of workers to desire the kind of society socialists envisaged.[5] Taken together, these novels suggest that 'pleasure' and 'desire' were central to the debates that took place between 1880 and 1914 about the meaning of popular culture, both in a capitalist society and under socialism.

Longing and performance

'In the beginning', wrote A. L. Morton, 'utopia is an image of desire.'[6] Morton was not the first student of utopian thought to posit some kind of relationship between utopia and desire. Annie Besant, writing in *Justice* in 1890, claimed that images of utopia were important because they rendered vague aspirations definite and pointed to the beauty of an ideal.

In so doing, she suggested, they made the 'man on the omnibus' all the more aware of current social ills, awakening the reader's desire to transform society. Once awakened, she wrote, that desire would propel individuals to struggle for the creation of a new society. As Besant put it, 'longing is halfway to performance'.[7]

Some notion of 'desire' permeated late Victorian socialist thought, although its meaning often remained vague. Moreover, the term has been central to the attempts made more recently to understand both socialist and utopian thought in the nineteenth century. Miguel Abensour, for example, has suggested that around the middle of the century an important change took place in utopian fiction: no longer did writers engage in concrete model-building; instead, they emphasised the importance of elaborating a series of alternative values. In other words, rather than focus on the details of a new social order, utopian thought became more speculative and open-ended, stressing the importance of the 'education of desire', or the cultivation of vague aspirations for a better society. According to Abensour, the new purpose of utopia was to 'teach desire to desire, to desire better, and to desire in a different way'.[8] Both Edward Thompson and Raymond Williams have been influenced by Abensour in their own analysis of the work of Morris. As Thompson has suggested, Morris 'saw it as a task of socialists . . . to help people to find out their wants, to encourage them to want more, to challenge them to want differently, and to envisage a society of the future in which people, freed at last of necessity, might choose between different wants'.[9]

Unlike Thompson, Perry Anderson has expressed numerous reservations about Abensour's work. He has argued that the concept of desire is full of 'metaphysical vacancy', being little more than an 'expression of a dejected post-lapsarian anarchism', a product of the disillusionment that followed the uprisings of 1968.[10] By rejecting the concept, however, Anderson overlooks the extent to which socialists in the late nineteenth century seemed to be obsessed with the problem of desire. It is thus necessary to ask what British socialists meant when they talked about desire; how they related their understanding of desire to their hopes for radical social change; and, finally, how they came to view the reorganisation of leisure as necessary for promoting both the development and the expression of 'correct' desires.

Jane Hume Clapperton, a feminist and a member of the ILP, offered one analysis of desire in her book, *A Vision of the Future* (1904), a popular work in socialist circles. She began her discussion by classifying all desires as primary or secondary. Each and every individual, she

45

suggested, experienced and expressed a desire for food, clothing, shelter, love, work and leisure. These, then, were the primary desires. By contrast, only individuals with some refinement of taste seemed to value the importance of 'cultured intellect', 'high moral and emotional attainments', 'aesthetic tastes' and 'spiritual life'; only a few seemed able to express these secondary desires for the higher pleasures. Inspired by the Fabians, Clapperton demanded a government run by enlightened experts who would be able to teach people how best to cultivate and satisfy their secondary desires.[11]

Clapperton was convinced that no individual was immune from the potential yearnings to satisfy his or her secondary desires. The problem, however, especially amongst workers, was that those desires were often dormant and in need of awakening. Clapperton believed that such an awakening was possible and hence she retained her faith in the improvability of the working class. This was a faith she shared with other socialists. Sidney Webb and Harold Cox, for example, once claimed that the battle fought by the working class for the eight-hour day demonstrated that most workers were at least vaguely aware of their secondary desires for culture and refinement: according to Webb and Cox, their struggle for fewer working hours was implicitly a struggle for the leisure in which they could satisfy those desires.[12] Most socialists, at least in the 1880s and 1890s, believed that workers could become conscious of their secondary desires and thus struggle for the leisure in which higher forms of pleasure might be developed and those desires satisfied. As one writer claimed in *Commonweal*, the organ of the Socialist League, in 1890, 'man is driven to the cultivation of himself, to the endeavour to shape himself in a way that is more desirable.'[13]

The most explicit, albeit indirect, analysis of what Clapperton termed the 'secondary desires' was offered by William Morris. Suggesting that the expression of individual needs and desires was blocked under capitalism, Morris, in *News from Nowhere*, depicted a society in which individual desire for the 'true pleasures of life' could be satisfied with ease. Following the revolution that abolished capitalism and the artificial desires that perpetuated it, the inhabitants of Morris's utopia once again 'found out what they were fit for' and 'work pleasure' grew up 'from a kind of instinct' amongst them.[14] An awareness of blocked desire was at the root of the revolutionary change central to *News from Nowhere*, for capitalism had not entirely extinguished the vision of a better society in which satisfaction of the more important desires could take place: 'I will not say that the people of that time foresaw the life we are leading now', said Hammond in Morris's novel, 'but there was a general instinct amongst them towards the essential part of that life.'[15] For Morris and his disciples, techniques were required to eradicate false consciousness and encourage individuals to become aware of what Clapperton termed their secondary desires or what Morris sometimes called their 'desire for Art'.[16]

'The rest of us', claimed Graham Wallas, 'are merely inventing methods of getting what we desire. William Morris taught us what to desire.'[17] But the process of teaching people what they actually desired, or what they should desire, remained an ambiguous one. At times Morris claimed he was merely awakening desires that already existed. But on other occasions he emphasised the 'feeble conception of the real pleasures of life' held by most workers and he stressed the importance of bringing to 'the mass of people some spirit of expectation, however vague, beyond the needs of the year'.[18] Did the secondary desires merely require cultivation and encouragement, then, or did they first have to be implanted in each individual? Morris usually believed the former to be the case and in this he was more consistent than many of his followers who, in their more pessimistic moments, believed that workers seldom exhibited any desire for genuine pleasure. As Ernest Bevin once wrote, the working class suffered from a 'poverty of desire'.[19] Bevin, moreover, was not alone in his convictions, for many other socialists had expressed similar ideas as early as the 1890s. In that decade Robert Blatchford complained that the 'earnest and efficient desire for the attainment by all of the best that human life can offer' was seldom evident in working-class life, while John Burns was even more adamant: 'The curse of the working class is the fewness of their wants, the poverty of their desires, the overloading of a few sensuous tastes, the absence of a varied set of elevated and healthy desires.'[20]

Morris believed that in his own society any poverty of desire was usually the result of an emerging consumer society which blocked the expression of the innate desire for genuine pleasure. But, as we saw in the last chapter, other critics were less sanguine. They suggested that the promise of immediate gratification offered by the new entrepreneurs of leisure appealed to a vast number of workers who, in seeking ephemeral pleasures, lost any desire they might once have expressed for the higher forms of pleasure. At the Social Science Congress in 1884, William Tuckwell asserted vehemently that the corruption of popular taste by mass entertainment led to the destruction of the desire for the higher pleasures.[21] By the end of the century some writers even began to oppose the building of public libraries, believing it was useless to 'provide for the masses something which they had no strong desire to possess'.[22]

Given this belief in the total eradication – rather than the mere blockage – of the secondary desires, many socialists believed that they should attempt to build those desires from scratch. The Keighley *ILP Journal*, advocating Sunday openings of museums and galleries, claimed, 'we must first create the desire for something better before we can raise any enthusiasm to endeavour to obtain it.'[23] The task socialists set themselves was enormous, although many of them encouraged the development of 'correct' desires fully confident that the results would be worth while. Most of all, they emphasised the importance of education, which would either establish or cultivate those desires they considered valuable. Formal institutions, such as the socialist Sunday schools, were particularly useful: in the process of socialisation they encouraged children to desire a richer life and they suggested how socialism could make that life possible.[24]

While socialist Sunday schools were useful in the education of desire they are also illustrative of socialists' faith in the mechanics of environmental determinism. With roots in the Enlightenment and its clearest nineteenth-century expression in the thought of Robert Owen, environmental determinism held that character was determined by the environment and that only by changing the environment could character itself be changed. At first glance, environmental determinism may seem far removed from our discussion of desire. But because socialists believed that personal desires were a constituent part of the very character that the environment was supposed to shape, they realised that the transformation of desire was related to a broader transformation of the environment. Institutions like Sunday schools were thus perceived as microcosmic environments in which the pernicious effects of capitalist society on the formation of individual character, and hence its component desires, could be thwarted.

Many socialists subscribed to a belief in environmental determinism. In so doing they often refrained from condemning workers for the poverty of their desires and instead attacked the environment which produced such a poverty of aspiration in the first place. Echoing William Morris, the Keighley *ILP Journal* once complained that the very conditions under which most people worked led to their exhaustion, encouraging them to seek a release from toil through the pursuit of commercial pleasures. Those pleasures, however, actively discouraged workers from cultivating their desire for the higher pleasures. Only a total reorganisation of society – a complete change of the environment – would allow the more base desires of the late Victorian worker to be replaced by the forms of desire most cherished by socialists.[25]

Environmental determinism is much more complicated than it first appears to be. If, on the one hand, it is characterised by fatalism (the individual is a mere product of his or her environment), it is also prone to voluntarism (certain individuals have the ability to change that environment). Many socialists were caught in this circular logic. Ben Tillett once claimed that 'good institutions create good desires, as well as right desires create good institutions'; while Dennis Hird wrote: 'Better men made a better world and . . . a better world would make better men.'[26]

Socialists who subscribed to this logic often conceived of their role in terms of the contribution they might make to the creation of 'good institutions'. But their belief that they were themselves in possession of 'good desires' suggests that voluntarism often smacked of elitism: those who could see how character was shaped by the environment and who knew how to alter that environment in order to encourage the development of 'good desires' in others had a special mission to lead those who were less privileged. As Morris wrote in *News from Nowhere*, certain individuals 'worked for the change because they could see further than other people'.[27] These individuals were responsible both for changing the environment which bred desire and for educating individuals to desire to change that environment themselves. This was put quite succinctly by Keighley's ILP paper in 1895: 'The Socialist . . . affirms . . . that to seek to alter the condition, at the same time that you seek to develop the personal character, is the only sure way to bring about "the Kingdom of Heaven upon Earth" for which all . . . so ardently long.'[28]

This passage is particularly interesting in so far as it suggests that not all desires were determined by the environment. Indeed, if they were then individuals might be expected to succumb to the desire for immediate gratification encouraged by the leisure industry. But some individuals seemed to resist that urge and appeared to 'ardently long' for a better world, thus expressing desires which seemed independent of their environment. Ben Tillett believed he had found the solution to this problem when he suggested that we 'adapt to our environment' but that our deep-seated desire for art and true pleasure always prevented us from adapting 'to a bad environment'.[29] This leads us back to Clapperton's notion of the secondary desires being innate and therefore not subject to determination by the environment. On the whole, socialists moved uneasily between their belief that desires were shaped by the environment and their faith in the innate character of the secondary desires. Because this faith was often deep-seated, most socialists tended to stress the importance of the voluntarist, rather than fatalist, aspects of environmental determinism. Until the decade prior to World War I, voluntarism usually triumphed over fatalism and socialists continued to emphasise the need to educate desire.

Central to socialist conceptions of desire was the belief that leisure offered one important site for the cultivation of 'correct' desires. Faith in the principles of environmental determinism thus led socialists to focus on the need both to introduce into present-day society particular pleasures that would encourage the desire for more of them and to work for the society of the future in which such pleasures would be abundant. As James Leatham wrote in 1897, the working class first had to desire the forms of pleasure that would develop under socialism if socialism itself were to be realised. Unfortunately, as things now stood, workers were sadly lacking in the 'intellectual and moral progress' necessary to develop those yearnings. While, he continued, socialists condemned the moral teachers of the people, they should instead assume the role of those moralists, educating recreational desires to desire in new ways.[30]

Robert Blatchford and his brother Montague were also convinced – at least in the 1890s and early 1900s – of the need to educate working-class desire through workers' uses of leisure. Montague once observed that 'while it is somebody's business to see that most of us work effectively, it is not considered to be anybody's business to see that we play equally effectively.'[31] He went on to claim that he had no interest in deciding how other people should amuse themselves, although, these protestations aside, leisure remained for Blatchford and for most other socialists who accepted environmental determinist arguments the site at which character could be reformed, pleasure managed and the desire for socialism encouraged. In short, leisure and desire would work hand in hand – the former in providing the necessary time, the latter the motivation – to develop those pleasures which would both offer a foretaste of socialism and assist in the struggle for its realisation. Morris summed up the whole process: 'The leisure which Socialism above all things aims at obtaining for the worker is also the very thing that breeds desire . . . desire for beauty, for knowledge, for more abundant life. [I]n short . . . leisure and desire are sure to produce art.'[32]

Work, pleasure and utopia

Many socialists considered social life in all its varied aspects to be one of the more accessible features of utopia. Moreover, they hoped that by discussing it in depth they could awaken working-class aspirations for a better society. When Robert Blatchford serialised his own utopian novel, *The Sorcery Shop*, in the *Clarion* in 1907, he claimed that he had written it for purposes of propaganda. Intended as a socialist tract, Blatchford hoped it would 'show what might be done by a united and cultured English people'.[33] One of the novel's reviewers went further, claiming that it might even awaken the innate desire for culture itself: 'If a few million copies of *The Sorcery Shop* could be distributed amongst these ignorant classes, a new light would dawn upon them, and their nobler natures would be aroused.'[34]

Socialists were perhaps aware of the importance of utopian writing because such forms of fiction had played a significant role in their own intellectual development. John Burns claimed that he had purchased a copy of Thomas More's *Utopia* as a child and that it had inspired many of his subsequent views. James Leatham was influenced by the picture of a decentralised society offered by Morris in *News from Nowhere* and this led him to encourage the publication of utopian fiction in the socialist press. Philip Frankford's *The Coming Day* first appeared in the Hudders-field *Worker* in 1908; Edward Bellamy's *Looking Backward* was serialised in the *Halifax and District Labour News* the following year; and Theodore Hertzka's *Freeland* appeared in the same paper in 1912 – all at a time when Leatham either edited those papers or worked closely with their publishers.[35]

Utopian writing was supposed to inspire workers, as it had Burns and Leatham. Some were indeed moved by the vision of the future they encountered in the socialist press. One correspondent to the *Woman Worker*, discussing Blatchford's novel on 'Our Prize Page' of that paper, claimed it offered insights into 'the highest social ideal a people could wish to attain'. This sentiment was shared by many women for whom utopian thought seemed to make a whole new world possible. A reader of Blatchford's *Clarion* wrote to Julia Dawson, the editor of the paper's women's column: 'We have read *News from Nowhere* and also *The Sorcery Shop*, and are filled with a hopeless longing. Might we not have just *one* day of it in reality? Here is a glorious opportunity of showing to a vast audience what socialism really means.'[36] 'Longing', to borrow from Besant, might indeed be 'halfway to performance'.

The portrayal of an ideal socialist society was supposed to

encourage the desire for socialism as nothing else could. Pleasure in such a society would be abundant, conceived of by socialists in terms of a far-reaching transformation not only of Victorian leisure patterns but also of work. But to understand socialist conceptions of pleasure in utopia it is first necessary to summarise their attitudes towards the relationship between work and leisure in their own society.

It was customary in the late nineteenth century to believe that work and play were separate spheres of activity and that the separation of the two had resulted from the experience of a century of industrialisation. Charles Charrington, speaking to the Fabian Society, expressed a widely held belief when he claimed that 'the great productive machines made life uglier and work more dreary; they fixed a sharper division between recreation and industry.'[37] For most critics, the division Charrington discussed was exacerbated by 'deskilling', resulting job dissatisfaction and the manner by which personal fulfilment came to be sought through leisure rather than work. The development of new machinery, the breakdown of traditional craft control, increased specialisation and standardisation in the work process, the lessening of status distinctions between the skilled and semi-skilled – all had enormous repercussions on working-class leisure patterns. Caught between the decline of older, craft-related leisure pursuits and the emergence of a fully developed mass culture, many workers were now confronted by a number of middle-class reformers who thought they knew best how workers could acquire forms of satisfaction from leisure that they no longer seemed to be acquiring from work.[38]

Recent scholarship has tended to play down the significance of deskilling and the routinisation of labour. Mechanisation did not necessarily lead to the loss of skill because new equipment required new forms of technical knowledge. Moreover, while apprenticeship declined in many trades, it developed in others such as shipbuilding, engineering and printing.[39] At the end of the nineteenth century, however, most critics perceived the changes as drastic, believing them to be responsible for transforming the work/leisure relationship. They feared a 'speeding up' of work, part of the 'speeding up' of life in general, and they suggested that this made the cultivation of desire for the higher pleasures more difficult.[40] As Thomas Wright claimed, the mechanic had been replaced by the 'machine-made man' who was 'cribbed, cabined, and confined, alike as to manual skill and intelligent self-resource'. Work had become so monotonous that it destroyed the male worker's ability to understand the entire process of production, thereby robbing him of his inquisitive nature. More important for Wright, once the worker's imaginative and intellectual faculties had been deadened he was left bereft of any desire for recreational pursuits other than those that stimulated the nerves.[41]

In drawing the connection between routinised labour and the reduced capacity for satisfying leisure, Wright was hardly alone. In fact, many social reformers were interested in leisure at the end of the century because they wished to promote recreational activities which might lessen the effects of alienation experienced at work. Liberals, in particular, suggested the need for more facilities for play and relaxation, hoping they might offset the effects of the new work processes: such was the thrust of numerous articles they wrote for the *Contemporary Review* and the *Nineteenth Century*. Conservative critics, by contrast, believed that the palliatives offered by liberals merely led to a desire for more of them, resulting in an undermining of all work discipline. This 'monomania for games', suggested *Blackwood's Edinburgh Magazine* in 1904, 'this modern lunacy', perpetuated the mistaken belief that work is a grievance and play a necessity.[42]

Analysis of the connections that existed between specific work practices and the leisure pursuits workers engaged in became central to late Victorian discussions of popular culture. Samuel Barnett, for example, believed that the recreations offered by the Toynbee Hall settlement would appeal to workers only if they were developed with the workers' interests in mind: hence the importance of studying how workers in various trades used their leisure.[43] Barnett's idea was not a new one, for rational recreation had always been concerned with the recreation of the worker for the tasks to be performed at work. But what was new in the 1880s and 1890s was the extent to which the perception of deskilling gave an added boost both to the study of the relationship between work and leisure and to the search for new recreational pursuits that would broaden workers' horizons. Some writers suggested that the Sunday opening of art galleries would fuel those 'natural and lawful desires' that were slowly being eradicated at work. Others suggested that outdoor recreation might lead to calmness of mind, a condition unattainable in a modern workshop. Still others suggested the necessity of reading, important if the worker 'is not himself to become a mere animated machine'.[44]

Many radicals were less sanguine about the value of such solutions. As the *Progressive Review* asked in 1897: 'Of what use is it to bid a man who has been toiling ten hours a day at some mechanical work to read or to improve himself by some rational amusement?'[45] By suggesting that

53

the degradation of work led workers to desire stimulating pleasures, these writers argued that most attempts at reform were in vain because they failed to address the question of why workers sought such pleasures in the first place. The Fabian, and Durham miner's son, Harry Lowerison believed that if workers demanded 'human conditions' at work desirable forms of play would emerge spontaneously and would not have to be cultivated by those worried about the effects of 'degrading toil' on the industrial workforce. The Aberdeen socialist William Diack also hoped for a transformation of pleasure, to be brought about by the mutual influence of satisfying labour and healthy recreation on each other: the worker's occupation, he wrote, 'must grow more like his recreation, his recreation more like his work. Only artificial pleasure and degrading toil have drawn the present line of demarcation between the two.'[46]

While recognising that palliatives were not enough and that lasting changes in popular culture would require a thorough reorganisation of work, few socialists were able to envisage a reorganised work process. Energies were often swallowed up by the demand of the Eight Hours' Movement for more leisure and were hence deflected from any consideration of work itself. As the *Labour Leader* suggested, one day socialists might be able to 'seize the machine' and change the nature of work, but meanwhile they could only 'endeavour to provide for the victims of the machine healthy interludes in the intervals of their toil'.[47]

By placing the question of work on some future agenda in order to concentrate on the reform of leisure in the present, such suggestions could have been found in many liberal periodicals. But not all socialists shared these sentiments: both Edward Carpenter and John Bruce Glasier believed that it was pointless to talk about the transformation of leisure while skirting the issue of work.[48] Most of all there was William Morris, for whom the 'Leisure Problem' was entirely artificial: it was not so much that empty, afterwork hours needed to be filled but rather that pleasure had to be reintroduced into the very heart of work itself.

Morris remained suspicious of the Eight Hours' Movement because he believed that it failed to address fundamental questions about the work process. As early as 1879 he asked: 'Shall all we can do . . . be to shorten the hours of . . . toil to the utmost, that the hours of leisure may be long and beyond what men used to hope for? [A]nd what then shall we do with the leisure, if we say that all toil is irksome?'[49] For Morris, not only was it impossible for workers to enjoy their leisure under current industrial conditions, but the promise of more leisure was little more than a bribe to induce greater effort at work – hence the need to alter the nature of work itself. Under socialism, he claimed, factories would be transformed, set in grounds large enough for healthy exercise and housing dining halls, libraries and schools which would assist workers comprehend all aspects of production. Factories would also be sites of social gatherings, places where music and dramatic entertainments would be encouraged and where 'all the resources for a refined and well occupied life' would be available.[50]

Despite Morris's suggestion that working hours in such a factory needed to be shorter than they were in his own society, he was most concerned to demonstrate how work under socialism would mark a qualitative break with that of late Victorian Britain. For Morris, genuine pleasure was not to be gained in idle leisure but in work which would offer 'hope of rest, hope of product, hope of pleasure in the work itself; and hope of these also in some abundance and of good quality'. In short, work was to be the source of pleasure, 'pleasure enough for all of us to be conscious of it while we are at work'.[51] Moreover, all of this would only be possible once workers controlled a reintegrated work process; only then would an entire system that encouraged production for profit give way to a new emphasis on the pleasurable production of use values. 'We do most certainly need happiness in our daily work', he wrote, and 'this cannot be if we hand over the whole responsibility of our daily lives to machines and their drivers'.[52]

Most of these themes were developed by Morris in *News from Nowhere*, which to some extent was a refutation of the society of the future envisaged by Edward Bellamy in his novel *Looking Backward*. In Bellamy's society, work would be undertaken by everybody between the ages of twenty-one and forty-five, all regimented by industrial officers under a system of state socialism far removed from Morris's own world of decentralised worker control. Unlike Morris, Bellamy was ambivalent about the pleasures that might actually be derived from work, and he suggested that work would simply be endured by workers, who understood that their desire for pleasure could be satisfied once they had completed their service in the industrial army. Only at the age of forty-five, when 'the physical forces begin to flag', would the worker 'become enfranchised from discipline and control', finally able to enjoy 'ease and agreeable recreation'.[53]

Morris believed that such a future was not worth struggling for and in a review of *Looking Backward* he complained that Bellamy was infatuated with machines simply because he wanted to reduce the hours of work, not transform its nature. Moreover, Morris asserted that while Bellamy could imagine the machinery of the future society he could not envisage the new social relations necessary to make it a happy society in which to live.[54] In his own novel, and in contrast to Bellamy, Morris asserted boldly that the transformation of personal relationships, along with the advent of social ownership, was not only possible but would turn work into a pleasure that most people would be afraid of losing.[55]

Significantly, Morris seldom discussed the organisation of leisure under socialism. He believed that genuine pleasure would somehow emerge spontaneously from each individual's innate desire for it once capitalism, presently responsible for inhibiting the expression of that desire, had been abolished. Like many middle-class observers of late Victorian popular culture, Morris was opposed to the 'hurried and anxious' pleasures which seemed to be a side-product of the degradation of work in his own society. Hence his call for 'an epoch of rest', to borrow from the subtitle of his novel. By focusing on 'rest' as an antidote to the hustle and bustle of late Victorian society, however, and by suggesting that the transformed practice of work would be virtually synonymous with the realm of pleasure, Morris avoided any discussion of the many varieties of pleasure that might actually exist under socialism. For Morris there would be an abundance of leisure in the society of the future and 'real leisure' would allow people to 'appreciate the pleasure of life'.[56] But Morris seldom went beyond such vague pronouncements and it was difficult for him to conceive of pleasure without ultimately returning to a discussion of work: 'And I may say that as to that leisure . . . I should often do some direct good to the community with it, by practicing arts or occupations for my hands or brain which would give pleasure to many of the citizens'.[57]

Morris did suggest that most of the recreations available to the late Victorian worker would disappear under socialism because they were mere substitutes for the pleasures to be derived from transformed practices of work. But if we put aside Morris's originality in his discussion of work, his analysis of leisure remains problematic. First, by focusing primarily on the organisation of work, Morris idealised a mythical past in which pleasure was supposedly derived from work. In so doing he shared with many contemporary social critics the belief that at some point in the past work and leisure had been interconnected to a much greater extent than they actually were. Secondly, although Morris was no backward-looking medievalist, totally rejecting modern machinery, he tended to romanticise the pleasures of a past popular culture. In *News from*

Nowhere, for example, a yearly festival is held in East London to celebrate 'The Clearing of Misery'. The ceremony is inspired by Morris's obvious enthusiasm for past customs and practices, such as the rituals of May Day. Under socialism those rituals have to some extent been infused with new life: there is the popular singing of revolutionary songs; there is communal celebration; and most of all there is fellowship. There is, indeed, pleasure outside of work. But the backward-looking medieval overtones that pervade the description of the celebration are obvious. More important, it is only in these passages that Morris actually deals – explicitly and concretely – with the details of formal, non-work pleasure.[58]

One of his critics has claimed that Morris's novel is merely a 'recreation of a dead past according to a romantically falsified memory', a 'testimony to the poverty of the creative imagination to deal with a living future'.[59] The judgement is too harsh, although, like the advocates of rational recreation, Morris was ultimately bound by a discourse that was unable to offer any scenarios of pleasure that did not rely heavily on images of a bowdlerised Merrie England. It is to his credit that Morris recognised – as no other socialist author of a utopian novel in Britain did – that the transformation of work was the necessary prerequisite for the attainment of 'genuine' pleasure. But once work had been transformed, the question of pleasure still remained. As Marx once wrote: 'The realm of freedom actually begins only where labour which is determined by necessity and mundane considerations ceases. . . . [Work] still remains a realm of necessity. Beyond it begins that development of human energy which is an end in itself, the true realm of freedom.'[60]

Authors of other socialist utopian novels attempted to deal with Marx's 'true realm of freedom', recognising that the transformation of work had to be accompanied by an equally important transformation of leisure. But they could scarcely conceive of that transformation except in terms of revitalised packages of rational recreation. Take, for example, Robert Blatchford's novel, *The Sorcery Shop*. On the surface it is similar to *News from Nowhere*. In both utopias the metropolis has disappeared, Morris's London resolved into its constituent communities, Blatchford's Manchester turned into a peculiar mixture of a garden city and Candleford Green.[61] But here the similarities end. What makes *News from Nowhere* possible, while *The Sorcery Shop* remains, as its subtitle suggests, 'an impossible romance', is 'the change' that leads to the establishment of socialism in Morris's work. In *News from Nowhere* the memory of past struggles and of the awakening of the desire for change gave a certain purpose to the lives of those in the new society. But Blatchford shrugged off the past and unlike Morris was unable to discuss how his utopian society came about, except via the transformation of the individual: 'The change', he wrote, 'is due to the changed ideal of the people.'[62]

In *The Sorcery Shop*, Blatchford discussed the character of the inhabitants of the new society in great detail. In so doing he was compelled to focus on leisure more than Morris had. As we have seen, leisure was, in Blatchford's own day, an important arena in which individual desire could be transformed. While Morris depicted the general contours of the society of the future in order to arouse the desire for it, Blatchford was more interested in studying the effects of recreations in that society on personal character within it. Utopian Manchester thus became for Blatchford a testing ground in which he could explore the social effects of rational recreation, depicting how a 'good' environment would ultimately create 'good' people.

In exploring these themes, Blatchford's novel shares much with other utopian novels written earlier in the nineteenth century. In *The Coming Race* (1871), for example, Edward Bulwer-Lytton envisaged a world in which the promotion of rational recreation was crucial for social harmony. Because their pleasures were so 'innocent', Bulwer-Lytton wrote of the inhabitants of his own utopia, they had 'an effect at once soothing and elevating upon the formation of character and the habits of thought'.[63] For Bulwer-Lytton, as for Blatchford, the cultivation of rational pleasures was important because such pleasures would breed 'correct' desires, thus enhancing the development of 'proper' character.

Rational pleasures were abundant in Blatchford's utopian society. In this it was very much unlike his own society:

> What do the labourers . . . ever see of art or hear of music? In our England the great bulk of the people have no artistic nor intellectual pleasures . . . . For our people there are the most banal music halls, the most fatuous plays, the most egregious novels, the cheapest music; . . . betting and the public house. . . . [T]he majority of our people do not know how to enjoy themselves.[64]

Or at least they did not know how to enjoy themselves in ways of which Blatchford approved. Morris could have written this passage, although unlike Blatchford he believed that an entire system of capitalist social relations blocked the expression of the desire for genuine pleasure: eradicate capitalism and that desire would emerge spontaneously. But Blatchford was less sanguine about human nature and he remained less optimistic about the existence of innate and worthy personal desires. Ultimately he believed that individual transformation was more important than social transformation. He thus took great pains in *The Sorcery Shop* to show how pleasure would be organised in such a way that it would encourage people to enjoy themselves rationally. Leisure remained important for Blatchford because he believed that its correct cultivation was necessary for the development of individuals worthy of his utopian society.

On the question of work Blatchford merely paraphrased Morris: workers need only be employed three or four hours a day in an enjoyable task that would be one of the 'chief amusements' in utopia.[65] But by no means did Blatchford believe that work would be the only amusement, for work alone did not create a truly 'cultured' and 'happy' race. When one of the visitors to Blatchford's Manchester notes that its inhabitants looked refined and intelligent, he is told that 'even the dustmen . . . are perfect gentlemen'.[66] To create perfect gentlemen rather than imagine a society which would liberate individual desire: this, in the final analysis, was Blatchford's task in *The Sorcery Shop*. To this end he prescribed a healthy dose of refined music and dancing, literature and science, games of cricket and football, theatres and festivals, all coherently articulated as part of a systematic programme of rational recreation.

In believing that 'correct' pleasures were necessary for the formation of the utopian character, Blatchford, along with other socialists, suggested that the state should play an important role in making those pleasures available. As Bellamy had suggested in *Looking Backward*, public funds would be used 'on a vast scale' for the recreations of the people because if 'bread is the first necessity of life, recreation is a close second'.[67] If recreations were indeed such a necessity, and if under capitalism they were unable to promote the development of those higher pleasures necessary for the success of socialism, then they were to be taken over and controlled by the state. This theme was developed in at least two socialist utopian novels written in Britain in the early twentieth century: Philip Frankford's *The Coming Day* and William Thompson's *A Prospectus of Socialism*.

Frankford's utopia is even less original than Blatchford's. A political columnist for Huddersfield's *Worker* and for the *Sheffield Guardian* and a pacifist in World War I, Frankford wrote *The Coming Day* for the *Worker*. The society it depicts – located in Croydon, of all places – emerges only after a struggle, the description of which is indebted to Morris. Unlike Morris, however, Frankford took elaborate pains to show how the provision of rational recreation would facilitate the improvement of character through the reshaping of desire. In utopian Croydon people would have 'ample leisure in which they could look a little higher' – in which, in fact, they would be encouraged to look a little higher each time they went to the palm houses, winter gardens, opera houses and other such places of entertainment provided by the municipality and the state. Frankford was quite specific about the social function of these institutions; they would elevate individual character because the recreations they offered would themselves be of an improving kind:

> After having enjoyed some really splendid music for awhile, the trio left the 'Tower Palace' and chartered an electric carriage, and proceeded to visit some of the features of the golden age. These included visits to parks, public gardens, museums, people's palaces and art galleries, where art, no longer trammelled under the foot of commercialism, was seen to have reached a higher level than it had attained ever before.[68]

The provision of opportunities for rational recreation was also important for William Thompson, who considered the promotion of 'correct' pleasures to be a major function of the state in his own blueprint for utopia. Even more than Blatchford or Frankford, Thompson deployed environmental determinist logic in his arguments about leisure, suggesting that the state should promote rational pleasures because an environment full of such pleasures would encourage the development of higher character:

> I hold . . . that if theatres and music halls be properly conducted, and the people educated to understand them, they might be made to stand in the front rank as a highly educating and refining influence among the people. If the people were only taught to look at them in a proper light, and free from all bigotry and prejudice, I cannot doubt that they would see in them sources of great usefulness and influence for good, if properly applied.[69]

The pursuit of rational recreation was thus central to Thompson's vision of a utopian society. In each co-operatively managed housing complex the state would construct a recreation centre. It would also manage outdoor recreation grounds and establish orchestras and theatre companies. At the local level, the municipality would operate the concert halls in which state-sponsored touring companies would perform. Although Thompson granted each community some autonomy in the provision of facilities for recreation, the notion that the state should provide 'every accessory' was central to his conception of leisure in a socialist society.

Thompson's *Prospectus of Socialism*, like *Looking Backward*, is the antithesis of the decentralised world pictured in *News from Nowhere*. Thompson, concerned with the cultivation of 'purity' and 'innocence', conceived of amusements that would be enjoyed under the benevolent gaze of the state, a state which had finally instituted those programmes of rational recreation that had appeared so elusive to many reformers in Britain in the second half of the nineteenth century. While rational recreation largely failed in its appointed task of transforming working-class leisure patterns in late Victorian society, here, in the socialist society of the future, the state promoted rational recreation and thereby guaranteed its success. As we shall see, many socialists called on municipal government in their own society to support those recreational activities that were supplied in abundance by the state in Thompson's utopia.

Thompson's novel is also important for the light it sheds on socialist attitudes towards working-class desire. Certain socialists, best represented by William Morris, were more often than not concerned with the education of desire, with drawing out those innate aspirations for a society in which individual yearnings for the secondary pleasures of life could be satisfied. Other socialists, however, exhibited less faith in human nature. They believed, to return to Bevin's cynical observations, that most workers suffered from a poverty of desire, and they stated that belief forthrightly in the utopian novels they wrote. They argued that workers required guidance from the state, which would henceforth be responsible for nurturing their every recreational whim. Desire, which in Morris's conception of things was to be encouraged, had in the hands of Thompson, and to a lesser extent Blatchford and Frankford, been rendered infantile: desire needed to be interpreted for, not by, the working class.

Anti-utopian fiction and the limits of proletarian desire

Not all socialists believed that utopian writing was useful in the struggle for socialism. E. Belfort Bax, expressing a sentiment shared by many of his colleagues in the SDF, thought that it was futile to attempt to describe the society of the future in any detail. While it might be possible to 'show the lines on which the new principle growing up within . . . [society] is going', wrote Bax in 1891, 'our imagination is quite incapable of envisaging the reality in its final and complete shape'. Writers of socialist utopias, Bax argued, offered merely an inversion – or a parody –

of their own society.[70] Judging by the novels discussed above, Bax might well have been correct: at least in terms of recreation, socialists seemed to focus either on the restoration of a golden past that supposedly had been lost; or on rational pursuits that were antithetical to the recreations of the late Victorian worker. By concerning himself with pleasure broadly defined, Morris is exempt from Bax's critique; other socialists, however, were locked into a particular mode of thought that made it next to impossible for them to conceive of a socialist society without a flowering of those rational recreations that were notably absent in their own society.

Despite Bax's belief that there were genuine difficulties in the very nature of the utopian project, the success of utopian novels as a literary genre around the turn of the century is well documented. Moreover, in the wake of the enormous popularity of Bellamy's *Looking Backward*, both in the USA and Britain, conservative critics became alarmed, fighting back with a number of anti-socialist and anti-utopian novels of their own. Eager to defend capitalism against the perceived menace of socialism, they also focused on the implications of socialists' conceptions of leisure in an ideal society. While most socialists seldom conceived of anything more than the triumph of rational recreation under socialism, their critics believed even that triumph would result in the suppression of personal liberty and the creation of an omnipresent state. As early as 1884 – long before socialism became equated with statism – one utopian novelist, author of *The Socialist Revolution of 1888*, exposed the dangers of a society in which the state regulated the affairs of daily life. Under the auspices of the Prince of Wales, deprived of his property and made Chief Commissioner of Public Pleasure, the state provided a comprehensive programme of recreation that not only undermined personal liberty but raised taxation to an unprecedented level.[71]

Eugene Richter, leader of the Liberal Party in the German Reichstag, also pointed to the weaknesses he believed were inherent in socialist utopian thought in his *Pictures of the Socialist Future*. First translated into English in 1893, the novel was debated in socialist circles and reprinted on several occasions during the following twenty years. The story of a socialist revolution as seen by a disillusioned radical, Richter's novel addressed the 'infraction of our liberties', as its English translator put it, under a regime primarily concerned with encouraging 'correct social conduct'.[72] In a chapter entitled 'Recreations of the People', Richter portrayed a 'well-devised organisation of the people's diversions', part of an attempt to ensure allegiance to the regime by shaping the character of those under its jurisdiction. Richter made it very clear, however, that leisure could be an arena for the formation of character only if individual liberties were ruthlessly suppressed by the state, which in this case sought the means to insure conformity to its dictates.

Like Richter, Ernest Bramah, in his own anti-utopian novel, *The Secret of the League*, feared state regulation of all aspects of life under socialism. Written during the conservative panic that followed the return of a number of Progressive and Labour MPs in the 1906 election, the novel opens during the 1916 election, which results in Labour's replacement by a socialist regime. The new government institutes a number of new taxes in order to fund a welfare state, eventually leading to mounting industrial bankruptcy and the final collapse of the state, unable to pay unemployment benefits to some 1.75 million workers. The enormous growth of the public debt was in part due to lavish expenditure on popular amusements, provided in a calculated attempt to secure the legitimacy of the regime. An 'open-minded Chancellor' in the new government was responsible for restricting interest on privately invested capital in order to direct funds to the state because he was, as Bramah wrote, 'in need of a few millions to spend on free amusements for the working class'.[73]

Bramah mocked such a policy because he believed that workers had no real desire for those amusements the state was bent on providing. In enjoying the leisure made available by the shortening of the working day, workers did not automatically seek to satisfy their desire for the higher pleasures of life, as many socialists imagined they would. On the contrary:

> While wages had remained particularly stationary, the leisure of the working man had been appreciably increased, and it was now being discovered that the working man had no way of passing his leisure except in spending money. Betting and drunkenness had increased in direct ratio to the lengthened hours of enforced idleness, and other disquieting indications of how the time was being spent were brought home to those who moved among the poor.[74]

Echoing this sentiment, Edward Herbert, author of *Newaera* – a parody of Blatchford's work, despite its play on the title of Morris's novel – suggested that in their leisure workers merely wanted to indulge in the luxuries enjoyed by the rich. If, as we saw in the last chapter, some socialists and new liberals feared that a more even distribution of wealth and leisure would encourage conspicuous consumption in the working class, Herbert's novel is testimony to the prevalence of that fear in conservative circles as well. More leisure and more disposable income, Herbert wrote, would merely encourage workers to pursue 'harmful luxuries'; working-class desire would always be expressed as an innate propensity towards dissipation. Even when Herbert described public festivals in *Newaera* – bowdlerised Merrie England days, similar to Frankford's account of the festival to celebrate 'The Emancipation of Humanity and Clearing of the Slums' (itself based on Morris's celebration of 'The Clearing of Misery') – his tone suggested that he believed workers to be incapable of desiring the kinds of festivities that socialists were so eager to promote.[75]

At the root of these anti-utopian sentiments was the belief that workers had no desire for the recreational pursuits cherished by socialists: 'It was useless to point out to workmen the number of gratis enjoyments open to them. They despised them. . . . What they wanted was more money *in their pockets*, to spend as their fancy dictated.'[76] The faith in human rationality that motivated many socialists, along with their belief that a socialist society could in part be brought about by encouraging individual desire for pleasure, was not shared by their critics.

By mapping their own personal desires onto a generalised image of the working class, many socialists convinced themselves that an innate desire for true pleasure existed in each and every individual. Writing about workers in an ideal socialist society, John Bruce Glasier once asked:

> Will they not wish to give a considerable part of their leisure hours to their gardens, to rebuilding, decorating and furnishing their homes, to building public halls for art and science, to working in municipal craft-workshops and scientific laboratories, or to getting up concerts, plays, and other means of education and entertainment? For you do not, I hope, really believe that the citizens in a Socialist community will want to spend one half of the day doing nothing except engaging in idle chatter, loafing at street corners, or watching other people make themselves happy by exercising their energies and abilities at games and other performances – as, alas, so many people do today, knowing no better way to pass the time.[77]

Socialists hoped that workers would devote their leisure hours to such edifying pursuits and it was this hope that fuelled much of their utopian thinking. But many critics of socialism believed that the hope was misplaced. And there were times when socialists themselves – even William Morris – failed to be convinced entirely by their own rhetoric.

CHAPTER THREE

Philanthropy
and the social utility of free time

It was often not enough for socialists to paint a picture of an alternative culture in some distant socialist future. If they feared the commercialisation of leisure for cultivating instincts they wished to see eradicated, they needed actively to encourage the development of recreational activities that would be a source of more desirable forms of behaviour in the present. Exhortation alone was inadequate for the task at hand, for workers needed to be provided with the kinds of cultural activities that would offer them a foretaste of a new, collective existence.

Many philanthropists and social reformers were also opposed to the commercialisation of leisure and they agreed with socialists about the need for immediate action. While Robert Blatchford outlined the contours of a shared, popular culture under socialism in *The Sorcery Shop*, Samuel Barnett prepared the ground for the emergence of a series of new relations between the classes through the cultural activities he developed at Toynbee Hall. Although socialists and philanthropists active in the work of cultural regeneration often viewed each other's efforts with suspicion, they shared a series of assumptions about the importance of 'culture' which resulted in many parallels between their varied efforts at social transformation. It is thus the purpose of this chapter to explore the links that existed between the cultural work of philanthropists and socialists prior to World War I.

Socialists often spoke out against philanthropy. One character in *On the Threshold*, a novel written by the Leeds feminist and socialist Isabella Ford in 1895, claimed 'philanthropy generally means giving away what you don't want, to people who would be much better without it'.[1] Nevertheless, many socialists had themselves been active in philanthropic organisations before joining the socialist movement and they never entirely rejected philanthropy in all its guises. Both Beatrice Webb and Emmeline Pethick-Lawrence became socialists after sensing that philanthropy and well-meaning liberal reform was incapable of dealing with the great social issues confronting late Victorian society. Webb, however, continued to support the work of Samuel Barnett, who, like Webb herself, came to realise that unrestricted and unregulated capitalism was a greater evil than indiscriminate charity. Long after she became suspicious of philanthropy in general, Webb remained supportive of Barnett's efforts to 'raise the condition of the working class'.[2]

Beatrice Webb and Samuel Barnett shared the belief that 'culture', in its broadest sense, could play an important role in the transformation of working-class life. They believed, as did Ben Tillett, that 'culture goes to work and purifies and enriches the mind'. Other socialists shared these sentiments and they welcomed the efforts to provide cultural facilities 'so that every man, woman, and child has places to go to spend a happy evening, and to enjoy art and music'.[3] So important was this kind of work that despite their opposition to philanthropy in general socialists often supported the efforts of a new breed of philanthropists who were themselves interested in the cultural life of the working class.

Philanthropy and popular culture

The reform of popular culture was an important aspect of philanthropic work in the nineteenth century. In the 1830s reformers realised that suppressing what was perceived to be a riotous and seemingly undisciplined popular culture was less effective than offering workers various counter-attractions. As we have seen, the provision of rational recreation was embraced enthusiastically by a large number of philanthropists in that decade. In the 1860s and 1870s, however, when the endemic problem of poverty came to be viewed in terms of the personal and moral failings of the individual, the mere provision of healthy recreational pursuits became less important than mounting a comprehensive effort to 'remoralise' and 'elevate' workers.[4] This meant a totally new approach to the 'problem' of the poor and their recreations, and led to a transformation of Victorian philanthropy. Benjamin Kirkman Gray, a member of the ILP and keen observer of Victorian philanthropy, noted the change that had taken place:

> The early philanthropist attacked particular abuses, and failed to remedy them because he treated them as particular; the modern sociological agitator regards every abuse in its relation to the whole range of social life, that is to say he adopts the method of science. But at the same time scientific method is given practical driving force by the infusion of the philanthropic mood.[5]

Late Victorian philanthropy was often distinguished from its 1830s antecedents by the greater attention it paid to the working-class environment and to the effects of that environment on working-class character. Indiscriminate charity – whether in the form of cash or concerts – dropped from favour as reformers began to sense that such 'gifts' seldom resulted in the noticeable moral 'improvement' of those who received them. For improvement to occur the entire character of the individual needed to be studied and reformed, a task which older forms of philanthropy had failed to pursue. Commenting on the failure of earlier forms of philanthropy, one observer noted in 1895 that there was 'a great deal of unreason and absurdity about the prescriptions of philanthropists for the recreations of the working classes, due to the ignorance of the ordinary conditions of their lives.'[6]

Late Victorian philanthropists were also concerned about the growing threat posed to their efforts by an emerging leisure industry. Beer, in particular, had always frustrated philanthropic attempts at moral regeneration, but in the 1880s and 1890s much discussion focused on how philanthropists might compete with the new cultural entrepreneurs for the recreational souls of the masses. Some writers hoped that philanthropists would engage in direct battle with the leisure industry. Others argued that the products of that industry attracted workers in stable employment and that philanthropy should therefore reach out to those unable to afford what entrepreneurs had to sell. Still others urged philanthropists to teach workers how to differentiate the good from the bad among the many recreational activities on offer.[7]

Although late Victorian philanthropic strategies of cultural intervention differed enormously, those strategies arose from the shared belief that philanthropy should play an active role in shaping and guiding working-class uses of leisure. Philanthropists' hostility to commercial leisure pursuits, coupled with their belief that workers could not resist the appeal of those pursuits, fuelled their desire to intervene directly in working-class life. Moreover, because most of them considered workers incapable of making 'correct' cultural choices, they believed their own efforts were both required and legitimate. Mary Jeune, who organised country holidays for working-class children in the 1890s, suggested there 'must be supervision everywhere', firmly believing in the importance of such a panoptical gaze because, as she put it, there 'is one thing we cannot expect the working-classes to provide for themselves, and that is their amusements'.[8]

Most of these themes – educating workers for leisure, supervising them in its uses, providing alternatives to commercial recreational pursuits – were brought together in the settlement house movement. The leaders of that movement hoped to re-make working-class culture through the cultivation of friendship between workers and their 'superiors' in the settlements themselves. By attempting to modify the whole environment in which recreation was enjoyed, settlement workers played a major role in transforming philanthropic activity in the 1880s and 1890s. The most prominent of them, and one of the most prolific writers on the subject of working-class culture and the social function of recreation in working-class life, was Samuel Barnett, vicar of St Jude's and first warden of Toynbee Hall. Barnett was convinced that the classes had become segregated in their pleasures, and that the poor were developing their own style of life which would eventually render them antagonistic to all established authority.[9] Barnett was also convinced that a complete breakdown of communication between the classes could be prevented only by the establishment of a shared, common culture. Toynbee Hall became for Barnett a place where that culture could, piece by piece, be constructed.

First and foremost, the educated residents of Toynbee Hall would teach workers how to use their leisure correctly. Such knowledge was particularly important because Barnett believed that workers had few of the necessary skills to select the best from the commercial recreational products available to them. As his wife wrote: 'We need some principles to enable us to advise this pleasure-seeking generation what to seek and what to avoid.'[10] The Barnetts also sought to provide those recreational pursuits they most approved of, from art exhibitions to concerts, from country outings to social teas in the settlement itself. In these settings, the 'refined' could mix with the less refined, thereby breaking down social barriers and enabling a process of cultural socialisation to take place.

Even when critics remained sceptical of philanthropists who claimed that their 'concerts for the people' or their country outings served to elevate the working class, they often praised the work of the Barnetts.[11] But not even the Barnetts were immune from the criticism that philanthropy failed to reach those most in need of its efforts. Various writers commented on the limited appeal of philanthropic activity, noting, for example, that the provision of clubs for workers in Bristol failed to attract those who wanted 'excitement other than they can get in such places'; that the People's Concert Society and many working lads' clubs did not reach out to 'the very lowest and most degraded class'; and that, in general, because of the limited success of philanthropy, the 'least worthy' still remained 'a menace to national morality, a . . . danger to rising generations'.[12]

Philanthropists were often unable to reach such individuals because they were unable to compete with the incipient mass culture they feared so much. In order to be popular they needed to offer their wholesome messages in glossy packages. As one observer of the mass-circulation press claimed, philanthropic papers like the *British Workman* were too didactic to appeal to most workers, while the editors of the *Leisure Hour*, published by the Religious Tract Society, knew how to blend entertainment with elevation, securing a wide readership in the process. In order to be successful, those papers aimed at moral elevation 'must be dealt with purely as a matter of business . . . [because no] surer way of missing the object in view could be devised than that of putting such a venture into the forcing-house of a philanthropic society'.[13]

Those who took their philanthropic responsibilities seriously, believing that it was their first duty to guide working-class uses of leisure, were annoyed by the need to compete with the captains of the leisure industry for working-class attention. Arnold Freeman was keenly aware of the dilemma when he wrote his study of working-class youth culture in Birmingham in 1914: 'The tragedy of the Club movement lies in the fact that in so far as it fails to provide amusement it will not attract boys; while in so far as it provides amusement, it is not assisting . . . the moral and mental unfoldment of the boy.'[14] This particular concern continually plagued philanthropists, especially as the new century ushered in a period of rapid growth in the leisure industry. Many of them found it more and more difficult to invade a working-class culture that was consolidating its own rituals and styles of life, often around commercially provided recreational pursuits.

It was not only the increasing appeal of commercial entertainment to workers that prevented philanthropists from being entirely successful in their endeavours. The very attitudes they held concerning the working class and its culture also made their task a difficult one. As George Sims, one of the more astute social observers of the 1880s and 1890s, claimed:

> The well-meaning efforts of societies which have endeavoured to attract the poor to hear countesses fiddle and baronets sing comic songs in temperance halls, have not been crowned with anything like success, for the simple reason that there is an air of charity and goody goody about the schemes, which the poor always regard with suspicion. They want their amusement as a right, not as a favour, and they decline to be patronised.[15]

Socialism and philanthropy

Socialists often had a great deal to say about philanthropy, largely because the boundaries between some of the work of the two movements were never that rigid and because individuals often traversed those boundaries with ease. Usually the journey they made took them from philanthropy to socialism; but the reverse journey was not uncommon. Just as Robert Blatchford became a socialist after reporting on the conditions of life in the slums of Manchester, conditions which philanthropy alone was unable to deal with, so Harry Nevinson found the policies of the SDF too radical and turned his attention to philanthropy and slum work before becoming a journalist for the *Nation*.[16] Moreover, a number of socialists argued that socialism merely extended the work of philanthropy. John Trevor believed that 'Socialism of any worthy sort includes philanthropy, but also goes far nearer to the root of our evils than philanthropy alone can do.'[17] If, for such individuals, philanthropy would not be required under socialism, under present social conditions its efforts were still better than nothing. As Stella Davies wrote of the members of the East Manchester Clarion Cycling Club, most were 'dyed-in-the-wool socialists' who seldom believed that philanthropic activity could alone solve the problems of society, but who were nevertheless pragmatic enough 'to take what [they] can get', as she put it, 'on the road to Socialism'.[18]

In 1896, Julia Dawson, editor of the women's column in the *Clarion*, attempted to assess what that paper's readers thought about philanthropy. She concluded, as did Davies, that while the motives of philanthropists were often suspect, and while education was required to show the poor that capitalism bred poverty, some philanthropic efforts at redressing social grievances were important. But even for Dawson, philanthropy was valuable only as an adjunct to socialist activity. After a lengthy discussion of the topic she posed the question: 'Ought Socialists to take part in any philanthropic work when they are absolutely prohibited from infusing any knowledge of Socialism?' A large number of readers responded to the question, and to her general dismay the 'ayes' won by a small majority of three votes.[19]

Socialists debated the merits of concrete philanthropic endeavours as well. In Bradford, for example, they argued endlessly about whether or not they should support the work of the Bradford branch of the Guild of Help. Established in 1904, the Guild soon became one of the leading organisations to encourage professional social work outside London; to consolidate and rationalise local charitable effort; and to urge the rejection of indiscriminate philanthropy. Working-class involvement in the formation of the Guild was negligible and in 1906 a Labour councillor in Bradford, E. R. Hartley, complained that the Guild was a mere dodge to keep the working class quiet. While Bradford's ILP and socialist paper, the *Forward*, also condemned the work of the Guild, there was a sprinkling of socialists active in the organisation itself, while three of the Guild's district heads were ILP members. One of them roundly attacked Hartley:

> We Socialist members of the Guild know perfectly well that we are dealing with the *effects* of a bad social organisation. In the good time coming the Guild's work will be unnecessary, but the time is not yet, and ... I am not so optimistic as to suppose it will come in my day. Socialist propaganda is good work, and I have always done a fair share of it, but meanwhile, what?[20]

Moderate members of the ILP usually supported the work of the Guild, while more doctrinaire socialists remained suspicious of its efforts. Overall, as Julia Dawson discovered, socialists eager to reject philanthropy in theory often alienated many rank-and-file socialists at the branch level, individuals who were more pragmatic when it came to the concrete work of philanthropy in dealing with social problems. But branch level support for various philanthropic efforts did not prevent socialist journalists from condemning philanthropy in general. As one writer in the *Socialist*, Sunderland's broad-based, ethical socialist paper, claimed in 'A word to philanthropists': 'You treat them as things to be amused, educated, restricted, lectured, advised, to have everything except fair play.' The author went on to assert the need for working-class independence, and claimed that 'we' are working out 'our own salvation', and consequently do not require the 'canting sympathy and foolish patronage' of philanthropists.[21]

This particular line of reasoning was not uncommon, but, as the debate over the Guild of Help suggests, members of the ILP remained especially ambivalent about the relationship between philanthropy and socialism. In the 1890s Keir Hardie saw as one of his missions the moral improvement of the working class, a task central to the work of the 'new' philanthropy. But Hardie also envisaged the ILP as a vanguard within the working class that would educate workers through the example of its members' own efforts at self-improvement. Well-disciplined ILPers, capable of organising others, were supposed to encourage all workers to take an active role in their own material and moral betterment, leading them to the point where they would be able to repudiate the work of well-meaning philanthropists.[22]

The SDF was the most adamant socialist organisation in its rejection of philanthropy. More than any other socialist paper, *Justice* condemned the work of philanthropists in forthright terms.[23] William Morris also put forward some of the most cogent arguments for the rejection of philanthropy. Recalling how he had become a socialist, Morris claimed that it was the 'consciousness of revolution' stirring in society that prevented him from wasting time supporting middle-class schemes to improve the lives of the workers.[24] In an article he wrote for *Justice*, Morris elaborated these ideas. In general, he argued that philanthropy was a palliative that dealt merely with the superficial symptoms of poverty and distress. But he also differentiated between two types of modern philanthropy. First, there was the 'preaching type', characterised by those individuals who gave away small pittances from their vast fortunes while preaching thrift and sobriety: Morris could not stomach these individuals. But there was another group of philanthropists, which Morris held in greater esteem, consisting of hard-working and dedicated people concerned with the great social problems of society. None the less, even these individuals had made up their minds that society could not be altered and thus had to satisfy themselves with the relatively minor changes they could bring about.[25]

Morris believed that workers would be better off when they took charge of their own destiny. But he seldom rejected outright the work of philanthropy in the cultural arena: even while the parks and gardens that philanthropists had managed to procure mostly benefited those with the money and leisure to enjoy them, Morris believed they were worthwhile ventures, although he rejected the ideological premises behind them. He repeatedly claimed that it was useless for philanthropists to try to impart their values to workers through the provision of works of art and literature, for most workers had neither the time, money nor education to appreciate them. Moreover, he also suggested that while the provision of formal cultural institutions was important, it was an inadequate compensation for the richer culture that would grow out of a more radical transformation of society: 'Though public libraries and museums and picture exhibitions are good, . . . if you are tempted to look upon them as substitutes for decent life in the workshop and the home . . . they may become dangerous snares to well-meaning, middle-class philanthropists.'[26]

Other socialists were so committed to the transformation of working-class culture that they tended to be less hostile than Morris to the cultural efforts of various philanthropists. In Sheffield, Edward Carpenter, appalled by the lack of facilities for healthy recreation, called for a 'public benefactor' to come forward and fund the construction of outdoor gymnasia. Likewise, the socialist *Sheffield Guardian* praised the beneficence of the Browning Settlement for lending reproductions of famous nineteenth-century paintings to members of the Working Men's Circulating Picture Gallery. And Arthur Ransom, writing in the Huddersfield *Worker*, called for more parks, recreation grounds and public halls, urging philanthropists to throw their support behind such schemes. Putting things more bluntly, one *Clarion* correspondent wrote: 'As Socialists, we shall welcome every attempt to provide the people with pure and healthy recreation.'[27]

Overall, socialists who wrote about philanthropy usually rejected its attempts to deal with poverty. But they were less hostile to its attempts to provide cultural facilities that would elevate working-class character. The concept of 'elevation' was a tricky one, however, and a relatively recent addition to the philanthropic lexicon. But certainly by the 1890s, the elevation of workers to middle-class standards of culture played an increasingly large role in the ideology of social reform. Moreover, there were some socialists, most notably the more zealous crusaders for the religion of socialism, who were entirely comfortable with the philanthropic rhetoric of elevation. James Leatham, for example, praised the work of the Barnetts at Toynbee Hall and complained that socialists, too involved with propaganda work, should, like the Barnetts, encourage the moral elevation of the working class. Likewise, William Diack claimed that socialism was a gospel of 'lifting up' that entailed the work of moral elevation: 'In these dull prosaic days we hardly realise that art and beauty are in themselves agents for uplifting mankind. They elevate because they purify. They purify because they are pure.'[28]

The *Clarion* was in the forefront of socialist discussions of 'elevation' in the 1890s. Without adopting the rhetoric of elevation endorsed by Leatham or Diack, the paper supported the efforts of philanthropists to offer recreational counter-attractions to drink and the new products of the leisure industry. It praised the efforts of the Sunday League and the National Temperance Café, Restaurants, Concert Hall and Music Hall Association in providing 'abstinence with recreation and sobriety with general amusement'. And it objected to the work of Sabbatarians, firmly establishing itself in the forefront of the battle to increase opportunities for working-class cultural and recreational fulfilment, even if that meant accepting the work of philanthropy.[29]

73

While the *Clarion* responded positively to such practical efforts, it usually rejected the ideology that accompanied them. The paper thus criticised the 'elevators of the people' on several counts. First, it suggested that in their passion for elevation such individuals overlooked the need to transform the environment, a necessary prerequisite for their tasks. Secondly, it argued that because philanthropists were wholly unaware of the conditions of working-class life, they tended to offer activities that most workers merely scoffed at on their way to the music hall or football match.[30] Thirdly, the paper pointed out that most attempts at elevation were in vain because philanthropists failed to provide the necessary education through which workers might appreciate and understand the cultural products they were offered. Finally, when the *Clarion* condemned philanthropists and their attempt to 'elevate the masses', it did so in the belief that the imposition of a common culture from above would, like the products of the leisure industry, prevent workers from advancing by their own efforts. The paper once carried a mock discussion between several wealthy philanthropists in which Cornelius Vanderbilt claimed that the masses could be raised only by men like themselves. This was a proposition the *Clarion* found unacceptable and it suggests that socialists rejected the moral diatribes and condescending attitudes of the 'elevators of the people' even while they found desirable the cultural and recreational monuments that philanthropists offered.[31]

Robert Blatchford set the tone for much of the discussion of 'elevation' that took place in the pages of the *Clarion*. Like other writers for that paper, he was suspicious of middle-class arguments in favour of moral elevation and he offered his own alternative in the form of 'self-culture', an idea he attributed to Samuel Smiles. Culture, for Blatchford, was not something that could be marketed or given away, either by commerce or by philanthropy. Instead, it was a state of being which could be achieved only through self-help: 'He who would get culture', wrote Blatchford, 'must learn self-reliance.' Blatchford thus tended to judge the schemes of the 'elevators of the people' according to his own assessment of whether or not they encouraged self-development.[32] Self-culture, rather than moral elevation, was central to Blatchford's thinking about the work of philanthropy in the cultural arena. While other socialists were less explicit than Blatchford in developing this concept, it nevertheless informed much of their discussion of the cultural work of philanthropists in the 1890s and early 1900s.

74

Elevating the masses

It is difficult to draw a firm line between those philanthropists who in the cultural sphere sought to reshape working-class character and those who encouraged workers to become more active in self-improvement, or self-culture as Blatchford called it. Most philanthropists and settlement house workers fell somewhere between the two extremes: they sought to impose their own wisdom on the worker, while hoping that the worker would be wise enough to use it for his or her own self-improvement. The complexity of philanthropic cultural work in the late nineteenth century was enormous and it prevented socialists from developing any uniform response to the programmes developed. By examining in some detail the complex links forged between socialists and five very different organisations aimed at elevating the masses we might better understand what socialists themselves meant when they spoke of 'elevation'.

Socialists were not alone in their condemnation of Blackpool. That recreation at seaside resorts encouraged hedonistic consumption rather than earnest self-discipline was also noted by a Church of England curate, T. A. Leonard, who offered his own solution to the problem: 'Better than all the whirligig holidays spent by the average north-country toiler at Blackpool . . . is a week spent with nature.'[33] Even before Blackpool became popular with workers, numerous philanthropists had organised country excursions, especially for working-class children. But with the rapid growth of resorts, the perceived need for such ventures grew accordingly. In 1890, William Booth proposed his 'Whitechapel-by-the-Sea', a veritable philanthropic Butlin's, a seaside settlement for the worker who would no longer be tempted by drink and sensational entertainment but who would instead be subjected to endless amounts of rational recreation, improved in a museum complete with 'a panorama and stuffed whale'.[34]

Booth's plans were not very popular with socialists. By contrast, those put forward by Leonard were – largely because Leonard did not advocate a heavy dose of middle-class patronage. Leonard was friendly with Keir Hardie and with the pioneer feminist and socialist lecturer Enid Stacy. He was also a member of the Colne Valley branch of the SDF, and it was in the North West in 1893 that he established his Co-operative Holiday Association (CHA). Urging workers to shun the popular resorts, Leonard encouraged them to provide their own recreation in the rural surroundings of his fellowship homes. The CHA published a magazine, *Comradeship*, which stressed the virtues of co-operative, rather than commercial, recreation: 'The Co-operative Holiday Association exists to apply the principle of co-operation to holiday making and to promote rational enjoyment in a healthy atmosphere.' Most of all, the CHA wanted to reach those who, 'for lack of the knowledge of how to do things better, will . . . fritter away their money and strength over the shoddy delights of some popular seaside town'.[35]

Leonard's work appealed to Robert Blatchford and to John Trevor. Both men shared his commitment to co-operative principles and both offered him space in their newspapers to discuss the CHA. Although Leonard was often disappointed that the workers he hoped to wean from Blackpool never came in great numbers to his holiday homes, he elicited a favourable response from socialists at the branch level. Many of them shared his desire for alternatives to the commercial resorts and the *Rochdale Labour News* enthusiastically advertised Leonard's holidays to its readers as a 'bargain' at a mere sixteen shillings per week.[36] So popular were his homes with readers of the *Clarion* that Leonard even suggested the need for a separate camp for them, hoping that Edward Carpenter might be able to offer hints for the cultivation of 'brotherhood' and simple living and perhaps discover a wealthy landowner who would be willing to back the scheme.[37] We will be returning to the desire felt by many socialists at the branch level to separate themselves from the recreational preferences of the 'masses' later. Meanwhile, it is worth noting that although Leonard's schemes were hardly original, they appealed to socialists who felt that any attempt to provide wholesome recreation – without middle-class cant – was to be welcomed.

Leonard's Co-operative Holiday Association appealed to socialists who were concerned about the phenomenal success of seaside resorts. But because the CHA spoke mostly to artisans who were already attuned to its message of self-help it failed to generate the support Leonard had hoped for. It also failed to offer inexpensive recreations to the slum-dweller. Socialists were thus forced to look elsewhere for schemes aimed at the recreational life of the urban poor. One such scheme was put forward by Stanton Coit. An American who had lived in the slums of New York and lectured for the New York Ethical Society, Coit moved to London, assumed control of the South Place Ethical Society and began to develop his own brand of ethical socialism. Prominent Fabians and their sympathisers, such as Graham Wallas and J. A. Hobson, lectured for Coit, while Ramsay MacDonald served as an ethical propagandist for him. By the turn of the century, Coit was increasingly involved in labour politics, standing as the Labour candidate for Wakefield in the 1906 election.

Like Wallas and Hobson, Coit was interested in working-class uses of leisure. Like them he believed that the shortening of the working day was a mixed blessing: 'The leisure the people now possess is well-nigh all wasted! The devil of anarchy now sweeps over in absolute sovereignty and claims ... the mighty kingdom of the people's leisure.' Coit suggested that an Education Party should be established which would teach workers how to use their leisure wisely and would inspire 'fellowship and democratic effort'. Coit put forward such ideas not because he thought that workers should be elevated to middle-class standards of culture but because he believed that leisure was currently used by workers in ways that robbed them of the desire to exercise control over the course of their own lives. Used correctly, leisure would lift the masses 'out of the ignorance and sordidness which now renders hopeless and friendless the cause of popular government'.[38]

Coit's interest in small-scale, participatory democracy led him to envisage a series of Neighbourhood Guilds that would develop in minia-ture a new order of society within the dominant culture. Each Guild would be the focus for the social life of the community. By drawing people together from several streets in the same neighbourhood, the Guild would serve to overcome the fragmentation of community life that many middle-class observers believed to be the result of the revolution in urban transport and the rise of the leisure industry. Each neighbourhood would have its own guild hall, where individuals could 'meet on the basis of friendship and common interest in the improvement of the conditions of themselves and those around them'. The Guilds would restore the life of the community, thwarting the various temptations that threatened working-class efforts at self-development.[39]

Each Neighbourhood Guild would organise its own recreational activities. Like Leonard's holiday homes, they would be relatively free of middle-class patronage. Coit often spoke out against the cultural endeavours of philanthropists, considering their efforts too moralistic. Most of all, he complained about their emphasis on 'instruction' and 'elevation', calling instead for self-made recreations. Coit argued that 'ordinary philanthropic workers' continued to ' "get up" entertainments for the people', instead of encouraging 'the people to getting up their own entertainments'. Only in settings such as those provided by his Neighbourhood Guilds, Coit claimed, could a genuine popular culture emerge from the rich associational life of the community, one in which

77

locally produced artistic productions would 'present before the people their own deepest struggles and highest aspirations'.[40]

Coit was convinced that community-based organisation was more important than programmes of elevation in contrived environments such as settlement houses. Moreover, he did not view the Guild movement as 'a mere patchwork of the dominant system', but instead considered it to be an anticipation of a new order of society – 'that order which men would still need to create, had the present industrial *régime* been swept away'.[41] Such arguments appealed to socialists who were also concerned with directing the working class away from dependent relationships encouraged by philanthropists. The *Fabian News* claimed that Coit's book, *Neighbourhood Guilds*, 'deserves the careful attention of social reformers and especially of Socialists', while Trevor tried to get the Labour Church to put many of Coit's ideas into practice.[42]

Charles Rowley was not unlike Stanton Coit in his suspicion of organised charity. But while Coit stressed the importance of democratic decision-making, Rowley, in his recreational work in the slums of Ancoats in Manchester, never escaped the didactic concerns that guided most middle-class cultural workers.

Like many settlement workers, Rowley believed that the modern city was a city of strangers, where rich and poor no longer met. It was, moreover, a city in which 'sentimental philanthropy', undertaken by those who believed that charity was a mere branch of social elegance, could not make up for the important social contacts that had once existed. While Rowley thus believed in the importance of bringing 'gentlemen' to live in the slums, he also believed the conditions under which most slum-dwellers existed needed to be improved. A staunch environmental determinist, Rowley claimed: 'If we can succeed in bettering the social condition . . . we may begin to talk about the things which are really worth living for – good health for all, reasonable surroundings . . . reasonable and rational amusements and so on.'[43] Despite the rhetoric, Rowley's schemes often fell short of his self-professed goals and he never received the whole-hearted support from socialists that Coit or Leonard did.

Rowley's efforts to improve the quality of working-class life in Manchester began in the early 1880s, when he established a popular Sunday lecture series, soon followed by rambling and cycle clubs. By the end of the decade, Rowley consolidated these activities under the auspices of the Ancoats Brotherhood, which, through its 'Hall of

Sweetness and Light', as Blatchford called it, and its associated recreational activities, attempted to brighten the lives of the residents of
Ancoats. Rowley claimed that he wanted to keep clear of religion and
merely desired amusement without elevation – 'simple fellowship without fuss or patronage', as he called it. But patronage was never entirely
absent in the Ancoats Brotherhood, for Rowley was convinced that the
working class was in need of culture, defined in middle-class terms.
Rowley suggested that culture was to be brought to the people and he
argued that 'a constant flow of fine quotations in a working- class district'
would somehow benefit its residents.[44]

By the turn of the century, the Ancoats Brotherhood was attracting
some 2,000 individuals per year, each paying a one shilling membership
fee. The recreational and educational activities sponsored by Rowley
were extensive. As early as 1893 there were Sunday morning reading
parties (rather severe gatherings at which Gardiner's *History of England*
was read), a book stall and lending library, a monthly 'At Home' and a
series of Wednesday lectures on 'Civic Life and Civic Duties'. During
the 1893–94 season, several socialists spoke at the Sunday gatherings,
including Ben Tillett ('The ideal we are trying to realise'), Peter Kropot-
kin ('The medieval city') and William Morris ('The dangers of restoration'). It is obvious from this roster of activities that despite his stated
ambivalence towards the idea of elevation, Rowley was as interested in
education as were most settlement house workers: the aim of the Ancoats
Recreation Committee, he once wrote, 'is to give the workers . . . some
taste of the best that has been thought, said, and done'.[45]

Although several socialists spoke in Ancoats, many remained sceptical of Rowley's work. In the 1890s he had alienated Blatchford when he
refused to support Blatchford's campaign for the Manchester Palace of
Varieties. Later, shortly after his 1906 Colne Valley electoral victory,
Victor Grayson lived in Ancoats, strongly resenting the charity work he
encountered there.[46] In commenting on Rowley's work, George
Bernard Shaw claimed that while Rowley attempted to popularise the
finest art of the nineteenth century he had barely managed to hold
together a small band of enthusiasts.[47] Shaw underestimated Rowley's
appeal, but he hit the mark in his assessment of Rowley's goals.

Rowley himself was enthusiastic about the work of many socialists.
He had nothing but admiration for Morris, who spoke in Ancoats on
several occasions; he praised the work of the Clarion Handicraft Guild;
and he lectured at the Labour Church. Moreover, despite Shaw's lack of
enthusiasm, a number of socialists were often as eager as Rowley for the

cultural elevation of the working class and they supported his efforts even while they repudiated the work of elevation undertaken by philanthropists in general. As the *Labour Annual* claimed in 1897, Rowley demanded 'the best in way of art and recreation for the people' and had 'done much to raise the intellectual tone of the workers in Manchester'.[48] The *Labour Prophet* echoed this sentiment, believing that the 'uncompromising socialist' disliked palliatives, but that such an individual 'forgets that before what is hideous can be done away with, the people must in some mysterious way become possessed of a desire for beauty'.[49] Bringing culture to the people was supposed to be one way of inspiring that desire. Unfortunately, neither Rowley nor those socialists who gave him their tentative support knew how to translate the desire for beauty into effective political activity. For them, the connection between middle-class culture and socialist politics indeed remained 'mysterious'.

Earlier in the nineteenth century, the Owenites demanded the provision of halls where workers might 'assemble with their wives and children, to acquire and communicate useful knowledge, and wherein they might have innocent recreation and rational amusement'.[50] Fifty years later, the novelist Walter Besant studied the recreations of workers in the East End of London and concluded that they, too, were in need of halls for amusement and instruction. Like the Owenites, he believed that the required halls should not be the 'tea-and-coffee make-believes set up by the well-meaning'.[51] But while the Owenites wanted their halls to be free of patronage, Besant, despite his opposition to middle-class 'make-believes', thought that workers required guidance in their uses of leisure and that he was ideally suited to provide it.

Walter Besant represents one particular – and not very original – variant of an extensive tradition in middle-class writing about working-class culture. His suggestion that the 'people' had no opportunities for play, nor the knowledge of how to play, was not a new one; while the voice had become more shrill, the sentiment had been around for decades. Each time a reformer claimed that workers had no culture, no opportunity for play, it legitimated that reformer's own plans for overhauling the recreation of the poor. Thus when Besant suggested that the 'young workman cannot play', he meant, like others who spoke about the poor, that he did not play the 'games which the young fellows in the class above him love so passionately'.[52] It was not that workers had no recreations but rather that they had few of which the middle class approved. It was to combat this perceived absence that Walter Besant developed plans for his People's Palace.

In 1882 Besant had written *All Sorts and Conditions of Men*, an important novel for the light it sheds both on his romantic interest in the social problems of the East End and on the way in which he formulated a solution to them. The novel centres on the lives of wealthy individuals who disguised themselves in order to live in the slums, came to some kind of understanding of the extreme monotony of everyday life and planned a Palace of Delight to make life more pleasurable. Knowledge of the actual material basis of poverty was less important in the novel than was an appreciation of the role culture might play in transforming the personal life of the slum dweller. Throughout the work Besant preached self-help, but because he believed in the power of 'culture' to reform the individual, self-help was not to interfere with the more important guidance offered from above. Moreover, as workers could never know what was best for them, Besant not only concocted a particular image of the working class but he also refused to let workers speak for themselves: 'First I drew what I saw; then my sympathy went out towards my models; the next step was to write for them, to speak for them.'[53] As one of his critics has astutely suggested, 'on the one hand, [the novel heralded] the misunderstood virtues of the working man, and on the other [took] away the genuine expression of those virtues'.[54]

Although Besant eagerly championed the idea of a Palace of Delight, it was Edmund Currie, the son of a wealthy gin distiller, along with the trustees of the Beaumont Institute, a philanthropic organisation, that brought his ideas to fruition. The People's Palace finally opened in 1887, offering extensive facilities for recreation, including a concert hall, gymnasium, library, winter garden, art gallery, theatre, reading room and dance hall. The recreations, of course, were to be rational, the music less sensational than that of the music hall, the dance less corrupting than that of the dance hall. The organisers hoped these activities would draw working-class youths off the streets and out of the music halls and would encourage 'the gentler pleasures which create and foster home life'.[55]

The sheer size of the People's Palace, coupled with the scope of its activities, led to an extensive discussion about its value in transforming life in the East End. The Palace was praised by Christian philanthropists, who envisaged an important role for such institutions in combating the attractions of an incipient mass culture. It also appealed to those who saw it as a first step in the development of municipal recreation, particularly after the London County Council began to contribute to its funding.[56] Even Herbert Burrows, opposed in principle to philanthropy, claimed that the Palace was important because it broke down the monopoly on culture enjoyed by the rich and allowed the working class to appreciate 'a little of the sweetness and light which have so long been the almost exclusive possession of the so-called cultured classes'. But Burrows also warned that the work of the Palace was little more than 'social chloroform': music, he wrote, 'is good, but not even the Moonlight Sonata can drown the wailing cries of starving children'. In short, he concluded, 'so long as nothing is done to mend the physical condition of the workers your palaces are really worse than useless'.[57]

Criticism of the Palace was extensive. One writer in the *Clarion* complained that it failed to attract the poorest of workers: 'The real palace is . . . a "some of the People's Palace". It is a palace whose advantages are on the whole only to be enjoyed by a privileged class. . . . I don't think the hundred thousand families existing on a guinea a week get much joy out of it.'[58] Writers for the Socialist League's *Commonweal* were less concerned about the ability of the Palace to reach the very poor, but they were alarmed that in attracting the skilled worker the Palace, like the model dwellings that philanthropists built, attempted to 'buy off' the labour aristocrat and thus push back 'the rising tide of discontent'.[59] Morris also disliked Besant's work:

> All this People's Palace business means that 'the people' are perforce such strangers to orderliness, cleanliness and decency, let alone art and beauty, in their own dwellings, that the upper classes, who force them into this life of degradation, do now and then bethink them if they cannot provide them with a place where they can play at being comfortable so long as they behave like good children, between the spells of their stupid weary work and their miserable and hideous 'homes'.[60]

This brings us back to the question of patronage and control. Besant would have disagreed with Morris's estimation of the motives behind the work of the People's Palace. He had argued that the Palace encouraged self-culture and, moreover, that it was 'to be governed by the people for themselves'.[61] Participatory democracy was at least characteristic of the rhetoric of the Palace: 'Let us . . . never be content until our own bands play our own music: our own singers sing our own songs: our own journal prints our own literature: our own novelists lie upon our own tables: . . . our own artists paint the pictures for our own exhibitions.'[62] To overcome the passivity that worried critics believed was characteristic of working-class life, Besant hoped workers would take an active role in shaping their own popular culture. On paper at least, Besant sounded much like Blatchford:

> Our working people want a public garden for the summer where their own flowers could be shown, where their own bands could play, where their own wives and daughters could dance, where their own choirs could sing. And they want a public hall for the winter, where they could study art and science, hold their own concerts and lectures, hold their own political and social gatherings, and read in their own libraries.[63]

Blatchford was merely reiterating what the Owenites had demanded in the 1830s. In a way, so was Besant. But the urge to improve and to elevate, to propagate middle-class values, never fully escaped him. Those urges were to be found in many socialists as well, although most of them failed to rally behind Besant and his People's Palace, or even to become as enthusiastic about the Palace as they were about Stanton Coit's Neighbourhood Guilds. As Coit had written, the People's Palace only appeared to embody what the Neighbourhood Guilds did embody – a people supplying and managing its own recreation.[64]

George Lansbury, in his much-quoted condemnation of Toynbee Hall, claimed that while settlement houses tried to bridge the gap between the classes with 'smooth words and ambiguous phrases', their greatest accomplishment was the education of settlement house workers for jobs in the government and civil service.[65] But not all settlements were suspect: in West Ham, where Percy Alden organised the Congregationalist Mansfield House settlement, the opposition voiced by Lansbury and his colleagues was muted.

Born in 1865, Alden was educated at Oxford, where he developed an interest in the relationship between religion and social reform. He played a major role in establishing Mansfield House in 1890, served as its warden for the next decade and became increasingly involved in local politics – first as a member of the West Ham Borough Council and later, in 1898, as deputy mayor. He worked with the first labour group to gain a majority on any local council in Britain and he continued to support labour and socialist causes after retiring from settlement work. An executive member of the Fabian Society between 1903 and 1907, Alden was elected as the Liberal/Progressive MP for Tottenham in 1906.

Alden wrote extensively about working-class culture, arguing, as had Walter Besant, that workers suffered from a paucity of wholesome amusement in their lives. In West Ham Alden noted the existence of an extensive street culture, but he believed that it produced little that was positive and much – like the hooligan – that was positively detrimental to working-class advance. Consequently, he believed that the poor needed to be offered rational recreation. As he wrote in 1905:

> The fact is, the working classes, and especially the very poor, need to be treated as children in the matter of amusements. They must be offered healthy and pure excitement. They must have good music given to them constantly. Free concerts, free lectures, free picture exhibitions will gradually make a difference . . . These things must, as far as possible, be brought to their very doors and carried out in no mean and stingy spirit.[66]

Will Reason, the secretary of Mansfield House, agreed with Alden, demanding the provision of those forms of recreation that workers could find neither in their own homes nor in the community at large. Alden, offering his own solution to the problem, called for settlements to engage in positive recreational work by providing a coffee club, a working men's club, a boys' club, a girls' club, choral societies, 'At Homes', Guilds of Play for children, a museum, concerts and a Pleasant Sunday Afternoon society. Eventually, Mansfield House came to provide all of these activities. If, as Alden believed, recreational opportunities in the community were scanty, then the corporate leisure offered in the settlement would more than make up for the lack.[67]

Given their opposition to Walter Besant's schemes for the 'elevation of the people', and given the similarities between the assertions of Besant and Alden, one might assume that socialists would have been as antagonistic to Alden's ideas as they were to Besant's. But Alden's emphasis on elevation was seldom expressed with the same degree of condescension encountered in the writing of those who had less faith in the working class than he did. Most would-be critics remained silent when Alden underestimated workers' propensity for self-improvement or when he complained of the lack of culture in their lives because they realised that his rhetorical emphasis on elevation was only a small part of his overall plan for social change in West Ham. For Alden, elevation always needed to be accompanied by more radical social reform.

Alden's ties with the labour movement were numerous and his support for socialist aspirations always genuine. He worked for Hardie's election campaign in the parliamentary constituency of West Ham South in 1892 and later backed Hardie's call for the establishment of local unemployment relief committees at a hearing of a House of Commons committee on unemployment in 1895. As the warden of Mansfield House, Alden made it the policy of the settlement to support all labour and socialist candidates in local elections and he played a central role in holding together the trade union/socialist alliance that was responsible for capturing the Borough Council in 1898. As early as 1895, when he paid a visit to Bradford, his ideas were considered 'startlingly Socialistic' by the *Bradford Labour Echo*. The paper praised both Alden and Reason and considered the work done at Mansfield House central to the cause of the labour movement in general.[68]

Largely because he played such an important role in local radical politics, Alden encountered a socialist movement favourably disposed to his settlement work. Moreover, Mansfield House offered socialists a forum in which they could address workers in West Ham. At various times, Will Crooks, Will Thorne, Herbert Burrows, G. B. Shaw and Edward Carpenter spoke at Alden's settlement, while the local branch of the ILP distributed copies of the *Mansfield House Magazine*. Other socialists came to many of their ideas through their contact with Alden. Frederick Pethick Lawrence, for example, met Alden at Cambridge and was convinced to work for Alden in West Ham, where he expanded the recreational facilities of Mansfield House, eventually becoming the settlement's treasurer. It was at Mansfield House that Pethick Lawrence met his future wife and became more involved in labour politics. When the Pethick Lawrences went on to become radical journalists, establishing both socialist and suffragette periodicals, they remained in close contact with Alden, who wrote for their publications.[69]

Alden, as a moral reformer, was thus acceptable to socialists because he also demanded widespread social reform, campaigning with labour and for labour's causes. Moreover, socialists seldom condemned Alden's work of moral regeneration outright because they believed that such work was useful in preparing the way for widespread participation in radical movements. On the other hand, those individuals who merely offered large doses of moral regeneration without any corresponding commitment to societal change were rejected by socialists for suggesting palliatives to prop up the system rather than the inspiration to change it. While socialists may have attacked the cultural missionary work of philanthropists and settlement house workers in general, their attitude always remained a pragmatic one: not only were they often willing to work for the immediate benefits such work might bestow on the working class but they also shared with those they often criticised the belief that the transformation of the individual was a necessary prerequisite for wider social change.

The Labour Church as philanthropist

When a flood struck Bristol in the 1880s, Helena Born and Miriam Daniell, two well-educated, middle-class members of the Bristol Socialist Society, went to help relieve the suffering. In a period when 'slumming' was fashionable, Born and Daniell moved into a working-class district of Bristol and attempted to organise its inhabitants. As one of their admirers wrote: 'Not in the guise of charity, but as co-workers, anxious to be of service, they sought to win the hearts of their less fortunate brothers and sisters.'[70] Although Born and Daniell rejected the suggestion that they were mere charity workers, much of their activity would have been familiar to less radical slum workers. On the whole, when socialists engaged in charity work they could seldom escape the ideological implications of such work. This was particularly true in the case of the Labour Church. In the 1890s, members of that organisation repudiated the efforts of many middle-class philanthropists and argued that socialists should assume the control of charity and break their ties with non-socialist, middle-class patronage. But could one be a philanthropist and a socialist? In undertaking the work of charity, the Labour Church often found its socialist gospel subject to dilution.

By the time Trevor decided that workers needed their own church, other churches were undertaking charity work in general and the provision of recreation in particular. As early as the 1870s, they felt the need to compete for the leisure time and income of the masses, often by becoming as entertaining as their competitors. It was no longer enough simply to attack the enemies of religious attendance: as the *Congregationalist* warned in 1879, 'We must offer recreative substitutes for that which we condemn.'[71] A large number of substitutes were offered and by the 1890s most churches had made some effort to stem the tide of commercial entertainment. The Church of England's Band of Hope provided uplifting recreations for the young, enjoying the support of over three million members by the end of the century. The Methodists also began to compete with commerce – and increasingly with rival sects – for the free time of the masses, leading one historian to refer to this process as the 'metamorphosis of religious act into entertainment'.[72]

In the 1880s John Trevor, who was raised as a Baptist and later converted to Unitarianism, was influenced by these developments. In 1890 he assumed control of the social and community work undertaken by a small chapel in a poor district of Manchester, where, after encountering Stanton Coit's plan for Neighbourhood Guilds, he began to repudiate the ideology that often accompanied the charity work undertaken by the more traditional churches. Not that he was opposed to the work of ameliorating conditions in the slums, nor even of elevating the character of those who dwelled in them. But for Trevor this was to be a political task: 'Somehow, the life of the people must be raised; and I believe that Politics must be the way.'[73]

If politics were to be the answer, traditional religion – and the kind of social work it increasingly generated – had to be rejected. Dubious of the efforts of the Pleasant Sunday Afternoon movement, Trevor disliked the condescending attitudes that seemed to him to be held by church leaders concerned with social and moral improvement. By the time Trevor considered establishing a Labour Church he had come to reject the philanthropy of the churches and had begun to suggest the need for working-class self-determination. In his autobiography he later speculated on the relationship between class, religion and philanthropy:

> I see very clearly that the whole Labour Movement is badly in need of the service of those who have had such advantages in life as are denied to the working man. What has hitherto made such service so objectionable, and even revolting, has been the element of patronage and leadership in it. All this must be given up. The superior person who goes to the East End to make the East Ender like himself is a mistake. . . . I think we reach to a higher level of service when we leave the working man to organise himself, and simply give such personal help as we can, without in the least lessening his independence and freedom.[74]

But what did it mean to 'leave the working man to organise himself' while still offering him help? Trevor sought the answer in a church where workers could chart their own destiny, occasionally assisted by middle-class sympathisers. Such a church would promote working-class self-help and would develop the spirit of egalitarianism and mutuality that was central to the religion of socialism. Important in this process was the development of recreational and cultural programmes. To some extent such programmes parallelled those developed by the other churches: all religious bodies, including Trevor's, designed recreations to compete with the attractions of an emerging mass culture. But Trevor hoped that his own recreational fare would also help workers in their quest to assert full control over their own lives, and he viewed the Labour Church as 'an intellectual, moral and religious school for the training of our highest faculties'.[75]

Resentful of patronage, Labour Church activists began to assume control of philanthropic activity themselves. The Manchester and Salford branch of the Church, for example, established a missionary class in which its members might learn about the kind of work they should undertake. Before long, however, the Labour Church seemed to be most supportive of the work of the Cinderella clubs, originally established by Robert Blatchford. The idea behind these clubs was simple: socialists would feed and entertain working-class children, offering their own 'truths' in order to counter the value-laden didacticism that characterised the charity work of the established churches. Entertainment at the Cinderellas was to be free of politics, or at least from the ideology implicit in middle-class charity. Politics, however, was never far removed from the process of entertaining and feeding impoverished children: 'Cinderella has been fed and clothed and entertained, and now she has been taken to church. Next she is to go to school . . . where she will be taught our principles.'[76]

Despite such assertions, many of those who were committed to the work of the Cinderella clubs soon found themselves engaged in traditional kinds of charity work, for which they felt they needed to apologise. In Rotherham, for example, the club attempted to justify its feeding and entertaining of 2,590 children by arguing that 'our main work as socialists is to abolish the need for charity by establishing a system of justice for the workers, and making it the duty of the State to care for the sick and the needy'. Meanwhile, in the absence of such a society, the work of the Cinderellas was viewed in Rotherham as important socialist activity.[77] Many Cinderella supporters thus viewed the work of the clubs to be one, and only one, of the many activities they undertook as committed socialists. But other socialists, particularly members of the SDF, felt that the clubs absorbed much of the energy that should have been devoted to those forms of political activity necessary for the realisation of a socialist society that would render all charity unnecessary.

Blatchford and Trevor might have convinced themselves that Cinderella work advanced the cause of socialism, that it was important political work because it offered children food and entertainment – and lessons in socialism. But it cost money to feed and entertain the poor and in attempting to raise the funds necessary for the work of the Cinderellas, labour leaders often turned to individuals who were less enthusiastic about the principles of socialism than they were. By 1913 the Earl and Countess of Derby, the Lord Mayors of Manchester and Salford and five MPs were all patrons of the Manchester Cinderella Club. Increasingly, club organisers were urged to tone down or eradicate the expression of socialist sentiments at their gatherings for fear of offending those in control of the purse strings.[78] While standard interpretations of the

Labour Church suggest that the organisation redirected energy from religion to politics, that it assisted individuals in their passage from a nonconformist, liberal radicalism to the Labour Party,[79] those individuals often brought with them a faith in charity and philanthropy that had been disseminated by the traditional churches. So widespread was that faith that many Cinderella workers remained torn between their desire to see a society where the efforts of philanthropy would not be required, and their belief that it was unrealistic to expect slum-dwellers to help themselves without the assistance not only of those who embraced their cause but also of those wealthy individuals who had always given generously to philanthropic causes.

Charity bazaars and socialism in Halifax

The elevation of the masses was a costly business. Sometimes wealthy philanthropists would come forward, offering their backing for a new public library or an addition to an art gallery or museum. When the proposed schemes were less grandiose, however, funding was often generated by holding fairs, festivals and bazaars: not only could such events raise money for the necessary work of elevation but they could also offer wholesome and improving entertainment. Moreover, such work was considered fit work for women. As one observer wrote: 'ordering, beautifying, and elevating the commonweal' was the special preserve of women.[80] Middle-class women discovered a lifetime of activity in 'getting up' the entertainments offered at such gatherings, playing an indispensable role both in the work of elevation and in raising the funds that made such work possible.

By the end of the century many socialists began to realise that they could adapt charitable fund-raising techniques to their own uses. In need of cash to pay for speakers, publicity, political campaigns and a growing radical press, socialist organisations were constantly in need of new sources of income. This was particularly true of the ILP in the 1890s; although many branches received support from local unions, substantial union backing of the Party was to emerge only later in its history. Socialist organisations thus relied on the generosity of a number of wealthy supporters. The Countess of Warwick, for example, eagerly bestowed her patronage on the *Clarion* propaganda vans in the 1890s. By 1911 she was also the largest single shareholder in the Twentieth Century Press, the SDF's publishing company.[81] But wealthy sponsors alone were often unable to provide the necessary funds for activities at the branch level. The movement thus adopted the charity bazaar and the provision of recreational extravaganzas as a popular way of raising funds.

By the 1890s most socialist organisations engaged in such fundraising activities. In 1895 the ILP held a bazaar – for 'pleasure and profit' – to raise funds for Fred Brocklehurst's campaign expenses.[82] That same year the local branches of the ILP, Fabian Society, SDF and Clarion Scouts joined forces in Liverpool, sponsoring a 'Merrie England Fayre and Arts and Crafts Exhibition', the proceeds of which would fund the Cinderella club, help finance the campaigns of local labour leaders and support the establishment of a local socialist newspaper. But the fair, like those sponsored by less-radical organisations, also offered entertainment. Believing 'that we should share our pleasures with those whose lives are not so bright as our own', its promoters set out to develop a series of edifying and wholesome amusements that ranged from lectures and concerts to a 'Cavern of Mysteries' and a 'Grand Shooting Jungle'.[83]

The financial records of the Halifax branch of the ILP offer valuable information about the increasing importance of such activities for the raising of funds for socialist causes in that town.[84] In 1894, the ILP sponsored the 'Merrie England bazaar and village' on the estate of the fifteenth-century manor of John Lister, the wealthy philanthropist and recent convert to socialism who served as the first treasurer of the national ILP. The success of the venture was attested to by its earnings, which amounted to over £100 on the first day alone and almost three times that by the time it was over. Not only did it raise badly needed funds for the ILP but it also provided a 'genuine picture of genuine socialism': 'Here, in Halifax, at the ILP Bazaar', wrote the *Clarion*, 'we have lived and moved in "Merrie England", and it is well with us.'[85] As in most bazaar work, women were responsible for organising the activities even though men presided over the opening ceremonies. Katharine Bruce Glasier praised the work done by socialists' wives in Halifax and suggested that women in other towns might engage in similar work for the cause of socialism.[86]

An examination of the annual balance sheets of the Halifax ILP (Table 3.1) suggests that such income-generating schemes were increasingly important for the financial success of the local ILP. In 1896, roughly 4 per cent of the ILP's total gross income came from the provision of bazaars, concerts and socials. The rest came from subscriptions – both from individuals and unions. The following year income raised through entertainment had climbed to 35 per cent of total income and by 1899 it stood at 55 per cent. Moreover, while income from

Table 3.1 *Halifax ILP, annual income*

	Year ending 31/1/1897			Year ending 31/1/1898			Year ending 31/1/1900		
	£	s	d	£	s	d	£	s	d
Income from entertainments									
Swimming club					3	0			
Gala				7	5	9			
May Day festival	4	2	2	6	14	5	39	7	5½
General entertainment							55	10	0
Clarion lantern show		12	9						
Clarion Vocal Union	1	6	4						
Sports day							101	10	5
Brotherhood tea party								13	6
Kingston social							3	0	11
Total	6	1	3	69	13	2	144	12	3½
Income in general									
Subscriptions	141	6	4	128	0	0	116	12	2
Entertainments	6	1	3	69	13	2	144	12	3½
Total	147	7	7	197	13	2	261	4	5½

Source: ILP directories, Halifax branch, annual report and balance sheets.

subscriptions declined slightly during the period, that from entertainment grew almost twenty-four-fold. Most of the additional income came not from small gatherings and concerts but from highly organised and publicised events such as May Day festivals or sports days: the 1899 sports day was alone responsible for more than one-third of ILP-reported income that year.

These figures point to the enormous importance of organised entertainments for the ILP. But they are also misleading because they do not take into consideration the expenses involved in staging such entertainments in the first place. Waxing lyrical about the 1894 bazaar, the *Clarion* claimed that the amusements were 'got up, managed, and executed by working people'.[87] But this was hardly the case. Throughout the 1890s, performers were often hired to provide entertainment at ILP functions and despite Lister's generosity in offering the use of his estate for the ILP's social events, private halls were also rented. While the May Day festivities in 1899, for example, were responsible for almost one-third of ILP entertainment-related gross income that year, the cost of providing those festivities was extensive (Table 3.2). The sale of ILP badges and refreshments was quite profitable, but were it not for the considerable amount raised through collections, the ILP would not have

Table 3.2 *Halifax May Day celebration, 1899*

	Income			Expenditure		
Social						
Tickets	£9	9s	3d			
Cloak room		4s	11d			
Refreshments	£1	4s	9½d		11s	3d
Hall rental				£2	2s	0d
Piano rental					10s	6d
Musicians					12s	0d
John Hunt					7s	8d
Soap						1d
Total	£10	18s	11½d	£4	3s	6d
Other activities						
Badges	£7	14s	10d	£3	15s	0d
Collections	£20	4s	8d			
Advertising		9s	0d		7s	0d
Hall rental				£1	5s	0d
Printing & posting				£4	8s	0d
Band rental				£7	0s	0d
Speakers				£5	5s	0d
Miscellaneous				£1	11s	5d
Total	£28	8s	6d	£23	11s	5d
Total profits*	£11	12s	6½d			

* Income minus expenditure from the social and other activities

Source: Account book of the ILP (Halifax) and socialist hall, pp. 9–10.

been able to afford the cost of hiring a public hall or the musicians who performed in it. Of the expenses incurred for the 1899 May Day celebrations, roughly 50 per cent went into the pockets of local entrepreneurs.

Many orchestras and bands prospered by offering their services to charity bazaars and political rallies. Given the fact that the established parties were also coming to recognise the importance of entertainment in their political campaigns, it was not uncommon for such groups to perform at a socialist gathering one day and a Conservative Party function the next. It was also not uncommon for the proprietors of public halls to refuse permission to socialists who wanted to use them for their gatherings. The rapid growth of the labour movement in West Ham scared many middle-class residents, who refused to allow radical groups to meet in their halls. While Percy Alden occasionally provided them with a meeting place at Mansfield House, a longer term solution was needed and a consortium of socialists and union leaders formed a company to build their own hall. In Halifax, the ILP was luckier, not only because of Lister's enthusiasm for its work but also because it could rent the Mechanics' Hall. But, as the statistics for the 1899 May Day celebration suggest, rental costs could still be exorbitant. In 1898 James Parker, the secretary of the Halifax ILP and a local town councillor, suggested that the *Clarion* should establish a nationwide fund for the construction of socialist halls.[88] Nothing came of the plan, but subscriptions were taken out for a hall in Halifax, which, when completed, generated income from the social activities it offered and from the rent it charged to the Clarion Vocal Union, the ILP café, the ILP Women's Group and other groups and private parties that used it.

Table 3.3 *Halifax ILP, profits from selected social activities*

Date/ Activity	Expenditure			Income			Profit			Profit as % of income
										%
1894/Bazaar							£300*			
1896/May Day				£4	2s	2d				
1897/May Day				£6	14s	5d				
1898/Bazaar	£93	0s	5½d	£489	5s	2d	£396	4s	8½d	81
1899/May Day	£27	14s	11d	£39	7s	5½d	£11	12s	6½d	30
1899/Sports	£77	4s	9d	£101	10s	5d	£24	5s	8d	24
1901/Bazaar	£83	11s	2d	£520	1s	6d	£436	10s	4d	84
1904/Sports	£107	7s	5d	£115	18s	7d	£8	11s	2d	7
1906/Tea	£3	12s	0d	£42	8s	6d	£38	16s	6d	91

* Approximate amount, estimated by *Clarion* reporters.

Sources: Clarion, 13 October 1894, p. 7; 26 November 1898, p. 381; 16 November 1901, p. 3; Halifax ILP account book, pp. 3, 13, 101–2, 117–18; account book of the ILP and socialist hall, pp. 9–10; annual report and balance sheets, 1900.

'Getting up' entertainments became big business and any entrepreneur in the leisure industry would have appreciated the sophisticated business acumen of the ILP pioneers. Certain activities, however, were more profitable than others (Table 3.3). May Days, for example, never seemed to yield as much gross income as sports days did. But the expenditure required to organise a successful sports day could be considerable. Thus, while the ILP balance sheet for the year ending 31 January 1900 shows that the income from the 1899 sports day accounted for well over one-third of that year's gross receipts, only 24 per cent was clear profit. By contrast, not only were bazaars responsible for a much higher gross income but the profit margin on that income was considerably greater than that of any other ILP-sponsored entertainment. Thus by the turn of the century the Halifax ILP bazaar had come to play a prominent role in the finances of the local socialist movement. Montague Blatchford wrote of the 1901 bazaar, opened by Keir Hardie, that there were 'two essentials' to a good bazaar, 'capable and untiring business management, and an artistic idea consistently carried out'.[89] Halifax seemed short of neither.

Enormous efforts were required to make bazaars, sports days and May Day festivities a financial success. Moreover, although the profit they generated was originally meant to fund the political work of the labour and socialist movement, increasingly it was swallowed up by the growing cost of providing those ancillary materials and services that allowed them to be successful in the first place. By constructing its own socialist hall, for example, the ILP in Halifax could dispense with the need to pay rent to the municipality or to a capitalist landlord. But in the short term the Party found itself saddled with enormous mortgage payments. And even if capitalist creditors could be dispensed with, socialist sympathisers could not. Although John Lister made no charge for the use of his estate, and although he never demanded repayment of many of the 'loans' he made to the Halifax ILP, the Party felt some obligation to repay him from the profits it made on its bazaars and related work.

ILP fund-raising activities, then, began to take on a life of their own and much of the profit they realised was plunged back into making them more elaborate and more independent of outside patronage and supervision. Like the Owenites two generations earlier, late nineteenth-century socialists wanted to be in full control of the activities they offered. But the socialist movement had to function within a capitalist society, and while it attempted to carve out a space in that society in order to develop an active branch life, it often reproduced many values of the dominant culture itself. As the socialist and feminist journalist Dora B. Montefiore wrote, socialists ought to oppose bazaars because they perpetuated the very aspects of capitalist exploitation that the movement so adamantly rejected: 'For Socialists and trade unionists to make profit out of unpaid labour which competes unfairly with paid labour is to show that they have not grasped in detail the principles for which they stand.' Montefiore also noted that bazaar work, while it drew many women into the socialist movement, seldom challenged traditional gender roles.

Rather than encouraging middle-class women to question their relationship to men in the struggle for socialism, male socialists merely urged them to continue providing the kind of services they had offered charities for decades. In short, Montefiore believed that bazaar work exploited women for the political advancement of men.[90]

Entertainment, originally seen as a means to an end, had, by 1900, often become an end in itself. Sometimes socialists justified their emphasis on making recreation a fund-raising activity by claiming that the entertainments they provided gave workers a foretaste of socialism. While the philanthropist and the socialist wanted the working class to benefit from the recreational activities they offered, the ends they had in mind differed enormously: the former often wanted to secure the status quo, to elevate workers to middle-class standards of taste in order to prevent social disorder; the latter wanted to prepare the ground for a new socialist culture by elevating workers so they could see the necessity of further developing that culture and hence begin to struggle for its realisation.[91]

Socialists opposed to various middle-class schemes for the 'elevation of the masses' began to recognise that class played a significant role in determining the distribution of knowledge in society, that a particular group's position within the social structure in part determined the extent to which it had access to 'culture', broadly defined. Through their settlement house 'At Homes' and related endeavours, philanthropists offered workers access to those cultural pursuits from which they had been excluded, albeit only as subordinate partners. Socialists rejected this work because they rejected subordination in general and because they realised that the relative position of workers in the class structure meant that they were at a disadvantage intellectually when confronted with the various schemes for their own elevation. They also realised that a genuine culture, germane to the life of the working class, had to be developed within the ranks of that class and could not be imposed by others operating with vastly different motives. To paraphrase the anthropologist Marcel Mauss, they concluded that the gift of culture wounded those who received it by undermining efforts at 'self-culture'.

One writer has suggested that the 'goal of a socialist welfare state must be . . . not to end the need for help, for there is no end to that, but to involve the needy in mutual help'.[92] In terms of their attitudes to moral reform, socialists in Britain prior to 1914 might have rephrased this statement: 'The goal is not to end the need for elevation, for socialism cannot be brought about without it, but to involve workers in their own mutual self-improvement.' Socialists thus supported philanthropic programmes that encouraged workers to advance by their own efforts. While they rejected the patronising attitudes of Walter Besant and his People's Palace, they praised the Neighbourhood Guilds proposed by Stanton Coit. Most of all, they praised Percy Alden for establishing a working men's club where 'respectable' workers could associate to make their own recreation.[93]

But what of the workers who were not so respectable in socialist eyes; those who failed to venture forth on a co-operative holiday and remained content with the pleasures sold them in the marketplace? While socialists often repudiated the intentions of philanthropists who wished to elevate workers to middle-class standards of culture, and while they stressed the need for working-class self-help, the work of elevation was too important to be left to workers themselves. Sadly, too many workers seemed impervious not only to the call of philanthropy but also to the call of socialism.

ILLUSTRATIONS A pictorial essay

I Spreading the word The ideas that led to the establishment of socialist propaganda vans came from Julia Dawson, editor of the women's column in the *Clarion*, who wanted to bring the socialist message to isolated rural districts. Sometimes they were well received. But on more than one occasion those who staffed them complained about the coarse manners of the workers they encountered. Joining a *Clarion* van, John Bruce Glasier once wrote in his diary, 'Evening meeting much disturbed by drunk men. Am shocked by the filthiness of their remarks.' Perhaps the vans were most valuable in providing the women who often accompanied them with useful experience in public speaking and organising.

1 The Clarion propaganda van, *c.*1898.

II The late Victorian leisure industry According to the *Clarion's* music critic, Georgia Pearce, 'A holiday should be a pause time, a breaking off to think.' When, however, socialists turned from the ideal holiday to the realities of late Victorian and Edwardian working-class holidaymaking they concluded that most workers were motivated by values that were vastly different from those cherished by Pearce: Blackpool, wrote Katharine Bruce Glasier, was full of 'unrest and fevered energy'. Hence they remained ambivalent about the 'holiday mania' of the period. While they were staunchly opposed to the work ethic and the bourgeois ideology of thrift, they were also critical of the new forms of consumer hedonism that appeared to them to be encouraged by entrepreneurs at resorts like Blackpool. Philip Snowden once remarked that workers cannot 'see others taking a holiday . . . to the seaside without desiring to do the same', and socialists in general wondered whether or not the 'holiday mania' might undermine the moral discipline necessary for the realisation of socialism.

2 'The Old Thrift and the New', cartoon from the *Labour Leader*, 23 September 1910, p. 1. 'Following the recent speech by Lord Rosebery, in which he deplored the general absence of "thrift", the Comptroller of the Post Office Savings Bank stated that "people nowadays save for the fine day, rather than for the rainy day".'   *facing* 3 The sands, Blackpool, early 1900s.

THE SANDS, BLACKPOOL.

4 May Day festivities, Rochdale area, early 1900s.

5 Walter Crane, 'The First of May', 1881.

III The transformation of public rituals In their attempts to develop an alternative culture, socialists often harnessed traditional festivities and modes of celebration to their own cause. The works' outing, for example, had for many decades brought workers together in forms of social intercourse and pleasure; socialist clubs often functioned in a similar manner, drawing like-minded individuals together in the pursuit of pleasure – and often in work for the cause. May Day celebrations, however, were perhaps the most important of the popular traditions that both inspired and conferred legitimacy on socialist struggles. Eric Hobsbawm has suggested that they became a 'regular public self-presentation of class, an assertion of power', and in their 'invasion of the establishment's social space, a symbolic conquest'. In the late nineteenth century many socialists might have agreed with this assessment, although others viewed the day as an exercise in pleasure for pleasure's sake, a one-day bout of healthy nostalgia: as Katharine Bruce Glasier once wrote, 'And surely there is nothing nearly so pretty and happy in our modern celebrations as the garlanding of the May-pole with real flowers, the crowning of the May Queen, and the . . . games and dancing on the village green.'

6 A works' outing from Portwood mill.

IV Children and the new moral order 'Scientific' studies of recreation in the late nineteenth century pointed to the importance of play in the socialisation of the young. Such ideas inspired the development of the Guild of Play, the working lads' club movement and various children's holiday schemes. Socialists also began to recognise the significance of the links being forged between play and socialisation: as one writer for *Women Folk* argued, 'to get hold of the children and organise them for sweet, wholesome play is a work of immeasurable value'. Such individuals attacked capitalists for exploiting child labour and were behind the movement to establish socialist Sunday schools, institutions that offered both opportunities for 'wholesome play' and 'lessons' in socialism. One writer for the *Labour Prophet*, commenting on the Labour Church's Cinderella clubs for poor children, wrote, 'Cinderella has been fed and clothed and entertained, and now she is to go to school . . . where she will be taught our principles'.

7 Punch and Judy show.

facing

8 'The Holiday Question', cartoon from the *Daily Herald*, 13 June 1913, p. 1. '[How many thousands of mere children must toil right through the summer in factory and mine and workshop in order to make a steady flow of profits for the Fat Man?] *CHILD LABOUR EMPLOYER: "Great guns. Playing! What a wicked waste of human energy."* '

9 'Our First National Birthday Card', Socialist Sunday Schools, late 1890s.

The Socialist Sunday School

Heartily wish you

many happy returns of

this your Birthday

There are little tasks awaiting you can do,
that only you can do,
There are little songs want singing,
that must be sung by you,
There's a little race wants running,
that only you can run,
There are little things you must do
or they will be undone

There are little words of kindness
that only you can say,
And little deeds set in between
the boughs of everyday;
There are little fights and difference
that only you can win
And child, nobody passing, oh, so fast,
had you better not begin?

10 Street orchestra, London SE10, 1884.

11 Street violinist outside a music hall, London SE10, *c.* 1885.

12 William Morris, *Chants for Socialists* (1885), title page.

V Music and socialist culture Socialists recognised that music was an important part of working-class culture and they attempted to develop an alternative musical culture that would harness the energies unleashed by working-class musical activity. Julie, the main character in Robert Blatchford's novel of that name, was 'transformed' after listening to a street orchestra, prompted to devote her life to the cause of music and the cause of the working class. Like others, however, Julie was unable to develop the connections between her twin passions. On the one hand socialists wanted to encourage workers to make their own music. But on the other they disliked many popular songs and compiled anthologies of works they believed were most suitable for workers to sing. Edward Carpenter liked to think that his *Chants of Labour* was 'A Songbook of the People'. Likewise, H. W. Hobart, the socialist responsible for cultural affairs in *Justice*, claimed: 'Few people can decide better what the workers want in the way of labour chants . . . than the toilers themselves.' But he added, 'or, at any rate, those who have an affinity with the working classes'. Hobart, like Carpenter, was never able to overcome the tension that existed between the forms of music that appealed to most workers and the 'chants' socialists wrote for them.

13 Edward Carpenter, *Chants of Labour* (4th ed., 1905), title page, designed by Walter Crane.

VI The Clarion Vocal Union was established by Montague Blatchford in Halifax, and by 1900 branches had been established throughout the country. Despite their explicitly socialist goals, however, most of them ended up as quasi-professional choirs dedicated to the performance of well-known Victorian choral works. Committed socialists believed the organisation was not political enough, while music lovers complained that it was too political. Nevertheless, Montague Blatchford was certainly correct when he suggested that the socialist choirs 'have attracted and held hundreds of adherents who would otherwise have kept aloof from the movement'.

14 Advertising poster for the Bradford branch of the Clarion Vocal Union, *c.* 1900.

PIONEER CHOIR

BRADFORD BRANCH OF THE C.V.U.

Bradford's Socialist Choir.

AIMS :

1. To practise the art of singing Glees, Madrigals and Part Songs.
2. To give Concerts.
3. Fellowship.

Members for all parts are wanted.
Soprano, Alto, Tenor and Bass.

Rehearsals are held each Tuesday at 7-45, in the Assembly Room of the General Union of Textile Workers, 84, Godwin Street.

Friends wishing to join please apply to members of the Choir, or to the Conductor any Tuesday at the Rehearsal Room.

Conductor : **Mr. F. W. BODDY.**
Hon Sec. : **Mrs. ALLEN, 174, High Street, Wibsey.**

IF YOU HAVE A SINGING VOICE, COME AND HELP.

15 Montague Blatchford.

VII Socialism as a whole way of life By 1900 the socialist movement offered a vast range of cultural and social activities that allowed converts to share their leisure with like-minded people. Annual Clarion Cycling Club meets brought together hundreds of individuals, while those who could afford it were able to enjoy their holidays at Clarion country retreats, modelled on the Rev. T. A. Leonard's Cooperative Holiday Association. By the First World War, however, the transformation of associational life – central to the 'religion of socialism' in the 1890s – was halted, partly because of the increasingly apolitical nature of recreational activity, partly because of the growing importance of legislative activity, and partly because of the extent to which club members isolated themselves from the needs and concerns of most workers. Those who participated fully in socialist club life, however, recalled it fondly long after its demise – an 'Enchanted Hall of Dreams' was the verdict of one socialist in Bristol.

16 Clarion Cycling Club, season's greetings card, 1895.

17 Group portrait, Clarion Cycling Club annual meet, Shrewsbury, 1914.

18 Clarion club house, Handforth, Cheshire, *c.* 1905.

A·SOUVENIR·FOR·MAY·DAY·1906: dedicated to the LABOUR PARTY by Walter Crane

THERE IS NO WEALTH BUT LIFE

OLD AGE PENSIONS

HOPE IN WORK & JOY IN LEISURE

MORAL & PHYSICAL REGENERATION UNDER SOCIALISM

SOC BEN

TRU COM WEA

LABOUR PARTY

FREE FOOD FOR THE CHILDREN

1906

"Now, children, our friend here has brought the provisions, & there are lots of good things coming, so we'll all have a good time!"

VIII The triumph of mass culture In his illustrations for the socialist press, Walter Crane offered a visual map of the aspirations central to the 'religion of socialism': the 'maiden' of May was wedded to the Labour Party, and they both marched forward under the banners of 'Hope in Work and Joy in Leisure' (the motto of the Clarion Handicraft Guild), the more practical demand for old-age pensions and the call – often made by Blatchford and Leatham – for 'moral regeneration'. But moral regeneration failed to appeal to most workers, while Crane's vision itself seemed anachronistic in the new century as workers became more and more accustomed to paying for their pleasures in the marketplace. Socialists grew disillusioned, unable to convince others of the need to share their own enthusiasm. Julia Dawson once claimed that the leaders of the movement had attempted to make 'gentlemen out of the multitude of hogs and clods', but workers increasingly resented such condescending attitudes, eager to define pleasure in their own terms. Meanwhile, socialists often continued to espouse their diatribes against working-class culture and by 1914 were attacking picture palaces as vociferously as they had attacked music halls a generation earlier. As one socialist critic would write in the mid-1920s, the picture palace was full of 'inane, vulgar and disappointingly trashy' Hollywood films. Socialism had become a minority cult, removed from the experience of most workers.

20 The Hackney Picture Palace, London, 1914.

IX Alternative cultures in a capitalist society The experiences of the women and men who joined socialist clubs were often recounted in glowing terms in their diaries and autobiographies. Many longed for an escape from a culture they did not approve of nor feel at home in. As Edward Carpenter wrote, 'The mental and physical depression of large town life, the want of sociability . . ., the void of personal affection trying to fill itself by the conviviality of the cup . . . all these things were to Tom Maguire, as they have been to many others, the kind of Hydra . . . with which he had to battle.' Salvation was often found amidst a rich associational life that offered fellowship and mutual dedication to the socialist cause. But self-imposed exclusion from a world marked by the 'conviviality of the cup' was often accompanied by forms of cultural elitism and the failure to reach those who shared very different values. Perhaps, as Raymond Williams has suggested, it is all too easy for an alternative culture to end up as a 'tolerated play area', especially when it is unable to challenge effectively the dominant culture of the period.

21 Group portrait, members of a Clarion Cycling Club.

CHAPTER FOUR

Music
and the construction of socialist culture

In 1898 the *Keighley Labour Journal* claimed that the work of the socialist Clarion Vocal Unions was 'a first promise of what enjoyment may be obtained from life when, under the socialism which . . . [they] are using their voices to promote, all men and women have leisure to devote to intellectual pleasures'.[1] This statement encapsulates several ideas central to socialist thinking about the importance of music in the cultural transformation that would be necessary for the realisation of a socialist society. First, implicit in the statement is the belief that intellectual pleasures – of which music was but one – were of the highest order. Secondly, the passage suggests that choral singing, a rational recreation if there ever was one, would be one of the more important pleasures in a socialist society. Finally, the *Journal* seemed to be arguing that the vocal unions were promoting the desire for the transformation that would bring such pleasures about and were thus central to the struggle for socialism.

So important was music for many socialists that even the SDF demanded that greater attention be paid to musical matters. As *Justice* once proclaimed: 'The one reproach to our movement is that we neglect music. Apart from the pleasure and refining influence of music, it is . . . or would be, if practiced, a great aid to us in our propagandist work.'[2] Other socialists agreed, devoting their energies to compiling songbooks and encouraging choral singing at their gatherings. By 1900 choirs had come to occupy such a prominent place in the rich associational life of the socialist movement that one historian has noted that the 'main cultural thrust of the early socialist movement was in music'.[3]

It was, however, a 'cultural thrust' full of contradictions. Montague Blatchford, founder of the Clarion Vocal Union (CVU), claimed that workers did not want 'high' art they did not understand: 'Formal classical coldness . . . and involved metaphysical art', he wrote, 'are no use to them at all. No, they must have art of their own, art that is built upon their lives.'[4] But despite his plea for 'popular' art, Blatchford also advocated the revival of Tudor madrigals, a form of music far removed from the lives of nineteenth-century industrial workers. The call for an 'art of their own' could serve as a rallying cry for those who sought a new popular culture. But it could also be an empty rhetorical device, deployed by those who sought to 'improve' workers by imposing their own cultural preferences on them. An examination of the role of music in socialist thought and associational life may elucidate some of these contradictions.

Music and Victorian social reform

Many Victorians assumed that music could exert a refining influence in society, elevating the passions and paving the way for social harmony. Any study of music in socialist thought must begin with this simple assumption. In its most elaborate form it was developed by the High Church theologian Hugh Haweis, a reformer who was seldom interested in the cause of labour and who was more concerned with bolstering religious orthodoxy than with fostering socialist unorthodoxy. His most influential book, *Music and Morals*, published in 1871 and in its twentieth edition by 1903, became the most important source of inspiration for individuals interested in the relationship between music and social reform. Moreover, the work was widely read in socialist circles. When Edward Carpenter delivered a lecture on 'Haydn, Mozart and Beethoven' to the Sheffield Secular Society in 1884, his material was drawn almost exclusively from Haweis. And when Montague Blatchford wrote an article, 'What is music?', for the *Clarion*, one correspondent suggested that music was both an expression of – and an important influence on – the emotions and that Blatchford could learn about the relationship if he read *Music and Morals*.[5]

Born in 1838, Haweis was ordained in 1861 and settled in Bethnal Green. It was there, after initiating a series of popular concerts, that Haweis became convinced that music could draw people together and awaken a spirit of 'sympathy'. 'Teach the people to sing', he wrote, 'and you will make them happy; teach them to listen to sweet sounds, and you will go far to render them harmless to themselves, if not a blessing to their fellows.'[6] His experiments in London led Haweis to offer the public his views on the relationship between music, the emotions and the social order in *Music and Morals*. The book not only contributed to the moral rhetoric of rational recreation but it also influenced the work of social reformers by suggesting that certain melodic forms could awaken socially desirable emotions. According to Haweis, the promotion of 'good' music would promote morality while the existence of 'bad' music would further demoralise the populace. Moreover, only after a systematic study of music and the emotions could the good be separated from the bad. A musical Benthamite, Haweis believed that social harmony could be brought about by awakening in each individual a love of 'true' pleasure through the cultivation of particular types of edifying music.[7]

Haweis justified the moral exhortations of rational recreation with what purported to be a scientific study of the emotions. But his work merely enhanced the confidence of those who already believed that music could be used to counter other, less desirable pastimes. As early as 1840, the Committee of Council on Education concluded that music could 'wean the mind from vicious and sensual indulgences', calling for a national system of music education that would stimulate feelings of loyalty and patriotism. Moreover, the temperance movement had recognised the value of music early in its history, and the Band of Hope Movement believed music to be among its most effective means of winning souls for the cause.[8] By the 1880s, the People's Concert Society, the People's Entertainment Society and the Kyrle Society were merely three of the more prominent agencies active in the attempted transformation of popular culture through various programmes of musical edification. Bolstered by the ideas advanced by Haweis, these organisations were dedicated to destroying workers' ties to 'lower forms of amusement' by training them to a 'very high standard of taste' which would secure their commitment to the established social order.[9]

Music, then, enjoyed a prominent place in the movement for rational recreation because it touched the emotions as well as the intellect: while rational, it was also inspirational.[10] As Sam Midgley, a miner's son, claimed in a lecture he delivered to the Bradford branch of the ILP in 1912, music could assist in building emotional bonds between individuals, bonds that would induce social harmony and inspire municipal pride.[11] Moreover, in an age when fears about the breakdown of contacts between the classes were widespread, settlement house workers were particularly apt to view music as a crucial weapon in their battle to overcome the perceived isolation and narrowness of working-class life. Samuel Barnett, who had presided at the initial meeting of the People's Concert Society, argued that music, 'which enfolds the passions that have never found utterance . . . will somehow appeal to [the worker] and make him recognise his true self and his true object'.[12]

The 'somehow' in Barnett's statement is important, for despite Haweis's 'scientific' study of music and the emotions, the belief that music could contribute to social harmony remained largely an article of faith. But it was a faith with many followers. Originally a weapon against the publican and other 'vicious allurements', 'good' music had, by the 1890s, become part of a much wider struggle for social regeneration, a panacea for numerous social ills that blended older notions of self-control and self-help with newer notions of social citizenship.

Music in the service of socialism

When socialists wrote about music they had at their disposal two intellectual traditions. First was that of middle-class social reform, a tradition subscribed to by many individuals who bridged the gap between socialism and philanthropy in the cultural arena. One such individual was Clement Templeton. Honorary secretary of the Harrow Music School in the 1870s, Templeton presided over that institution's efforts to popularise good music through the provision of inexpensive concerts. The success of the venture led to the formation of the People's Concert Society and the appointment of Templeton as its honorary secretary. Later, in Bradford, he became popular for his 'Musical Evenings With the Great Masters', prompting the *Clarion*'s theatre critic to claim that Templeton, 'with his great love for music and great goodwill towards working people', was inspired by socialism. Not only did Templeton establish singing classes for members of the Labour Church in Bradford but he also assisted Trevor in compiling the *Labour Church Songbook*, to which he contributed several tunes.[13]

Links such as these, however, should not obscure the importance of music in earlier nineteenth-century radical movements. Music had always enjoyed a prominent place in utopian socialist thought and it was this heritage that formed the second important intellectual tradition that late Victorian socialists drew upon. Working from environmental determinist principles, they believed that human passions could be harnessed to the cause of radical reform and that music could encourage intense feelings of shared identity, important in developing the spirit necessary for entry into the new moral world. For the Owenites, music was no mere form of amusement, nor was it simply a means of attracting new members to their cause. Rather, it was a means of awakening in individuals new 'universal sympathies', developing their understanding of the homology that existed 'between the universal laws of harmony and the orderly arrangement of mankind in society'.[14]

These two traditions – the philanthropic and the utopian socialist – were by no means exclusive. Both had roots in Enlightenment assumptions about rationality and the social order, and both held that music could be important in the transformation of character. But it was the *ends* for which character was to be reformed that differentiated them. While the philanthropists often saw personal reform as a means of strengthening allegiance to the status quo, Owenites viewed it as important in the development of the new personality that would overthrow the status quo and establish a socialist community. By the time Haweis wrote *Music and Morals*, however, the ends to which music might be applied were often lost sight of, buried under hymns of praise to the transformative potential of music in general.

That socialists were enamoured of the idea of using music to assist in the moral reform of the individual is attested to by the number of articles they wrote on the subject. Robert Blatchford doubted 'if there is any art so refining, so elevating or so delightful as the art of music'; while John Trevor claimed that music in the Labour Church was 'calculated to uplift all those who are capable of being moved by sweet sounds into quite a new world of beauty, romance, purity and power'.[15] The enthusiasm expressed by these socialists knew no bounds, although it often led them to lose sight of their long-term political objectives, urging the moral reform of the individual for its own sake. In part, this was because socialists valued the importance of personal transformation; in part it was because they shared the enthusiasm of more conservative, middle-class reformers. But it also grew from socialists' own awareness that music played an important role in working-class life and could, they hoped, be harnessed to the struggle for socialism. The only problem was that for most socialists workers no longer seemed to appreciate 'good' music. One writer, urging the Labour Church to counter the appeal of music-hall fare, claimed that while workers were indeed musical few of them could differentiate the 'good' from the 'bad'. This writer suggested that the Labour Church might provide its members with 'first-class' music so that they might learn to develop a distaste for music-hall fare. But this required practice: 'It is like the study of Socialism', he wrote, 'you must go into it again and again – it will conquer you in the end.'[16]

Few socialists admitted that their own taste preferences informed their classification of 'good' music. Moreover, a number of them remained ambivalent about using music in the attempted moral uplift of the masses. George Bernard Shaw, for example, despaired of those philanthropists who stressed the virtues of 'music for the people' while sidestepping issues of social reform, and he suggested that workers wanted bread, rest and respect more than they wanted 'good' music. But he also argued that every centre of population should have a competent symphony orchestra and an opera theatre, and that until the state assumed a greater role in organising the arts philanthropists should be turned to for support. More than concerts *for* the people, however, Shaw suggested that workers needed to make their own music. All of the efforts of the People's Palace to provide concerts for the people were in vain, wrote Shaw, urging the directors of the Palace to 'invite the East End to come in and play for itself'.[17]

The importance of working-class music-making was a central theme in Robert Blatchford's novel, *Julie*. The story recounts the life of an East End slum child who sought to drown her sorrows in the music she heard in a local pub. Listening to a street orchestra one day, Julie was noticed by Melton Guineagold, a minor composer of independent means who offered her piano lessons in the hope of making 'a lady out of her'.[18] Receiving a moral as well as a musical education, Julie began to perform in the People's Palace. After her first appearance, Chigwin, the secretary of the Coal Porters' Union, asked her to perform at a strike meeting, complaining that she had been filled with 'middle-class unction' and taught to 'look down on the proletariat' (p. 95). Julie agreed to play at the meeting, convinced of her duty to work among 'her own' people. Blatchford's novel shared much with contemporary philanthropic thinking, particularly in its emphasis on the importance of women as the moral regenerators of the nation. But Blatchford remained suspicious of philanthropic meddling in working-class life: while he agreed with Walter Besant that music was an important source of moral elevation, he hoped that efforts at reform would emanate from the ranks of the working class itself. Hence he was eager to portray Julie as a working-class musician: 'Her music is our music', Chigwin once observed (p. 131).

Despite Blatchford's claims, Julie's musical preferences separated her from many workers, forcing one to conclude that the novel is most concerned with depicting the marginality of the trained working-class artist and examining the complexity of class relations in the cultural arena. Like so many late Victorian novels of working-class life, *Julie* focuses on the harmony of middle-class and artisanal tastes, legitimating upward (cultural) mobility.[19] This is clearly exhibited by Julie's fear of returning to the slums: 'They might not like her playing', she thought, they 'might resent her visit as an impertinence. . . . They would think she was giving herself airs and patronising them' (p. 124). These fears proved so great that Julie began to doubt her ability to work with the poor, seeking an escape from her dilemma through marriage to a dashing young lieutenant. This provoked a storm of protest from *Clarion* readers, most of whom felt that Julie was shirking her responsibilities to her own class. Blatchford said he would change the novel's ending, although he maintained that Julie's working-class background, coupled with the musical education she received, made her uncomfortable performing either in the slums or 'to a mob of well-dressed philistines'.[20] Despite his rhetoric about the need to encourage the love of 'good' music in working-class circles, Blatchford remained uncertain about whether or not musical tastes could actually be transformed, either by middle-class reformers or by working-class autodidacts. As we shall see, this uncertainty permeated socialist thought, becoming even more intense during the decade prior to World War I.

The desire for a musical culture developed by workers themselves was thus fraught with contradictions. Such contradictions are apparent in the work of Rutland Boughton, a composer with strong links to the socialist movement. Boughton studied at the Royal College of Music, became the music critic for the *Daily Mail* and for labour's *Daily Citizen*, assumed control of the Clarion Vocal Unions following the death of Montague Blatchford in 1910 and eventually joined the British Communist Party. Boughton believed that all genuine art emanated from the 'people' and he suggested, much as Matthew Arnold had, that the 'tyrannic idling' class merely 'consumed' the art of others while the 'parasitic trading' class had no artistic understanding of its own. But 'the music of the common people in a simple condition', he wrote, 'is as lovely and true as the world will ever know'.[21] Boughton romanticised 'the people', with their 'true appreciation of music'. But he also believed that popular art was in decline and thus needed to be encouraged by socialists like himself, individuals aware of the extent to which the commercial revolution had eradicated a viable popular musical culture.[22]

The tendency of musicians and socialists alike to deplore contemporary musical taste while romanticising popular creativity was also evident in the work of Edgar Bainton. A professor of piano and composition in Newcastle Upon Tyne, Bainton developed an interest in the work of the local branch of the ILP, speaking to its members in 1910 on the subject of music and socialism. Bainton argued that music had once expressed the aspirations of the people. But, as early as the Middle Ages, wandering minstrels were already beginning to turn music into a profession, creating a gulf between the 'people' and the performers. As was the case in much of the cultural thought of the period, Bainton contrasted the popular culture of an earlier Merrie England with what he perceived to be the cultural barrenness of nineteenth-century life:

> The beautiful, simple music which had burst forth out of the hearts of the people . . . full to overflowing with joy or sorrow, was now degraded from its true purpose, which should have been the spreading of the band of sympathy between men and women, and was made the trade of adventurers and mountebacks who dished up the people's songs as an accessory to the riotous feasting of a dissolute nobility.[23]

Bainton concluded his lecture on a more optimistic note, praising the work of the Clarion choirs and suggesting that socialism would restore a genuinely popular art by inspiring the people to create their own music once again.

But what did it mean to call on the 'people' to create their own music, holding up to them a mirror of their own artistic creativity in the Middle Ages? Did Boughton and Bainton really desire a self-made, 'popular' culture, or simply a romanticised version of such a culture, orchestrated by people like themselves? While Blatchford's novel, *Julie*, at least deals with the colossal problems of culture and class relations, the work of Boughton and Bainton – despite its rhetorical façade – trivialises late nineteenth-century working-class musical tastes and thereby creates a role for individuals with professional training and a classical background.

Although Boughton and Bainton called on workers to assume the mantle of artistic creativity once again, they often did so in an attempt to shatter the connection between music and commerce, thereby weakening workers' attachments to music-hall fare. While Boughton, in particular, blamed the 'commercial music' of the halls for subverting any desire workers might have to make their own music, he also believed that it had reduced their awareness of what constituted a genuinely 'popular' musical culture. Likewise, when Cecil Sharp began collecting material for his *Folk Songs from Somerset*, he was appalled at those who passed off music-hall songs and composed songs of all types as the authentic artefact for which he was looking. This led Sharp to suggest that most workers were unable to comprehend the very essence of folk music, and hence of an authentic popular culture.[24] Socialists were concerned that workers who drew on various traditions in expressing their own musical

preferences had become oblivious to the importance of a shared vocabulary, important in cementing working-class solidarity. Thus, when the
music critic for the *Clarion* discovered that her readers enjoyed a largo by
Handel, along with the melodies accompanying 'Annie Laurie' and
Carpenter's 'England, Arise!', she concluded that such a confusion of
musical genres stood in the way of furthering the socialist project of
generating a common musical heritage, germane to working-class life.[25]

For many socialists, a new, national repertoire of songs was one
means of giving a common focus to the musical life of the nation.
Clement Templeton used C. V. Stanford's *Collection of Old English Songs*
to prevent the musical good sense that he assumed lay dormant in the
children he taught in Bradford from becoming 'irreclaimably lost or
corrupted'. He also praised John Trevor's *Labour Church Songbook* as an
important vehicle for the creation of a national musical culture.[26] Montague Blatchford shared these sentiments: 'We socialists are all for
"nationalising" the national wealth', he wrote in 1895, claiming that 'a
magnificent heritage of pleasure and refinement' was to be found in
English glees, madrigals and part-songs. According to Blatchford, this
heritage could awaken workers' 'musical capacity' and sever their ties to
those commercial forms of music he so despised.[27]

Cecil Sharp, along with other folksong collectors, also suggested
the need for a national musical culture and he devoted much of his life to
concocting a musical tradition *for* the people, selecting songs that would
purify national life and elevate popular taste. Sharp, who called himself a
'conservative socialist', shared these sentiments with Charles Marson, a
Christian Socialist, Fabian and fellow folksong collector. In a lecture to
the Fabian Society, Marson once argued that the vitality of cultural forms
depended on their independence from 'commercial bondage' and that
because folk music was 'authentic' it could become the basis for a genuine
popular culture.[28] The lack of authenticity in late Victorian folksong
collections has recently been documented, although most socialists welcomed the folksong movement with open arms. As Rutland Boughton
wrote: 'Folksongs are tunes which have been evolved by the simple
people of the countryside, and there is a very real fitness in our singing
them.'[29]

Even more tireless than Boughton in crusading for the folksong
revival was Georgia Pearce, author of the *Clarion*'s 'Musical Notes' and
editor of *The Clarion Songbook*. Pearce praised Sharp for providing the
people with a sense of their own heritage and for attempting to undo the
harm the music hall had done to popular taste. Like Sharp, she was often

more interested in imposing a unity on working-class taste than in encouraging popular expression and she hoped that her comrades, while urging the 'people' to make their own music, would carefully construct a cultural heritage for the working class. A perusal of her column in the *Clarion* suggests that Pearce was most concerned with the systematic education of working-class tastes, offering workers an image of a unitary culture which they could claim as their own.[30]

Occasionally Pearce was chastised by her readers for writing too technically or for suggesting attendance at concerts few of them could afford. But she was also praised, particularly by those workers who felt that she managed to make some sense out of the numerous forms of music available to them:

> I enjoy reading about the music in your column, only it makes one feel how poor we working people are. The music you describe in the *Clarion* is just the kind of music I like, I know it is though I never heard it. You give me the right feeling I want when I sit to hear music, but not often get. And it is so with scores of working people.[31]

Pearce did not see her task merely as a philanthropic one of bringing 'good' music to the people, despite her belief in the ability of such music to elevate the listener. On the contrary, she felt that music could be an important component of a socialist culture and she saw her task as one of suggesting to workers the richness of the various musical traditions they could draw upon in constructing that culture. In this she was not alone: 'Don', the music correspondent for the ILP's *Bradford Pioneer* for several months in 1913, conceived of his role in similar terms. He urged his readers to become aware of the evils of 'commercial music' and to agitate for the public provision of 'good' music. But most of all he tried, like Pearce, to give workers a sense of possessing their own musical heritage by constructing a selective tradition for them, one that drew from folk music, songs of the English renaissance and 'classical' concert pieces.

Unlike Sharp, these critics did not simply call for the dissemination of folksongs in working-class life. Instead, they attempted to bring together what they considered to be the better elements of several musical traditions in ways that might permit them to be perceived as 'popular'. Behind the rhetoric of participation, behind the call for a 'music-of-the-people', behind the fervent desire for workers to make their own music, socialists attempted to exert a subtle – and sometimes not so subtle – influence on working-class musical preferences. Their real object was less to 'return' music to the people than to give coherence to a fragmented musical taste, to displace the perceived prominence of music-hall entertainment in working-class communities and to appropriate material from various musical genres for an emergent socialist culture that workers might begin to consider as their own. Various aspects of English musical traditions were to play a role in this new 'culture of the people'. Overall, the object was seldom to impose a totally alien taste on the working class. But taste was still to be 'improved', and this was usually the most important of the contradictory goals socialists set themselves in the musical arena.

Composing socialist songs

An examination of the contents of socialist songbooks can illuminate the traditions that socialists sought to draw upon in their attempts to develop an alternative, socialist culture. While almost forgotten today, socialist songbooks published prior to 1914 played a prominent role in the movement's associational life. Edward Carpenter's *Chants of Labour*, for example, was to be found in socialist circles for more than thirty years. First published by Swan Sonnenschein in 1888, it was reissued in 1892, 1897 and 1905, while further editions appeared in 1912, 1916 and 1922 under the imprint of George Allen and Unwin. Even at the local level, branches of various socialist organisations published their own anthologies of songs that remained in print for many years.

Several anthologies have been selected for the purposes of the following analysis: Carpenter's *Chants of Labour*, one of the earliest of the songbooks, which came to serve as a model for later compilations; *The Labour Songbook* (1888?), published by the Bristol Socialist Society; the collection of *Socialist Songs* (1889) issued by the Aberdeen Branch of the Socialist League; *Songs for Socialists* (3rd ed., 1890), compiled by James Leatham; *The Labour Church Hymnbook* (1892); John Bruce Glasier's *Socialist Songs* (1893); *The Clarion Songbook* (1906), edited by Georgia Pearce; *The SDF Songbook* (1910?); and, finally, *Songs for Socialists* (1912), compiled by a subcommittee of the publishing committee of the Fabian Society.

These songbooks shared the goal of fashioning a general literary and musical culture for the socialist movement. While the emphasis in each songbook differed, their contents overlapped at many points. Of the fifty-one songs in *The SDF Songbook*, twenty-three had appeared in Carpenter's *Chants* over twenty years earlier; and of the 532 pieces in all nine songbooks there were only 246 different titles. Each organisation felt that it was contributing to an evolving socialist tradition. The compilers of the Fabian collection, for example, claimed that their work was not solely a 'lyrical expression of Fabian Socialism' (to which one reviewer responded: 'We should think not – and what the "lyrical expression of Fabian Socialism" would be like is truly tantalising to the imagination'[32]), but a 'representative' collection of revolutionary songs and of works popular 'with the socialist movement in England during its formative years' (preface).

Each of the anthologies offered socialists material drawn from a number of different intellectual traditions and none relied solely on propaganda songs written for the movement. But differentiating the various works that editors believed were important in representing and cultivating socialist sentiments is a difficult undertaking. When the songbook committee reported to the Fabian Society's publishing committee in 1911, it suggested a collection of 131 titles, divided into three categories: the socialist and revolutionary (seventy-two titles); the ethical and devotional (twenty-three); and the popular and traditional (twenty-six). The first category was to consist of earlier radical songs, mostly written by Chartists, and more recent works, often written by Fabians themselves. Then there were the ethical hymns to be sung at Sunday meetings, followed by songs, usually of a non-political character, that, because they were popular, would enliven socialist gatherings.[33] While the tripartite classification devised by the Fabian Society is illustrative of how certain socialists conceived of the ideological roots of their own musical offerings, it is less useful in a discussion of those offerings. For example, given the emotional rhetoric of the religion of socialism, it is difficult to distinguish a purely 'socialist' from an 'ethical' song. Moreover, the category 'popular and traditional' is too broad to be of much analytical use, especially when works such as 'England, Arise!' became traditional favourites at socialist gatherings.

The establishment of six categories, based on each song-writer's relationship to a particular intellectual or political tradition, can be of some help in attempting to understand the diverse sources that were drawn upon in fashioning this aspect of socialist culture (Table 4.1). Category I consists of pieces written by trade union, labour and socialist activists between 1880 and 1914. Category II consists of works written by Chartists and champions of various radical causes in the middle third of the nineteenth century. A third category consists of songs written by middle-class advocates of radical causes between 1880 and 1914 who,

Table 4.1 *Authorship in selected socialist songbooks*

Type of author	Number of titles in songbooks*									Total number of songs in category (%)	
	EC	BSS	SLA	JL	LC	JBG	GP	SDF	FS		
I Socialist, labour or trade union activist	27	24	18	22	4	43	20	33	23	214	40.2
II Earlier nineteenth-century radical	2	3	1	1	5	6	4	1	5	28	5.3
III Supporter of reform or radical movements	8	5	3	4	4	6	8	4	9	51	9.6
IV Prominent poet (British & American)	9	6	1	1	9	14	10	5	25	80	15.0
V Lesser known writer, often religious	2	0	1	1	25	1	6	0	6	42	7.9
VI Foreign author of patriotic/revolutionary songs	4	0	1	3	0	8	2	6	9	33	6.2
VII Unknown (no author listed)	3	4	4	4	37	10	10	2	10	84	15.8
Total	55	42	29	36	84	88	60	51	87	532	100.0

* Songbooks:
EC Edward Carpenter, *Chants of Labour* (1888)
BSS Bristol Socialist Society, *The Labour Songbook* (1888?)
SLA Socialist League (Aberdeen), *Socialist Songs* (1889)
JL James Leatham, *Songs for Socialists* (1890)
LC *The Labour Church Hymnbook* (1892)
JBG John Bruce Glasier, *Socialist Songs* (1893)
GP Georgia Pearce, *The Clarion Songbook* (1906)
SDF *The SDF Songbook* (1910?)
FS Fabian Society, *Songs for Socialists* (1912)

while often socialist in their sympathies, were not primarily engaged in work for the cause. (While the songs of Carpenter, Glasier and Morris, for example, fall within category I, those of Edith Nesbit and H. S. Salt would be found in category III.) Category IV consists of material drawn from the work of canonical Anglo-American poets, such as Blake, Burns, Lowell, Shelley and Whitman. Another category consists of material drawn from that vast repertoire of songs written by lesser known Victorians, often minor poets and hymn-writers. Finally, a sixth category can be established, consisting of songs written for foreign struggles, such as the French Revolution or the revolutions of 1848.

Songs written by late nineteenth-century socialists and labour activists predominated in the anthologies under discussion. Of the 532 titles in the nine songbooks, 214 (40.2 per cent) were written explicity for the movement by its activists. Excluding the *Labour Church Hymnbook* (discussed more fully below), such pieces account for between 26.4 per cent of the contents of the Fabian collection and 64.7 per cent of the anthology compiled by the SDF. A survey of the fourteen most prominent titles (those that appeared in at least six of the nine songbooks) also suggests that songs written by late nineteenth-century socialists and their sympathisers dominated these works (Table 4.2). Seven of the fourteen titles were written by activists in the movement (Carpenter, Connell, Morris and Scheu), while an additional four were written by individuals sympathetic to the cause of socialism, although perhaps better known for their other work: Havelock Ellis, the pioneer sexologist; Edith Nesbit, the children's writer; and H. S. Salt, founder of the Humanitarian League.

Table 4.2 *Most common titles in selected socialist songbooks*

Category	Author	Title	No. of songbooks
I	Edward Carpenter	'England, arise!'	9
IV	James Russell Lowell	'True freedom'	9
I	William Morris	'The march of the workers'	8
III	Edith Nesbit	'Come gather, O people'	8
III	H. S. Salt	'Hark! The battle cry is ringing'	8
III	Havelock Ellis	'Onward, brothers'	7
I	William Morris	'The voice of toil'	7
III	Edith Nesbit	'The hope of ages'	7
I	Jim Connell	'Workers of England'	6
II	Ernest Jones	'Song of the lower classes'	6
I	William Morris	'All for the cause'	6
I	William Morris	'Come, comrades, come'	6
IV	Percy B. Shelley	'Men of England'	6
I	Andreas Scheu	'Song of labour'	6

With four of the fourteen titles to his name, William Morris stands out as the most well-represented poet of socialism in the anthologies. Most of his songs were written between 1883 and 1886 for *Commonweal* and *Justice*, and were later published as a pamphlet by the Socialist League, *Chants for Socialists*. Their popularity rested less on their expression of socialist convictions than on the way in which they conveyed those convictions through forms of imagery that would have been familiar to those knowledgeable of romantic verse. By far the most complex of the socialist songs, they not only portrayed in vivid tones the future socialist society but also offered a historical analysis of those forms of oppression that would ultimately be overthrown. 'The Day is Coming' is characteristic of a whole genre of romantic verse that envisaged a better world: 'Come hither lads, and hearken, for a tale there is to tell / Of the wonderful days a coming when all shall be better than well'. While John Bruce Glasier viewed this work as 'almost the most beautiful socialists utterance',[34] 'All for the Cause', like *News from Nowhere*, went on to focus on the struggle that would be necessary to bring the new society about. By contrast, in the 'March of the Workers' Morris asserts his confidence in the outcome of that struggle, loudly proclaiming the victory that will ultimately be achieved: 'Come and live! for life awaketh, and the world shall never tire; And hope is marching on'.

The purpose of these songbooks was not merely to circulate the battle hymns of the movement, such as those by Morris, but to appropriate material from other traditions that could be placed in the service of socialism. H. S. Salt, who edited his own radical songbook, justified the inclusion of material written by individuals outside the mainstream of late nineteenth-century labour and socialist politics. Only by seeing how the 'revolutionary ideal' had developed in the past, he wrote, could a feeling for the historical and ideological richness of the radical tradition be generated. Salt's own collection began with songs of the French Revolution and continued with the 'poets of democracy', such as Burns and Shelley. In Shelley, wrote Salt, the socialist movement had 'as strenuous and sustained a vindication of human freedom, as determined a protest against conventional authority, as can be found in English literature'. Other socialists agreed and Shelley's 'Men of England' appeared in two-thirds of the anthologies.[35]

The desire to capitalise on past radical traditions can be seen most markedly in the prominent place afforded the work of the Chartists. Chartist poetry appeared in all the songbooks, although not without some significant gaps depending on the ideological predilections of their compilers. For example, one of the most radical of the Chartist songs was Ernest Jones's 'Song of the Lower Classes', an explicit attack on capitalist exploitation:

> We're low, we're low – we're very, very low –
> And yet from our fingers glide
> The silken flow and the robes that glow
> Around the limbs of the sons of pride;

And what we get, and what we give,
We know, and we know our share;
We're not too low the cloth to weave,
But too low the cloth to wear.

The forthright analysis of exploitation in the 'Song of the Lower Classes' clashed with the more general ethical tone stressed in the Labour Church, Clarion and Fabian anthologies, although the editors of those collections made available other, vaguely utopian Chartist works such as Thomas Cooper's 'Truth is Growing' and John Mackay Peacock's 'Sons of Labour'. By contrast, the SDF anthologists made a special effort to transcend utopian abstractions and reprinted the more revolutionary of the Chartist pieces, including those by Jones.[36]

The emphasis on legitimating socialist aspirations in terms of recognisable political struggles and through familiar poetic imagery meant that few foreign works were included in the anthologies. Glasier once wrote of the ILP (equally applicable to the songbooks compiled by organisations such as the ILP) that it 'has been the means . . . of restoring the English tradition into our socialist agitation – a tradition which was lost by the usurpation of the Marxists and Communards'.[37] Of all the organisations that compiled anthologies, the Fabian Society was most concerned with representing this 'English tradition'. Over 28 per cent of the works in the Society's *Songs for Socialists* were written by major Romantic poets – almost double the average – perhaps indicative of the Fabians' search for legitimacy in terms of a native, and often non-threatening, intellectual heritage.

Policies of inclusion or exclusion, however, often had less to do with the political sentiments of the poet than with the emotional rhetoric and romantic imagery conveyed by their poetry. So captivating were some images that many compilers emphasised the poetry that utilised them at the expense of the more explicit critiques of industrial society written towards the end of the century. As both Glasier and Salt noted in the prefaces to their anthologies, it was whether or not particular poems shared an emotional affinity with the whole apparatus of socialist imagery they desired to cultivate that dictated their utility. Hence the popularity of Charles Mackay, the well-known poet and editor of the *London Illustrated News*, whose poem 'There's a Good Time Coming' – a work that sold over 400,000 copies in the 1850s – appeared in several songbooks because it appealed to those who wished to stress a vague yearning for a more just social order:

> There's a good time coming, boys,
> A good time coming;
> We may not live to see the day,
> But earth shall glisten in the ray
> Of the good time coming.

Images of the 'good time coming' were central to the religion of socialism. As we have seen, they were also prevalent in socialist utopian writing, although only Morris, in poems such as 'The Day is Coming', was capable of linking such imagery to an explicitly socialist politics in a fully effective manner. But although Mackay's poem was divorced from any radical political understanding, it was, none the less, part of a genre that socialists found inspirational because of its lyrical utopianism. Moreover, music itself was seen as an inspirational vehicle for conveying such sentiments: as one socialist put it, music of use to the movement 'must represent an aspiration after the ideal beauty, an attempt to express in a tone-picture something beyond the rays of verbal description or realistic experience'.[38] Collective singing of Mackay's work, or of similar pieces by a host of other writers, might allow workers – or so it was hoped – temporarily to feel transported to the promised land. As John Bruce Glasier claimed, the desires awakened by such utopian imagery were an important source of energy in the movement as a whole.[39]

Some socialists attempted to develop the imagery of the 'coming day' in new directions by suggesting that the society of the future was merely a restoration of what had once been, a golden age in some indeterminate past. At times this was expressed in terms of the 'Norman Yoke', of a world of free-born citizens who were robbed of their birthright in 1066. The theme of exile from the promised land, in which the industrialist had come to assume the role of the Norman conqueror, can be seen in Carpenter's song, 'The People to Their Land':

> A robber band has seized the land,
> And we are all exiles here.

It is also an important theme in Tom Maguire's 'Mammon Land':

> Weep for the fallen, alas for them all,
> The daughters and the sons of men!
> Accurst was the hour that told of their fall –
> Accurst every hour since then –
> When they wandered away into Mammon Land,
> To be slaves of the god of gold;
> Weep for the fallen, alas for the fallen
> From worthier ways of old.[40]

The romantic imagery of the 'coming day', when wedded to such an analysis of oppression, would, it was hoped, intensify the desire to struggle for the better world that many songs depicted. Moreover, the romantic yearning for a new society was often accompanied by a belief in the inevitability of its arrival, as in Sparling's 'A Socialist Marching Song':

> Too long the wolves of capital
> Have drunk our blood and filched our all,
> But from their power they'll have to fall,
> The People's day is coming.

Despite such proclamations of inevitability, few works managed to transcend the superficial optimism of the 'coming day' poems and offer an analysis of oppression and a call for revolutionary change. The vague utopian yearning that characterised the majority of the songs in the anthologies may have encouraged a surge of optimism among those who sang them, but ultimately the sheer number of such pieces overwhelmed the more revolutionary works. None the less, writers like Morris, and to a lesser extent Carpenter, Maguire and Sparling, attempted – and to some extent succeeded – in harnessing the energy of the 'coming day' poems to their own cause. In the process they showed the strengths of a movement which looked to the past for various kinds of material that could be drawn upon, often in an eclectic manner, in the construction of a new political culture.

The Labour Church Hymnbook shared material with other socialist songbooks, although it differed substantially from them. Explicitly political songs were largely absent from the collection – even William Morris finds no place in the first Labour Church hymnbook. Moreover, unlike the other anthologies, Trevor's contained many works written by Victorian religious figures. On first glance, this religious emphasis supports Trevor's contention that the purpose of the Labour Church was to appeal 'to those who have abandoned the Traditional Religion of the day without having found satisfaction in abandoning Religion altogether'.[41] Trevor's claim also substantiates the more recent suggestion that the chief function of the organisation 'was to lubricate the passage of Northern workers from Liberal Radicalism to an Independent Labour Party', by offering socialist ideology through the familiar imagery, rhetoric and rituals of nonconformity.[42] There is much evidence to lend credibility to this assessment. In Leicester, for example, a stronghold of Liberalism and nonconformity, the Labour

Church continued to flourish long after other branches began to wane.[43]

Theories of 'lubrication', however, vastly underestimate the originality of the Labour Church. Like the Primitive Methodists, the Labour Church stressed democratic decision-making and encouraged workers to play an active role in their own advance. Moreover, a perusal of *The Labour Church Hymnbook* suggests that Trevor's hymnal has little in common with those of either the Church of England or the traditional nonconformist sects. Of the eighty-four titles in Trevor's work, none appears in the Anglican *Hymns Ancient and Modern* (1885 ed.) and only two appear in the *Congregational Hymnary* (1916 ed.). By contrast, *The Labour Church Hymnbook* shares a number of titles with the anthologies compiled by quasi-religious institutions explicitly concerned with social problems, such as the settlement houses. *The Mansfield House Songbook*, for example, offered 106 songs for settlement house meetings, including hymns focusing on social issues, along with the poetry of Carpenter, Ellis and Whittier.[44] Such material also enjoyed a prominent place in the Labour Church anthology. Fifteen titles in Trevor's work can also be found in the hymnal of the Pleasant Sunday Afternoon Association, an organisation which, like Trevor's, regarded its meetings neither as 'mission services nor meetings of practical churchgoers', but advertisements for the 'practical side of Christianity', thus requiring new material for congregational singing.[45]

Trevor's anthology shares with such works an emphasis on the connection between personal salvation and social emancipation. Song writers such as Malcolm Quin, who dealt with both themes, figured prominently in *The Labour Church Hymnbook*. Secularist, Comtean Positivist and member of the Newcastle upon Tyne branch of the ILP, Quin wrote 'hymns of ethical platitude' as he called them,[46] which, aside from appealing to Trevor, also appeared in the Clarion, Fabian and South Place Ethical Society songbooks.

Although Trevor was not immune from selecting pieces written by traditional hymn-writers, he selected only those works that explicitly endorsed the optimism and self-help he believed was central to the philosophy of the Labour Church. While *The Labour Church Hymnbook* and the *Methodist Free Church Hymns* shared only two titles, seven writers provided material for the two collections, although the material they provided for the one differed from that provided for the other. The most important theme to emerge in the religious hymns in Trevor's anthology is one of hope, of God's assistance in the realisation of the inevitable 'good time coming'. Where the same writers provided material for the

115

Methodist collection, the themes developed were more of resignation, of turning to God not for inspiration and courage but for sustenance and rest. Compare, for example, the work of Horatio Bonar in Trevor's anthology with that in the Methodist hymnbook. Trevor selected a work by Bonar that emphasised hope:

> Sow love, and taste its fruitage pure;
> Sow peace, and reap its harvest bright;
> Sow sunbeams on the rock and the moor,
> And find a harvest-home of light.

By contrast, the Methodist hymnal offered a more resigned work:

> My refuge and my rest,
> As on father's breast,
> I lean on Thee;
> From faintness and from fear,
> When foes and ill are near
> Deliver me.[47]

The Labour Church Hymnbook can be seen as ignoring much of the traditional content of nonconformity even while deploying its principle vehicle of congregational singing for the generation of socialist optimism. Not merely a paving stone on the road from nonconformity to socialism, the Labour Church and its songbook made an important contribution to the development of an alternative, socialist culture by transforming and extending specific cultural idioms with which many workers were already familiar. Although other songbooks appropriated material for the cause from romantic and radical critiques of industrial society, Trevor's collection was more subtle, carving out a new space for the growth of socialist sentiment from the work of hymn-writers who – unlike Jones and Shelley – might well have felt uncomfortable in the socialist movement themselves.

While the lyrics in socialist songbooks were often new, the tunes to which they were set were usually well known. Those who compiled the anthologies believed, along with Haweis, that the tune was a 'powerful secondary agent to deepen and intensify the emotion already awakened by the words of the song'.[48] But selecting the appropriate tune for a particular work was often difficult. It was most convenient for socialists to write new words to existing melodies, thereby facilitating communal singing by individuals unable to read music. On the other hand, the familiar tune might not 'deepen and intensify' the emotion aroused by the new words if that tune was too strongly associated with other lyrics that contradicted the new, socialist message.

Dissatisfaction with the setting of new poetry to existing tunes was extensive. Sometimes, good poetry had to be disregarded because no familiar tunes could be found to accompany it. As members of the Aberdeen Socialist League claimed, they had selected songs for their anthology 'not necessarily because they are the best specimens of revolutionary poetry, but because we had managed to secure well-known tunes for them'.[49] But complaints often focused on the incongruities that were perceived to exist between a given song and its accompanying tune. When Jim Connell wrote 'The Red Flag' in 1889, he meant it to be sung to the familiar tune of 'The White Cockade'. Such a combination, however, made the performance of the work difficult and when the SDF selected the song for inclusion in its own songbook it rejected 'The White Cockade' in favour of the German 'Tannenbaum'. Connell was indignant, complaining that the new tune was 'calculated to remind people of their sins and frighten them into repentance'.[50]

So unsatisfactory were some combinations that H. W. Hobart, the SDF writer on cultural matters, claimed that in many of the songs in Carpenter's *Chants* the words were chopped in order to fit the music or a slur was introduced to the music in order to squeeze all the words in. Like other critics, Hobart felt that the attempt to fit the 'Hymn of the Proletariat' by the Austrian anarchist Johann Most to the tune of the 'British Grenadiers' was an exercise in futility, not only because of the technical difficulties of the combination but also because of the ideological conflict between the radical lyrics and the conservative feelings to which the music gave rise.[51]

Complaints about poorly selected tunes were so numerous that many a song was printed without any suggestions for a tune to accompany it. Justifying the fact that he offered no tunes in his own anthology, John Bruce Glasier wrote: 'I did not think it wise . . . to fix down songs breathing the spirit of a new social life to airs of the past, many of which are instinct with feelings of . . . an anti-socialist character.'[52] Socialists thus began to call for the provision of new tunes for the movement. Writing on behalf of the Glasgow and District Socialist Sunday Schools about that organisation's plan to select material from the SDF collection for a new Sunday school anthology, one socialist hoped that composers would come forward with new melodies so that children would have a songbook free of those tunes that gave rise to sentiments antithetical to the spirit of socialism. When the book was finally completed, it contained over thirty new tunes, including one for Connell's 'Red Flag'.[53]

The attempt to discover new tunes often led the compilers of socialist songbooks to turn to working-class amateur composers. In Bristol, Edward Carpenter struck up a friendship with Robert Sharland, who had been instrumental in the formation of the Bristol branch of the SDF and whose musical work Carpenter praised. As early as the 1870s, Sharland rewrote radical poems of freedom and liberty so they could be sung to available melodies, and he also adapted traditional melodies to accompany the newer songs of freedom. Carpenter also admired J. Percival Jones, a working-class composer from Bristol who provided more than thirty new tunes for the poetry of the socialist movement, several of which appeared in Carpenter's anthology.[54] But Georgia Pearce felt that Carpenter's attempt to acquire new melodies was largely unsuccessful and when she compiled *The Clarion Songbook*, almost thirty years later, she made a greater effort to secure tunes that actually 'worked'. Some were provided by worker-musicians such as Jones. But most were written by middle-class socialists like Pearce herself (eleven), or by professional composers with socialist sympathies, such as Edgar Bainton (four) and Rutland Boughton (four).[55]

The difficulty of tune selection is illustrative of larger problems faced by socialists in the cultural arena. On the one hand, they demanded new forms of expression developed within the ranks of the socialist movement. But on the other, they recognised the importance of older and familiar forms through which they might convey their message with ease. Increasingly, as the socialist movement grew to maturity, a new song culture began to emerge, and it is important to note that the songbooks compiled in the early years of the twentieth century included a greater number of new tunes than those compiled in the 1880s and 1890s. And yet socialists remained aware of the fact that in order to succeed in their endeavours they needed to build on familiar forms of expression in working-class life. The 'new' culture they claimed to be generating was thus inevitably indebted to a number of familiar poetic and musical traditions which socialists attempted to shape in imaginative and creative ways.

The problem of selecting tunes to accompany socialist poetry was related to the problem of building a culture around the experiences of workers themselves. While Edward Carpenter believed socialism to be the cause of the working class, like others he overestimated the role played by that class in the emergence of a socialist culture. When he proclaimed that the songs in his anthology were for, and mostly by, 'the people', he was as guilty as Cecil Sharp of confusing a tradition that developed from the people with one manufactured and imposed on them. Hobart was more aware of the problem in his review of Carpenter's work: 'Few people can decide better what the workers want in the way of labour chants . . . than the toilers themselves', he wrote, adding parenthetically, 'or, at any rate, those who have an affinity with the working classes.'[56] While Carpenter's *Chants* included several pieces written by workers, the majority of songs composed for the movement flowed from the pens of middle-class leaders or sympathisers. The exceptions to this were few, although George Meek, who organised Clarion groups on the south coast; Fred Henderson, who wrote several books of verse and whose 'Song of the Springtide' appeared in four of the anthologies; and John Gregory, a shoemaker who wrote *Idylls of Labour* and served as the vice-president of the Bristol Trades Council were workers who each provided a small number of songs for the movement.[57]

Only a few songs in the anthologies describe the experience of work itself. In a letter to the *Labour Leader*, one correspondent claimed that men and women who worked in a mill or in the fields once sang fine songs, but that did not seem to be the case anymore.[58] Indeed, the songs the movement did provide differed substantially from those termed 'industrial folksongs'; overall they 'had little influence on the sort of thing the singing miners, mill-hands and foundry workers made for themselves'.[59] This is not to suggest that the theme of work had absolutely no place in socialist songs, for a few writers attempted to discuss work in terms of the general aspirations of socialism. One such individual was William Wilson. As a blacksmith's apprentice, Wilson wrote about work in his *Echoes from the Anvil*. Later, active in the Amalgamated Society of Engineers, Wilson became a convert to socialism and wrote poems, such as 'King Labour', that emphasised the connection between the consciousness of exploitation developed at work and the struggle for socialism.[60] But the best-known socialist to write explicitly about the experience of work was Tom Maguire, whose *Machine Room Chants* was written as a direct result of his role in organising the tailoresses in Leeds. When the book appeared, the *Church Reformer* claimed that Maguire's poems portrayed 'the inner workings of the mind of the average working girl'.[61] More recently it has been suggested that Maguire's work represents 'the point of juncture between the theoretical understanding of national leaders, the moral teaching of Morris and Carpenter, and the needs and aspirations of his own people'.[62]

Poets like Maguire were rare among the ranks of those who wrote socialist songs. Thus, despite their occasional reluctance to do so, socialists looked more to middle-class writers for their material than to workers. In part this was because they were concerned with fashioning a general socialist culture – through the deployment of familiar romantic imagery – that might transcend occupational specificity and unite workers in all parts of the country behind the struggle for socialism. But this entailed relying on educated writers most capable of drawing on a number of diverse traditions, individuals who, in attempting to provide a shared vocabulary of struggle, ended up remaining aloof from workers and their immediate concerns. Take, for example, the work of Francis Adams. A member of the SDF who moved to Australia and published a book of verse, *Songs of the Army of the Night* (1888), Adams was championed as a poet of the labour movement and enjoyed a small, albeit enthusiastic, following after his return to England. Early in his career, Adams praised the poetry of Goethe and upheld the claims of 'art'. Later, he championed the cause of labour. But in his own work the claims of art were never fully reconciled with the claims of labour. While suggesting that workers should emancipate themselves through their own efforts, Adams attempted to inspire and cultivate those efforts through his poems. But his poetry often remained esoteric, distanced from the concerns of daily working-class life, full of metaphors that would have made little sense to the uneducated.[63]

The work of Francis Adams points to the problems encountered by socialists in their attempt to build a new culture, a culture that was supposed to inspire political activism by erecting bonds of comradeship between workers and legitimate their struggle through the provision of a recognisable intellectual heritage. Writers like Adams seemed more concerned with bringing workers into the orbit of serious poetry than anything else. Others, like Maguire, were more successful in their attempt to speak to the concrete needs of the working class. But even if socialists songbooks cannot be viewed as entirely successful, the efforts that went into them were prodigious. Socialists were not only aware of the need to fashion a new, explicitly political, culture but they were often imaginative in their attempts to do so.

Radical politics and Victorian choral music

It is by no means certain that socialist songbooks played the important role in the movement for which their compilers hoped. While certain works, such as Carpenter's 'England, Arise!', did become part of the shared vocabulary of socialists, many workers in the movement sang non-political songs. Stella Davies, recalling her experiences as a participant in the Openshaw Socialist Society, claimed that although its members sometimes sang revolutionary songs, they were also devoted followers of William Paul, a member of the Society who was an expert in folksong. Likewise, while meetings of Will Sharland's Bristol Socialist Choir were 'enlivened by the singing of socialist songs', its members also sang popular Victorian choral works on their summer rambles.[64]

The Clarion Vocal Union (CVU) affords a unique opportunity to study the type of music that was popular in the largest of the socialist choral bodies in Britain. The CVU was established by Montague Blatchford, one-time Halifax town councillor, honorary conductor of the choir of the Halifax Industrial Society and composer of several light operas.[65] In October 1894, Blatchford spoke to the congregation of the Halifax Labour Church on the need for a socialist choir. Some 150 people responded to his call and branches of the Clarion Vocal Union were soon formed in Glasgow, Halifax, Hull, Keighley, Manchester, Nottingham, Oldham, Rochdale, Salford and Sheffield.[66]

From the beginning, the CVU was called upon to provide its services at socialist gatherings. As May Day festivals, socials and bazaars became important means of fund-raising, greater pressure was placed on the talents of socialists as entertainers. The CVU thus came to play a major role in providing entertainment and raising funds at one socialist assembly after another. Montague Blatchford also suggested that in addition to providing entertainment the CVU should encourage the revival of interest in madrigals, glees and part-songs. According to Blatchford, the music of the English renaissance was a genuine 'people's' music, which, if cultivated once again, would 'appeal straight to the hearts of those most benighted people whose highest musical ideal is the singing of the "Rickety-Rackety Crew", by a third-rate music-hall comedian'.[67]

The belief that all would be well if workers could be drawn from the halls, learning to appreciate what socialists believed was rightly their heritage, made Blatchford sound very similar to the philanthropists whom he often attacked. In this sense the CVU was no different from other organisations that attempted to develop an appreciation of traditional English music. Writing about the Home Music Study Union, one supporter claimed that the music it offered both elevated the individual and 'makes the being elevated thoroughly enjoyable'. Writing about the

CVU, Blatchford wrote, in a similar vein: 'I really don't know any method by which I could do so much towards "raising" the masses as by . . . cultivating a love of good English music.'[68]

Much of the music sung at CVU meetings was not the 'good English music' Blatchford hoped it might be, as a study of the sheet music collection of the Halifax and Bradford branches of the organisation indicates. Several hundred pieces of music belonging to these two prominent branches are still in existence, offering a good idea of the type of music that Clarion vocalists sang. The significance of the collection cannot be underestimated, for while it may give only a partial glimpse into the repertoire of these working-class choral groups we have little other quantifiable evidence of the musical activities of British socialists.

Table 4.3 *Contents of the sheet music collection of the Clarion Vocal Union, Halifax and Bradford branches*

Type of song	Number of different titles	% of total
Victorian choral works	86	61.0
Traditional folksongs	23	16.3
English songs of the 16th & 17th centuries	16	11.4
'Classical' choral works	10	7.0
Political songs, written by socialists & their supporters	6	4.3
Total	141	100.0

Source: Clarion Vocal Union Collection.

While songs written by socialists and their supporters dominated the songbooks, explicitly political songs accounted for less than 5 per cent of the contents of the Halifax and Bradford sheet music collection (Table 4.3). Unlike most of the songbooks, which were published by socialist presses, the sheet music used by the CVU came from the houses of major music publishers; the CVU relied on what was commercially 'popular', and the music it purchased was thus representative of the various works found in the catalogues of the industry. Songs of the Tudor and Stuart period, consisting mostly of madrigals by Dowland, Gibbons, Morley and Wilbye, accounted for slightly more than 11 per cent of the collection; 'traditional' folksongs made up some 16 per cent; and 'classical' choral pieces, such as Mendelssohn's 'Hunting Song' and 'Hail, Bright Abode' from Wagner's *Tannhaüser*, formed 7 per cent. By contrast, the bulk of the collection (61 per cent) consisted of Victorian part-songs.

William Sterndale Bennett (1816-75) and Charles Villiers Stanford (1852-1924) had an enormous impact on choral composition in Victorian Britain: together they provided the Halifax and Bradford vocal unions with 10 per cent of their titles. 'Technically easy and aesthetically timid',[69] their songs were ideal for singing by those with little or no musical training. So were the works of Dudley Buck, an American organist and composer whose 'Hymn to Music' was a favourite at CVU choral gatherings.[70] Moreover, the more the unions opted for public performance the more they were forced to select from the limited range of music that served as the mainstay of the choral movement. Thus the songs of Buck, Stanford, Sterndale Bennett and a host of others overshadowed those written by socialists at CVU concerts. For this reason, the *Yorkshire Musical Record* could ignore the socialist roots of the CVU, instead praising that organisation's attempt to draw workers into the burgeoning choral movement, a process it considered to be 'a most encouraging feature of our national life'.[71]

The choral movement encouraged the sophisticated public performance of vocal music, and eventually the Clarion unions succumbed to the competitive spirit the movement fostered. John Spencer Curwen is credited with being the founder of the modern festival movement, the man behind those massive late Victorian musical gatherings at which various choirs would perform a series of works before a judge, hoping to be rewarded for their efforts. In 1897 the CVU began its own annual music festivals. But the more successful they became, the less they attracted a working-class audience. While claiming to 'lighten the dull monotony of our not too Merrie England', the 1898 competition drew an audience 'of mayors, aldermen, and presidents of musical societies, and other kindly-disposed people who are interested in musical culture'.[72] The following year, at the competition held in Manchester's Free Trade Hall, all claims to being primarily a socialist body were dropped: 'The Clarion Vocal Union', claimed the programme, 'was established for the cultivation of the musical taste of those to whom the wealth of unaccompanied English choral music was almost unknown.'[73] The emphasis was on technical competence, and the songs performed would have been familiar to those with some knowledge of choral music in the 1890s: Danby's 'Awake Aeolian Lyre', Pinsuti's 'Good Night Beloved' and Eaton Faning's 'Moonlight', a favourite at choral competitions.

Despite the competitive nature of the festivals, they did offer fellowship to CVU members and they also encouraged the growth of shared, regional loyalties. As the *Sheffield Guardian* claimed: 'Naturally we look to the Sheffield . . . Union to uphold the reputation of Sheffield as a musical town.'[74] Nevertheless, the festivals gradually came under attack, both for the aesthetic poverty of the pieces performed and for the competitive spirit they fostered. Just as the *Sheffield Guardian* criticised Montague Blatchford's competition piece 'Hark! A New Song Ringing' for being unimaginative, so George Bernard Shaw believed that the part-songs of Cowen, Macfarren, Parry, Stanford and Sterndale Bennett were characterised by an 'extra-special dulness'.[75] Moreover, T. A. Barrett, a musical entrepreneur in Manchester, warned his *Clarion* readers in 1902 that festivals were too competitive to 'admit of much genuine musical culture', and that the 'contests are rather in the nature of athletics than of music'.[76]

Montague Blatchford defended the competition movement, drawing an analogy between the CVU and socialism in terms of the standards of excellence both sought to encourage:

> There is an immense difference between competition for profit and emulation for advancement. The Socialist ideal is not to pull down, but to lift up. To get from everyone their *best*, believing that it is only by arriving at the highest excellence attainable for *each* that we can have a really great and happy country for all.[77]

But not everybody shared his enthusiasm. Moreover, getting the 'best' from members entailed the development of musical expertise, and this discouraged participation by those who merely looked for 'fellowship' in the unions. Success at competitions also required trained music teachers, and this demanded a stable membership able to contribute financially to the unions. Blatchford recommended that a charge of sixpence per month be levied on Clarion vocalists, while the Keighley branch fined its members for arriving late or missing rehearsals.[78] In addition, inexpensive teachers were hard to find, although the unions did give rise to a number of quasi-professional musicians, like William Scott Wilkinson, who contributed valuable time and expertise to the choirs. A member of the ILP, Wilkinson worked in a cotton mill in Keighley, played trombone in the company band and received a diploma from the college that encouraged the tonic sol-fa method of sight-singing before establishing the Keighley branch of the CVU and becoming the music master of the Keighley Trade and Grammar School.[79]

Most branches of the CVU adopted the tonic sol-fa sight-singing method of music notation. This appealed to workers, who had little or no formal music training, but it further limited the musical repertoire available to the movement. Eighty-three titles, or 55 per cent of the works in the Bradford and Halifax CVU sheet music collection, are in tonic rather than staff notation (Table 4.4). Moreover, thirty-nine are from one publisher's catalogue: Novello's Tonic Sol-Fa Series. Music publishers were clearly able to profit from the growing working-class interest in choral music to which the vocal unions contributed, and Novello once offered a two-guinea prize to the conductor of the winning choir at an upcoming Clarion competition.[80]

Table 4.4 *Music in tonic sol-fa and staff notation in the sheet music collection of the Clarion Vocal Union, Halifax and Bradford branches*

Branch	No. of songs in tonic notation	No. of songs in staff notation	Total
	%	%	
Bradford	23 (64)	13 (36)	36
Halifax	36 (72)	14 (28)	50
Unidentified	24 (37)	41 (63)	65
Total	83 (55)	68 (45)	151*

* There are only 141 different titles in the collection, but ten of them exist both in tonic and staff versions.

Source: Clarion Vocal Union collection.

Professional musicians also profited from the activities of the CVU. While Rutland Boughton's socialist sympathies cannot be doubted, he also viewed the vocal unions – which he led after Montague Blatchford's death in 1910 – as a means of supplementing the income he derived from his music criticism, work that eventually led to his appointment as music critic for labour's *Daily Citizen*. Boughton despised the increasing reliance of the musician on the market, once claiming that it 'is abominable to think that the products of a man's deepest emotions should be carried to market like a pound of butter.'[81] Yet to market he went, hoping to create a demand for his talents by appealing to socialists. Ideological conviction and self-interest were never that separate in Boughton's career, but in attempting to become a guardian of socialist music-making he made many enemies. While he despised the middle class for rejecting his work on aesthetic grounds, he also became annoyed when addressing the 'people' in whom 'true' musical talent was supposed to reside. Discussing workers' lack of interest in his own choral composition, he once complained: 'You won't have it because you have long ago renounced all jolly, lively, meaty tunes, and taken to yourself the dull, dry bones of music they serve up to you in those cathedrals of yours – the music halls.' Small wonder, then, that when Boughton spoke to members of the Labour Church in Stockport his audience consisted of serious music-lovers, few of whom were manual labourers.[82]

Boughton's experience is illustrative of the extent to which the Clarion vocal unions were marginal to mainstream late Victorian and Edwardian working-class culture. Perhaps they were also marginal to the struggle for socialism and the creation of a socialist culture: as one historian has concluded, they 'tried to accomplish their task largely within the confines of an existing repertoire, making only a limited effort to create an alternative socialist musical culture'.[83] Moreover, they often failed to appeal to those individuals their promoters hoped to reach: while the Liverpool branch advertised in the *Clarion* and several local papers, it never attracted any members from either the ILP or the SDF. Participants in the CVU were usually more interested in music than politics and many abandoned the organisation when they discovered it was going to perform at socialist gatherings.[84]

Most committed socialists believed that the CVU was not political enough, while many workers with an interest in music condemned it as too political. But aside from the important fund-raising role it played, the CVU did contribute to the business of 'making socialists', drawing at least some individuals into the practical and political work of the move-ment. This point needs to be stressed, for there were a number of workers who claimed that they had become committed socialists after joining a branch of the CVU. The choirs, wrote Montague Blatchford, attesting to the importance of this, 'have attracted and held hundreds of adherents who would otherwise have kept aloof from the movement'.[85]

The Clarion Vocal Union did 'convert' some individuals to the socialist cause. It also offered friendship and comradeship and perhaps even a foretaste of 'the good time coming'. But while enthusiasts argued that the structure of the choral movement and that of a potential lived socialism were homologous – that both were based on principles of harmony – they were unable to relate the singing of Victorian part-songs to the political battles in which they were engaged. This was not for want of trying, for there were some (usually unsuccessful) attempts to link socialist struggle with particular musical practices. One musician claimed in a lecture, 'The relation of music to socialism', that socialism was an economic and political movement with an artistic side. Hence the importance of the CVU, which 'endeavoured to inculcate [in workers] a desire for good music'.[86] But this author was unable to show how the desire for good music was related to politics. In short, socialist advocates of choral singing were more concerned with training workers in accepted standards of musical taste than they were in delineating the components of an explicitly socialist culture. While the compilers of socialist songbooks were aware of the need to construct a selective tradition that could be deployed in the struggle for socialism, Clarion vocal unionists succumbed to the desire for success measured in choral competition victories.

Building a socialist culture

In his study of the relationship between music and democratic culture in Britain, Ian Watson has offered a useful approach to the analysis of alternative cultural forms by suggesting the existence of a 'first', or dominant, culture and a 'second', or alternative, culture. He defines the latter as consisting of 'those elements inside specific historical, cultural and ideological relations which express opposition to exploitation and ... the right to a happy and meaningful existence free of oppression'.[87] By no means entirely autonomous, this second culture has always been related to the dominant culture, from which it appropriates specific forms through which to give expression to its concerns. Prior to World War I, socialist musical culture made an important contribution to the development of this second culture. But while the revolutionary material in its songbooks confronted the dominant culture – often standing in opposition to it even while appropriating material from it – the choral music that was performed by the Clarion Vocal Union was seldom more than a minor variant of tastes inscribed within the dominant culture itself.

Central to socialist cultural thought was the belief that workers should have access to the musical heritage of the nation. The components of this heritage varied according to the ideological assumptions of those who spoke in its favour. But all agreed that 'English' music was important, whether of the sixteenth and seventeenth centuries or of the 'folk'. The poetry of earlier radical and romantic critiques of industrial society was also significant, for while it was a 'national' asset it was also considered to be rooted in the experience of the 'people'.[88] The culture socialists encouraged was thus not merely part of the national heritage, but a heritage that workers might be convinced they had a stake

127

in, a national culture as well as a workers' culture. Moreover, while socialists desired the revival of cultural forms rooted firmly in the national past, they also sought to encourage a more explicitly political culture that could express the contemporary aspirations of the movement. Many of those aspirations were implicit in the heritage socialists sought for workers, although socialists also wrote new songs to inspire the struggle in which they were engaged.

In theory, socialist cultural forms were supposed to emanate from the initiatives of the people themselves:

> Socialism had to come from the volition of the people, not as something that was administered externally. Thus on the cultural front, it was not simply a matter of making the working class familiar with the received, traditional culture and to draw enrichment and hope from the best it had to offer; they had to be awakened to the possibility of making their own culture as fully conscious human beings.[89]

But there remained a problem: while socialism 'had to come from the volition of the people', the people also 'had to be awakened', inspired to create their own, alternative culture. Moreover, the process of awakening required cultural missionaries who would educate workers about the need for a socialist culture. Activists in the movement thus became like the philanthropists whom they disliked, trying to impose their own desires about the importance of music-making on the working class. In so doing, they often adopted the educational methods of philanthropy and social reform.

But how could such methods be divorced from the ideological baggage that accompanied them? The choral movement was as much a social phenomenon as anything else, aimed at encouraging discipline and promoting social harmony. By emphasising the importance of choral singing, socialists could not evade the socially integrative functions central to the choral movement. Likewise, the tonic sol-fa system of music notation was originally intended as a means of moral training for workers, giving the illusion of unsupervised participation without threatening middle-class cultural hegemony. Although socialists used tonic sol-fa notation, the equation of the system with the improvement of musical aptitude within well-defined boundaries made it hard for socialists to overcome its conservative connotations. In short, while they demanded that workers help construct a socialist culture, socialists hoped to develop workers' consciousness of this need by using methods that, by definition, could subvert their own goals.

The songs of the German socialist choral movement functioned in similar ways to those of its British counterpart. First, many of them acted as a powerful mechanism for the transmission of the ideas and beliefs of the movement. Secondly, by emphasising the disadvantaged position of the working class, some songs encouraged workers' understanding of the social distance that existed between them and other groups in society. Finally, many traditional songs served a socially integrative function, binding workers to the values and aspirations of the dominant culture.[90] Moreover, in Germany as in Britain socialists stressed the importance of linking present struggles to a cultural heritage derived from past experience, implicitly advocating Lenin's argument that any successful socialist culture must build on the triumphs of pre-socialist cultural forms.[91] But in Germany the dominant culture was more fragmented than in Britain, making it easier for German socialists to conceive of an extensive socialist subculture that did not always function to bring workers into the framework of the national culture. By contrast, constructing a cultural heritage for would-be socialists in Britain was a more dangerous proposition, for it could blunt the desire for an oppositional, socialist culture. In possession of an 'art of their own', to borrow from Montague Blatchford, workers might find themselves satisfied with their place in the established social and cultural order. The socialist choral movement in Britain was thus implicitly conservative in so far as it suggested to its participants that they shared a musical vocabulary with members of all classes.

For men like Blatchford and Trevor, socialism sometimes meant little more than making socialists and convincing them of the universal harmony to be enjoyed in the 'good time coming'. Thus the appeal of the CVU, which could offer individuals in the present an example of the kind of social harmony that a socialist order might offer in some distant future. But other socialists, like Hyndman and Morris, believed that class struggle was also important and revolutionary change necessary. The gap between these positions was enormous. Moreover, it was paralleled by divisions in the musical arena. On the one hand, there was an emergent political culture which stressed the necessity of conflict and struggle. Writers like Morris, along with other contributors to socialist songbooks, contributed to this culture. But songbook culture had to contend with a series of beliefs and assumptions about the elevating power of 'good' music that was part of an entirely different cultural vocabulary.

All of this did not matter much to most workers. They went their own way, unaware of the dilemmas faced by socialists in their attempt to develop a culture for the movement that remained familiar while being oppositional, that had roots in the past while being alive to the concerns of the present. Some workers may have enjoyed a few folksongs or madrigals, and some may have become more familiar with a large number of Victorian part-songs. There were even some who sang a few socialist songs beyond the obligatory 'England, Arise!' But the goal of uniting fragmented working-class tastes in a shared, socialist culture remained an elusive one.

CHAPTER FIVE

Municipal socialism
and the production of pleasure

It has been suggested that by the early twentieth century Robert Blatchford was growing weary of waiting for 'John Smith', the 'typical' worker to whom he addressed *Merrie England*, to see the world as he saw it.[1] Utopian aspiration had failed to generate widespread enthusiasm for the socialist community Blatchford envisaged, while workers seemed to be flocking in greater numbers to commercial recreational haunts. In the late 1890s and early 1900s, however, socialists began to sit on municipal councils, using their powers to enact reforms that promised a foretaste of socialism in one city. Moreover, recreation became a part of the legislative programme of these new, municipal socialists.

Municipal socialism was often associated with the Fabian Society. The term itself appeared in the Webbs' pamphlet, *Socialism in England* (1890) and it was in the following year the focus of Sidney Webb's *London Programme*. From their initial calls for municipal control of the gas and water supplies, of the docks and local transport, the Webbs went on to urge the municipalisation of the drink trade, pawn shops, slaughter houses, bakeries, hospitals, insurance agencies and the Thames steamboats. Although the Fabians often initiated discussion of the benefits to be derived from such policies, other socialists shared their enthusiasm. By the early 1900s, a number of national and local socialist newspapers had initiated columns devoted to municipal politics and it was here that attention was also paid to the benefits to be derived from the municipalisation of pleasure. But socialists were certainly not in the forefront of discussing the role the municipality might play in providing recreational and cultural facilities, for others also envisaged a role for the state in combatting the perceived menace of commercial recreation. Praising the activities of T. A. Leonard's Co-operative Holidays Association, for example, one reformer urged local government to make such initiatives their own: in the future, he wrote, holidays would 'not be left to the accidents of private initiative or individual philanthropy, but will be a recognised duty of the public authority responsible for the administration of all public affairs'.[2]

By 1900, the optimism associated with the religion of socialism was beginning to wear thin and socialists began to turn in greater numbers to more immediate and pragmatic concerns connected with their role as local councillors. Moreover, as the Bradford socialist Fred Jowett claimed, if utopian vision had failed to generate much working-class support for the cause of socialism, more practical measures might:

> however much the earnest seeker of a new social order, based on goodwill and fellowship, may be inspired or influenced by the vision of a transformed society such as he thinks possible and right, the general public is not moved by the same influence to any great extent. It is the next step only to which the majority can see their way, and hence such ideas as we may have of a future near enough for us to live in must shape themselves in some sort of conformity with the institutions and customs amid which we now find ourselves.[3]

Socialists began to turn away from their faith in the innate goodness of working-class desires and suggest that the state and the municipality could play a role in initiating the cultural changes they viewed as important in preparing the ground for the socialist transformation of Britain.

Leisure and the state

While socialists began to encourage the state to concern itself with the cultural and recreational affairs of the nation, few of their suggestions were entirely new. As early as the 1840s, in his introduction to Leon Faucher's study of Manchester, J. P. Culverwell claimed that there was nothing 'connected with the health and morals of a dense community like ours . . . beneath the notice of a municipal body', and that it was better 'that the pursuits of the masses should be influenced and guided by a reputable body, like the corporation', than left 'to the management of publicans and gamblers'.[4] Culverwell was one of the first writers to consider the role the municipality might play in supervising public recreation. But such suggestions, isolated as they were in the 1840s, were made more frequently during the subsequent fifty years. Gladstone argued that the state should assist in the 'cultivation and improvement' of the people, while others claimed that 'improvement' was central to their call for public libraries, art galleries and museums.[5] By the 1890s individuals were drawing up elaborate plans for advancing still further the role of the state in the cultural arena. The drama critic Clement Scott, for example, suggested the need for 'a separate department of the state to control amusements' under the control of a 'Director General of Public Amusements'.[6] Such ideas were widespread by 1900, indicative of the extent to which the state was increasingly viewed as a guardian of popular culture and public morality.

Initial intervention by the state in the cultural arena developed less from widespread theoretical concerns than from the practical necessity of maintaining urban order and securing public health. The 1833 Select Committee on Public Walks offered suggestions concerning the provision of playgrounds and parks that were later embodied in the Towns' Improvement Act (1847) and the Public Health Act (1848). Although open spaces were first justified on medical grounds (especially after the cholera epidemics of the period), their advocates soon stressed the recreational benefits to be derived from them. The Museums Act of 1845 and the libraries Acts of 1850, 1853 and 1855 empowered municipalities to construct museums and libraries; in so doing they further encouraged civic responsibility for the edification of the populace. Acts of 1875 and 1896 allowed such institutions to remain open for longer hours and permitted Sunday openings of galleries and museums. And in one of the most comprehensive acts, the Public Health Amendment Act of 1907, earlier policies were codified and municipalities were finally permitted to erect entertainment pavilions and refreshment rooms in parks, and provide free, public concerts.

Despite the passage of these Acts, an extensive debate took place over the legitimacy of state intervention in such matters. While many reformers supported the public provision of museums and libraries, others believed that gymnasia, refreshment rooms and public concerts were beyond the purview of the state.[7] Consequently, many towns lagged behind others in implementing the measures made possible by the various Acts. In the 1890s, despite the attention that was focused on the achievements of the London County Council (LCC), other towns had already led the way in the provision of cultural and recreational facilities. Birmingham was the most important of these. There Joseph Chamberlain's 'Civic Gospel' of the 1870s had led to the establishment of an extensive network of parks, libraries, museums and art schools. Other localities emulated Birmingham's policies, and by the 1890s towns competed with each other for the accolades that usually accompanied the municipal provision of opportunities for recreation and culture.[8]

Concern about the rapid development of the leisure industry in the

1880s and 1890s intensified pressure on the municipality and the state both to regulate and provide facilities for culture and recreation. Fearing the corruption of popular taste, especially by the new music halls, reformers urged the state to combat the perceived menace by establishing centres of cultural excellence that would serve as a bulwark against the new, commercial trends. Not only was the state assigned the role of protecting 'culture' but it was also called upon to compete directly with the recreational entrepreneur. As early as 1877 one writer argued that in addition to supporting public libraries the state should 'subsidize amusements which enter . . . copiously into the veins of a nation's life'.[9]

Philanthropists and settlement house workers who feared the growth of the new leisure pursuits and the breakdown of social contact between the classes were especially prone to favour state provision in the cultural sphere. The ideas of these individuals have been outlined in an earlier chapter, but it is important to add that most of them actively encouraged the state to assume some of their cultural and recreational responsibilities, or at least provide a recreational infrastructure that would make their task an easier one. As early as the 1870s, Charles Rowley was elected to the Manchester City Council on the pledge of 'Baths and Washhouses, and Public-rooms for Ancoats', the district he represented, and a generation later Percy Alden wrote: 'In these days of artificially organised society, when the citizen is removed from the . . . healthy influences of country life, it is the duty of the state to intervene and provide opportunities for healthy recreation.'[10] Influenced by the Garden City Movement, with its own call for the public provision of all kinds of cultural facilities, Samuel Barnett voiced similar concerns in *The Ideal City* (1894). By stressing the importance of collectivist measures, individuals like Rowley, Alden and Barnett not only influenced legislation, particularly at the local level, but also contributed to a thorough reassessment of traditional liberal aims in late Victorian society.

The pleasures of municipal socialism

As Benjamin Kirkman Gray, the prominent social reformer and historian of philanthropy, noted approvingly in 1908, the state was slowly beginning to assume responsibility for the recreational work that philanthropists had initiated but were unable to extend further.[11] Socialists encouraged such activity. Not only did they contribute to intellectual debates about the legitimate sphere of state activity but they also demanded that the state identify, protect and make available various cultural forms that they deemed important – n >t only for the cause of socialism but also for the well-being of the nation.

Until 1906, when the Labour Party made a significant break-through at the parliamentary level, it was to the local boards of guardians, school boards and councils that socialists looked for electoral victory.[12] And it was in terms of their local successes that socialists first began to specify the duties of the state in the cultural arena. As early as 1884 H. M. Hyndman called for the municipal provision of gardens and playgrounds and in 1887, in his comprehensive plan for London, he conceived of an extensive municipal machinery through which Londoners would control their gas and water supplies, roads, lighting, police, tramways, buses, drainage, sanitation, markets, poor relief, parks, baths and libraries.[13] By the 1890s many socialists and trade unionists at the local level were making similar suggestions. In Halifax the election committee of the local trades council advanced a broad municipal programme that included the call for the 'opening of a news room and museums on Sundays as a counter-inducement to the temptation of intemperance'.[14] Fabians, however, were especially active in suggesting the need for socialist municipal policies. In 1891 the Rev. Joseph Wood of Birmingham delivered a lecture to the Society in which he argued for the municipal construction of playgrounds, gymnasia and swimming baths, and for the provision of band, orchestral and choral concerts.[15] In the socialist constitution they later drafted, the Webbs codified such demands, calling for a ' "National Minimum" of subsistence and leisure', to be guaranteed by a standing committee in the Social Parliament on 'Common Amenity and Public Beauty'.[16]

Many socialists rallied to such calls. Fred Brocklehurst, member of the National Administrative Council of the ILP, secretary of the Labour Church and town councillor in Manchester, believed that 'municipal pleasures' were 'at least as valuable as municipal utilities' because they cultivated 'the social qualities of the citizen'.[17] In 1900 Brocklehurst initiated a weekly column of 'Progressive news and notes' in the *Clarion*, attempting to popularise his views. Moreover, his call for 'municipal pleasures' found an eager audience amongst socialists, in part because they were increasingly frustrated in the cultural arena: philanthropy had failed to advance the cause of rational recreation to any appreciable extent, while the threat posed by the commercialisation of leisure had tended to drive the goal of a more rational organisation of leisure into some distant future. Brocklehurst believed that weapons forged in the municipality could become part of the increasingly sophisticated arsenal required to transform working-class behaviour. 'Outlaw' echoed these sentiments, telling his *Clarion* readers: 'Your municipality should restore the means of recreation of which you have been robbed.' He proceeded to outline a comprehensive plan for the provision of bowling greens, tennis courts, football grounds, swimming baths, libraries, club rooms, theatres and free public concerts. Taken together, he suggested, they would encourage more 'desirable' forms of pleasure.[18]

Central to this polemic was the belief that the boldest of measures were required to 'rescue' working-class taste before it was too late. As the Scottish ILPer Willie Stewart argued, desirable forms of pleasure had to be encouraged by the municipality in order to displace less worthy – and often commercial – activities and thus contribute to the education and refinement of recreational desires.[19] Stewart's belief that valuable character traits could be developed through the regulation of pleasure had always been a central article of faith in the socialist movement, although it was only towards the end of the century that socialists began explicitly to conceive of a role for the state in the reformation of individual character. In short, the state offered socialists yet another means of making available the kinds of activity they both valued in their own lives and wished to encourage in working-class communities. But while Stewart and 'Outlaw' were genuinely enthusiastic about the potential for redirecting personal tastes through municipal action, conservative thinkers, as we have seen, soon seized upon such programmes in order to fuel their own attack on the anti-libertarian sentiments they associated with the socialist movement and wrote about in their anti-socialist novels.

In their discussion of specific 'municipal pleasures', socialists focused on the need for the state or the municipality to assume control of the theatre, to provide edifying music and to rescue the drink trade from the clutch of the brewers. As one writer claimed in the *Labour Leader*: 'If the joy of life is to come back to us in its fullness, the arts, too, must be rescued from the grip of callous and hateful commercialism.'[20] Implicit in such calls was the assumption, discussed in Chapter one, that despite their claims capitalists were more interested in profit than in edifying entertainment. This was central to the arguments made by the Fabian and drama critic Charles Charrington in support of the provision of municipal theatres. It also surfaced in the writings of worker-socialists like Dan Irving, a warehouseman active in the Bristol Socialist Society who later became a member of the Burnley branch of the SDF and served on the Burnley town council. Irving believed that a municipal theatre 'would remove most, if not all, of the objectionable features' of the theatre, would be effective in 'the inculcation of high moral and ethical ideals', and would lead to the production of plays that were 'elevating and instructive in tone'.[21]

Socialists also argued that concerts and concert halls were ripe for municipalisation. Sam Midgley claimed before an ILP audience in 1912 that only music could 'help in cultivating a taste for pure pleasures', and he called for an addition to the rates of a farthing in the pound for the establishment of a municipal orchestra. Such schemes would have appealed to the individuals who had little sympathy with socialism and yet had already supported Bournemouth's creation of a municipal orchestra. But under the guise of attacking commerce for thwarting the goals of rational recreation, Midgley advanced schemes for municipal intervention in the cultural arena because existing working-class pleasures were so distasteful to him: workers 'given up to frivolity will not make a city prosperous; for that purpose sobriety and seriousness of aim are needed. Healthy drama and good music will undoubtedly be of service in this direction.'[22]

Many articles appeared in the socialist press extolling the virtues of 'municipal music' in Glasgow, for it was there that a number of local initiatives were implemented. The arguments put forward by Glaswegian socialists for the municipal provision of music are familiar ones: municipal concerts would 'enliven and elevate the moody masses from the dull apathy created by their dismal environment', resulting in 'their expressed desire to get more healthy surroundings and better conditions of life'.[23] By 1898 Glasgow was spending some £3,000 per year on open-air band concerts and Saturday afternoon concerts in public halls. Such experiments led many individuals to suggest the expansion of such activities. Although municipal concerts were well attended, writers suggested that they did not draw workers from the music halls and that municipalities thus ought to provide music-hall entertainment to accompany their other offerings.[24]

Although they demanded 'municipal music', socialists were often more concerned with municipalising the sale of alcohol. One of them wrote: 'If we want a big field for our first fight with capital we shall find it . . . in the drink trade.'[25] The ensuing battle was waged on many fronts. For strict teetotallers, it was fought by urging the suppression of drink altogether. But despite the strength of teetotal feeling in the socialist movement, many believed that lecturing workers on the evils of drink did not strike at the heart of the problem.[26] Hence the appeal of experiments in municipalisation, such as the 'Gothenberg System' in Scandinavia. By vesting control of public houses in community groups that were limited to an annual return of 5 per cent, the System gave public-house managers little incentive to encourage excessive drinking.[27]

The Fabian Society surveyed the drink problem in Britain in order to bolster such arguments for the control of the industry. As Edward Pease, the Society's secretary, wrote: 'The slum-dweller must have his liquor, but there is no reason why the state should not see that he is given a lesson in decency and comfort every time he takes his glass.'[28] A shot of whisky was to be followed by a chaser of rational recreation. Like Pease, most socialists who urged municipalisation suggested the need to provide public houses with facilities for recreation and entertainment. The total suppression of the drink trade remained an elusive goal, and socialists came to accept that the best that could be hoped for was careful supervision of the public house. As socialists in Rochdale put it, urging the council to erect a municipal pub: 'All things are demoralising when they are abused, therefore proper control is the most essential rule.'[29]

Although socialists wrote a number of pamphlets and articles on the municipalisation of the public house, their thinking cannot be divorced from their desire for the transformation of pleasure in general, for by controlling such an important site of working-class culture they hoped they would be able to encourage more 'worthy' forms of recreation. In one of the more elaborate schemes put forward in the pages of the *Labour Leader*, the ageing activist Frederick Rogers suggested that communities should take control of public houses and hand over the profits to Westminster. Once a year the state would grant each community a share of the profits (the amount being determined by the size of that community) for the 'establishment and maintenance of creative centres, the primary object of which shall be to counteract the influence of the drink traffic'. This, according to Rogers, was a 'sane' temperance policy because it vested in an 'enlightened municipality' the power to regulate 'whatever evils grow out of drinking'.[30] But what if the municipality was not so enlightened, or if the municipalisation of the drink trade was resented as an attempt by do-gooders to regulate the pleasures of the people? This was indeed the fear of some socialists, aware of the tension that existed between the desire to encourage working-class co-operation and self-help and the deployment of the coercive arm of the state to regulate working-class behaviour.

Municipal socialism at work

One cannot study municipal socialism in the 1890s and early 1900s, particularly in London, without examining the Progressive Movement, of which it was a vital component. By 1900 Progressive thought was so widespread that the Progressive label was attached to policies that had been advanced under the guise of municipal socialism a decade earlier. Characterised by its emphasis on the rational determination of social progress and the persuasion of a democratic electorate, Progressive thought assigned an important place to ideas in its quest for progress. In so doing it brought together many socialists and 'new liberals' who shared the belief that the state – which for them represented the desire of the whole community – could will progress to predetermined ends.[31]

The Progressives predominated in the chambers of the LCC after the creation of that body in 1889, and by developing a radical programme of social reform they forestalled the emergence of an autonomous socialist presence. But socialists generally supported and contributed to Progressive policy and were often elected under the Progressive banner. In 1892 the Labour Representation League was influential in the election of nine labour councillors, including John Burns (Battersea), Fred Henderson (Clapham) and Will Crooks (Poplar). For almost two decades the alliance between the working class and the middle class, between liberals, radicals and socialists, was largely a success. Moreover, as early as 1889 the Progressive victory was heralded by *Justice* as a triumph for social democracy and the beginning of progress towards the London commune that Hyndman had called for. Until doctrinal disputes and a conservative backlash finally led to its fragmentation in 1907, the Progressive Alliance was in the forefront of plans for the extension of municipal services.[32]

While Progressive influence on LCC policy has been the object of analysis, the Council's work in the cultural arena has escaped such treatment. Although it is beyond the scope of this study to explore the evolution of the LCC's cultural policy in detail,[33] the Progressive programme in London both illuminates the practical application of many of the ideas outlined above and suggests the importance of the role played by socialists in contributing to their implementation. In Poplar, for example, Will Crooks became a major Progressive presence. In the 1880s, working as a cooper in an East End brewery, Crooks and his co-workers agitated for the construction of a public gymnasium, library and technical institute. With the backing of the Poplar Labour League and a number of middle-class Progressives, Crooks was elected to the

LCC and became a leading member of the Parks Committee, soon playing a major role in the establishment of a greater number of parks and open spaces in the East End. A staunch teetotaller, Crooks also argued for the municipal control of music halls and the drink trade. Like many socialists, Crooks was a firm believer in the role local government might play in shaping popular culture: the LCC, he once wrote, 'showed the people . . . what great powers for good lay in the hands of the municipalities'.[34]

Those 'powers for good' were also cultivated by labour leaders in other parts of London, especially in Battersea. There John Burns played a major role in the development of Progressive policy, even though he was still a member of the SDF when elected to the LCC in 1892. With a population of 169,000 in 1902, mostly working class, the borough was the centre of an extensive labour movement that generally supported the Progressives. Burns voiced their aspirations on the LCC, while the local Labour League and Trades Council urged workers to vote for Progressive candidates and support their reforming efforts.[35] Burns was no friend of popular culture in the 1890s and he urged the state to encourage more rational recreation. He had little faith in workers' ability to use their leisure wisely and he believed that shorter working hours and higher wages were responsible for an increase in drinking and gambling. Between the wars, echoing points he had made in the 1890s, Burns suggested that additional libraries and galleries would 'give men and women . . . an alternative to the monotonies and frivolities too frequently imposed upon them'.[36] While Burns had his own ideas about the kinds of activity that should be 'imposed' on workers, in his later years he began to realise that although government legislation might encourage more 'healthy' pleasures, this by no means guaranteed widespread public support of them. But in the 1890s, at least, Burns's faith in the municipality and in its attempt to detach workers from the perils he associated with gambling, drink and the music hall remained undiminished.

Besides supporting municipal libraries, museums and galleries, Progressives in Battersea pioneered the public provision of music. Burns once praised 'municipal music', arguing that free concerts were 'delightful counter-attractions' to the public house and that the LCC should follow Battersea's lead and establish a municipal orchestra, opera house and academy of music.[37] Despite his enthusiasm, however, much of the impetus for the municipal provision of music in Battersea came not from Burns but from his colleague W. Lethbridge. Through his efforts on the borough council, Lethbridge managed to establish a municipal choir and orchestra, erect an organ in the town hall, hire an official borough organist and institute free public concerts. As Fred Brocklehurst approvingly noted, Lethbridge was the father of 'healthful recreation' in Battersea.[38]

Such policies were not without their critics, and though Progressives in Battersea eagerly called for the expansion of municipal activity in the cultural arena their ideas were often challenged. Moreover, Lethbridge's achievements were actually overturned. Under his tutelage, the local council began to offer free public concerts in the town hall on Tuesday evenings at a cost of £650 per year. From October 1901 to March 1902 additional performances took place on Fridays and Sundays, at a cost of an additional £400. The growing expense associated with these concerts alarmed many conservatives who, under the auspices of the Municipal Alliance, concluded that the borough had no statutory power to use the rates for the provision of free concerts. A £278 surcharge was thus imposed on members of the council.[39] Competing with the purveyors of commercial recreations in an attempt to reshape working-class culture was a costly business and few ratepayers were willing to foot the bill. Despite widespread enthusiasm on the left, the promise of music and morals in Battersea failed to be realised, and one of the earliest attempts made by socialists and labour leaders to use the municipality to improve working-class taste ended in failure.

The municipal provision of culture was also advocated in West Ham, largely by members of the majority socialist and labour group on the borough council. The population of West Ham grew rapidly in the late nineteenth century, a result of the expansion of the docks and heavy industry in East London. From 128,953 inhabitants in 1881, it rose to 288,425 in 1904. West Ham became an independent county borough in 1888 and was thus not a part of the LCC. Moreover, while the LCC was active in municipalising various services and amenities, West Ham lagged behind, mostly on account of the rapidity of its growth and its consequent inability to provide even the most rudimentary services. But individuals like Will Thorne devoted a considerable amount of their energy in the 1890s to organising workers in order to press for municipal programmes like those being developed by the LCC. The son of a brickmaker and a sweated labourer, Thorne came to London in 1881 and worked for the Beckton Gas Works in the Canning Town district of the borough. He played a major role in the formation of the National Union of Gas Workers, served as the secretary of the Canning Town branch of the SDF and was elected to the borough council in 1891, a post he held (for all but three weeks) until 1910, when he became an alderman. From his seat on the council he argued for the municipalisation of various services, although when, as early as 1891, he called for the municipal provision of baths and washhouses, as well as for municipal control of the tramways, he was branded as a 'revolutionary'.[40]

Labour presence on the West Ham borough council grew rapidly in the 1890s. Moreover, it was an independent presence and not part of a general Progressive Alliance. A strong trade union and socialist movement under the leadership of the SDF had worked hard with the ILP and various Christian Socialist bodies to secure representation on the council. In 1896 they gained seven of the thirty-six council seats and two years later, after the division of the borough into twelve wards, they secured ten of the twelve new seats and also managed to elect several aldermen. This was the first time that any borough council in Britain had come under the control of a socialist and labour majority, consisting of a number of individuals who put aside their doctrinal differences in order to develop a coherent policy of municipal reform.[41] As such West Ham affords a unique opportunity to study socialist cultural policy independently of the Progressive label.

Percy Alden was an active member of the labour group on the council, convinced that his settlement work at Mansfield House had to be supplemented by political activity: 'in no direction', he wrote, 'has democracy made greater headway in England than in connection with our city life.'[42] Elected to the borough council in 1892, becoming West Ham's deputy mayor in 1898, Alden made it the policy of his settlement to support labour politicians. It was in part due to the efforts of Alden and Will Reason, the secretary of Mansfield House, that the labour and socialist representatives on the council were cemented together. Although settlements were often more popular with their middle-class enthusiasts than with the workers they attempted to influence, Mansfield House set out to develop the civic pride of workers in West Ham by encouraging their participation in public bodies. As Alden wrote in 1898, settlements can 'assist in educating the civic conscience, in forming and crystallising public opinion, [and] in supplying men to initiate and carry out various social reforms'.[43]

This particular aspect of settlement work was praised by local labour leaders. While middle-class programmes of moral elevation were rejected – Will Thorne, for example, complained that the 'East End of London has never taken kindly to the "high-brows" ' – Alden's attempt to educate workers and prepare them for the affairs of local government was always welcomed. Thorne, himself an autodidact encouraged in his endeavours by Eleanor Marx, claimed that 'the growth of education is gradually permitting the submerged workers of this crowded over-worked and over-populated district to appreciate the finer things of life.'[44] Will Crooks also considered education to be central to working-class struggle and like Thorne he praised Alden for linking education with a concept of political democracy and social citizenship that avoided middle-class cant. Moreover, he claimed that working-class mistrust of middle-class reformers seldom extended to Alden, again suggesting the important links that were forged between various middle-class reformers and labour leaders at the local level.[45]

In his capacity as borough councillor, Alden worked to secure the provision of the cultural facilities important for the kind of educated municipal citizenship he envisaged. He was influenced by Samuel Barnett's experiments in art education at the Whitechapel Gallery, persuading the council to mount an annual free picture exhibition. At the height of its popularity it attracted 130,000 visitors. Alden also supported moves 'to bring the country into the city' through the provision of parks and playgrounds; he induced the philanthropist J. Passmore Edwards to provide funds for a municipally owned museum; and he worked to secure a greater number of public baths, libraries and public concerts.[46] But despite his enthusiasm, the cultural policies enacted were by no means innovative or extensive. While members of the labour group on the council worked hard to bring West Ham in line with the LCC, they merely speeded up a process that had been initiated earlier in the 1890s. Socialists and labour leaders did vote for the Sunday opening of reading rooms, for an annual fortnight's holiday and the cessation of labour on May Day for all municipal workers, and for the provision of free concerts. But the Public Library Act, for example, had already been adopted in 1890 and the first libraries had been opened before socialists gained a significant voice on the council.

Moreover, when socialists did develop plans for a more far-reaching policy of municipalisation, ratepayers grew alarmed, as they had in Battersea, establishing the West Ham Municipal Alliance to halt the tide of reform. One member of the borough council claimed that the promise of concerts and clubs for the working class was merely an attempt to bribe the electorate. Moreover, even if all the promises made by socialists were to result in concrete policies, this writer continued, the higher rates necessary to fund them would scare employers out of the borough and would thus entail 'a great amount of suffering upon the very men for whose benefit the new order of things has been introduced'.[47] Municipal socialism may have envisaged a cultural renaissance in West Ham but it could do nothing to alter the nature of capitalist relations that shaped the very community in which that renaissance was to occur.

Despite the barriers to success, municipal socialism was an appealing proposition in the 1890s, offering many a tantalising glimpse of socialism in one city. And yet the cultural policies advanced by socialists could have been accepted – and often were – by liberals, and even by a few conservatives. It was thus easy for such proposals to be put forward under the general Progressive umbrella, not only in London but also in many provincial towns.[48] Taken together, the cultural policies developed by advocates of municipal activity, no matter what their political persuasion, contributed most of all to the establishment of a more extensive role for the state and the municipality in the cultural arena, a role that had come about with the provision of parks, playgrounds and museums in the 1830s and 1840s, and that would become institutionalised through such post-1945 creations as the Arts Council and the Sports Council.

On the one hand, municipal socialism merely extended the cultural work of philanthropists by other means. On the other, it allowed socialists to claim control of such work for themselves, thereby allowing them to repudiate philanthropic paternalism. Sometimes socialists merely advocated 'improving' recreations for their own sake; on other occasions, as was certainly the case in West Ham, municipal cultural endeavours were explicitly linked to the encouragement of working-class co-operation for mutual improvement through the municipality. But this alarmed many adamant critics of socialism in Britain, while the radical rhetoric often employed by municipal socialists alienated many would-be supporters and ratepayers, thus reducing the amount of room socialists had in which to develop the policies they considered important.

The battle for the control of municipal cultural policy, and over the direction that policy should take, was often a bitter one. In Bradford, for example, the spectre of municipal socialism scared many council members, even though they were prone to accept many of the policies socialists put forward when shorn of their radical rhetoric. Heated debates took place in the council chambers for months over the request of £100 for the provision of free public concerts. Most councillors agreed that the sum requested was a mere trifle and that municipally sponsored rational recreation was a worthy goal. Nevertheless, because the initiative was so eagerly supported by socialists and labour leaders it was seen as the thin edge of the socialist wedge: 'For are not free concerts the same in principle as free theatres, free music halls, gratis pleasures of all sorts?'[49] Most of the labour and socialist councillors voted in favour of the initiative and funds for free concerts were made available. But the measure was later rescinded, in part because of pressure from the Bradford ratepayers' league. For many members of the middle class, personal material well-being came to outweigh the desire for a publicly funded realm of rational recreation, while their mistrust of socialists' motives propelled them into the forefront of the attack on municipal socialism.

Municipal puritanism

While they contributed to carving out a municipal space for the development of more-radical forms of association and collective development, the cultural policies advanced by municipal socialists often attempted to wed workers to a system of cultural preferences that was part of the dominant culture. 'Municipal pleasures' did offer workers a semblance of control over facilities, institutions and activities they may well have rejected if provided by middle-class do-gooders and philanthropists. But despite the appearance of control that accompanied the ballot-box, decisions were still made in the council chambers. And here there were many socialists and labour leaders who experimented with cultural policy because they found existing working-class culture distasteful and had as strong an axe to grind with many working-class leisure pursuits as had a number of philanthropists. Activists like Will Crooks and John Burns, respectable and temperate, moral and virtuous, hoped that their cultural preferences could be imprinted on the rest of society and they viewed the state as the tool for the eradication of pleasures they so disliked. For this they were dubbed 'municipal puritans' by their critics, individuals who began to doubt the virtue of using the state to impose a rigid cultural conformity on the populace.

Municipal puritanism was subscribed to on the right as well as on the left. It can be seen at work in Sheffield, where it was often the policy of those opposed to socialism. In 1907 the local branch of the Labour Representation Committee applied to the council for a permit to hold a demonstration in Firth Park on the first Sunday in May. A majority of the council members voted against the request. The arguments they put forward were ostensibly Sabbatarian ones, although, as the socialist *Sheffield Guardian* suggested, perhaps there was something more to their decision than this: 'It all comes down to a question of Sabbatarianism behind which there probably lurks a dislike of the Labour Movement.' The paper was appalled by the decision, claiming that the puritanical spirit of Oliver Cromwell was alive and well on the council. According to the *Sheffield Guardian*, the councillors were attempting to suppress the rights of the people, particularly their right to choose from a variety of pleasures on Sundays.[50]

What occurred in Sheffield in 1907 was not unusual, for similar battles took place throughout Britain. Nor was it uncommon for the critics of such municipal policies to label their advocates 'puritans', a term that came to be attached to all individuals who attempted to use the state in their struggle against popular pleasures. Obviously, the *Sheffield Guardian* had a vested interest in gaining council support for its demonstration. But the language it used in its attack on council members was also deployed by other socialists in their own attempts to thwart legal interference with the pursuit of pleasure. Moreover, as the Protestant work ethic gave way to a new emphasis on pleasure and consumption – and indeed to the pleasures of consumption – some socialists actually saw the people's 'right to pleasure' as the first line of defence against capitalist exploitation. Ernest Belfort Bax, for example, was convinced that the work ethic – which had created a world in 'which we are all "puritans", despising pleasure as frivolous and [a] waste of time' – had to be dismantled if workers were to be liberated from capitalism.[51]

The attack on puritanism grew rapidly in the nineteenth century. As early as 1828 one writer spoke out against middle-class puritans who do not allow 'the natural privilege of both mind and movement belonging to the operations of nature', and who fail to realise that 'the poor are ... entitled to the rational enjoyment of the pleasures and amusements such people are addicted to'.[52] Such beliefs became widespread later in the century. If, as socialists often believed, individuals had an innate desire for pleasure, then desire needed to be educated. The problem with philanthropists was that they attempted to elevate workers before properly understanding their needs. Even worse, the problem with puritans was that they attempted to suppress the desire for pleasure altogether, often by legally restricting access to those pleasures they deemed undesirable.

While the term 'puritan' was rooted in the religious struggles of the sixteenth and seventeenth centuries, it meant something quite different in the nineteenth. By 1900 puritanism was associated less with the explicitly religious opposition to popular culture that had triumphed under Cromwell than with a more general desire to cleanse recreation of its less-savoury aspects. But despite the differences, critics of puritanism were eager to discredit its nineteenth-century manifestations by tracing their origins back to the policy of the Commonwealth. Socialists often contrasted the Merrie England of the Middle Ages with the Dismal England of their own day, placing the blame for the present state of affairs squarely on the shoulders of the Puritans. As William Diack wrote in 1895: 'With the rise of Puritanism, the first effective blow was dealt at ... merry rites and customs. The Puritans caused the Maypoles to be destroyed, and also forbade the continuance of the annual merry makings.'[53] While recent historians have argued that Cromwellians were not as puritinical in regard to popular culture as their nineteenth-century critics suggested, the myth of a Merrie England destroyed by puritanical fanaticism fuelled socialist attacks on those forms of puritanism that operated in a very different context in their own society.

The debates that took place over puritanism in the late nineteenth century do not represent a clearly demarcated conflict between 'socialists' and 'puritans'; as we have seen in the case of Burns and Crooks, puritans were to be found in the ranks of the socialist movement itself. Such individuals were often attacked by the *Clarion*, which always claimed to rally to the defence of popular pleasures. Not only did the paper defend the Manchester Palace of Varieties against its detractors but its music critic, Georgia Pearce, condemned those 'puritanical beings' who thought music a frivolity that socialists should devote no time to. Moreover, Leonard Hall once argued in the paper that although the socialist movement 'has been cursed by its dismal Calvinism', the Clarion Fellowship – the organisation that brought *Clarion* readers together – encouraged an anti-puritan spirit in the movement. Many workers from puritanical backgrounds agreed with Hall's assessment, suggesting that their own participation in Clarion activities had a liberating effect on their lives.[54] The *Clarion* also became the mouthpiece for Robert Blatchford's personal vendetta against Keir Hardie and the ILP, a body he viewed as having much in common with the roundheads of the seventeenth century. As he wrote to a friend concerning Hardie and his colleagues on the *Labour Leader*: 'They were nonconformist, self-righteous ascetics, out for the class war and the dictation of the proletariat. We loved the humour and colour of the old English tradition.'[55]

The success of the *Clarion*, along with Blatchford's popularity (particularly in Lancashire), can in part be attributed to a widespread distaste for Hardie's puritanism and a desire among many workers for the

147

'cakes and ale culture' that Blatchford admired and claimed to offer.[56] But what was on offer were cakes to be eaten in moderation and ale to be imbibed sparingly, for Blatchford could often be as puritanical as Hardie himself. One of his biographers quoted him as saying: 'I was rather strait-laced and perhaps ... inclined to a certain ... self-righteous Puritanism.' George Bernard Shaw noted the puritanical streak in Blatchford, complaining of the way in which he imposed his 'trumpery little moral system' on the world.[57] Blatchford's puritanism also permeates his novel, *The Sorcery Shop*, in which one of the visitors to utopia claims that its inhabitants 'are all vegetarians and non-smokers, and teetotallers who don't know the meaning of the word "damn"'. Such passages forced Blatchford's biographer to conclude that *The Sorcery Shop* was unsuccessful because Blatchford concocted a world that demanded strict, ascetic behaviour.[58] Thus, despite Blatchford's own claims, a subtle form of puritanism even pervaded the Clarion movement. In 1912, one writer recognised that this would need to be overcome if the socialist movement was ever going to appeal to a large number of workers:

> The preaching of the Play Spirit, the cult of the Right to Play, is just the very thing that the Labour and Trade Union movement needs in order to make it healthy and effective. I think that our movement is too much bound up with a kind of puritanism for it to be really successful.[59]

In the 1880s and 1890s, socialist anti-puritan activity often centred on debates over the Sabbath, and in these Christian Socialists played a major role. But their appeals did not convince all workers, for the working class was itself divided over the issue. One argument put forward by Sabbatarians was seized upon by many workers who suggested that if Sundays were to be given over to pleasure-seekers a number of workers would have to face Sunday employment in their service. These claims were voiced by many working-class Lib-Labs, including Henry Broadhurst, who voted against a Sunday opening bill for museums and galleries. Only two labour societies in London supported Broadhurst (sixty-one opposed him). Nevertheless, workers like Robert Mackintosh, president of the Glasgow Workingmen's Sabbath Protection Society, shared Broadhurst's concerns: 'Turn the Sabbath into a pleasure day, and instantly you fasten the yoke of labour on the necks of myriads of unwilling workmen.'[60] But despite their prevalence, such arguments were seldom voiced in the socialist press. Both the *Labour Leader* and the *Clarion* claimed that while they were opposed to profit-making they were even more opposed to Sabbatarianism. In practice, compromises were required to satisfy those who feared that Sunday openings would lead to the further exploitation of labour. Thus, when the West Ham council voted to allow picture palaces to be opened on Sundays, it added the proviso that workers should still only have to labour six days per week.[61]

The legacy of puritanical opposition to popular culture lingered on, and the desire to eradicate it united socialists like Blatchford and Bax with settlement house workers like Barnett and Christian Socialists like Stewart Headlam. These individuals shared, to varying degrees, the belief that any opportunity for Sunday recreation was better than no opportunity at all. But, as Conrad Noel suggested, Sunday pleasures were still to be carefully supervised rational pleasures. A prominent figure in the Christian Socialist revival, Noel was also a member of the SDF, a slum worker in Paddington, a prominent speaker in Northern socialist circles and, after 1911, a member of the executive of the British Socialist Party. In a pamphlet, *The Day of the Sun*, he claimed that while puritanism had to be eradicated, the promised kingdom of pleasure should not result in uncontrolled licence. Noel spoke out against those who advocated unbridled pleasures at any cost:

> [timid] . . . of preaching the Puritan's hell, they dwell *ad infinitum* upon the sugary joys of an immediate and easily gained heaven for all. Repudiating the asceticism of their ancestors, they yet give us no principle of guidance in the matter of the bodily appetites. How seldom we hear any definite theory of control in place of the old-time theory of suppression.[62]

Noel went on to suggest that religion, assisted by the state, should guide the uses of pleasure.

The debate over the Sabbath was thus a complicated one, for it was seldom a question of fun-loving socialists opposed to the stern morality of puritanical church leaders. Christian Socialists could be as anti-puritanical as those socialists who, like Belfort Bax, repudiated traditional religion. On the other hand, many self-professed socialists, like John Burns in the 1890s, could be as puritanical as any traditional church leader. Moreover, debates about puritanism ultimately became debates about the legitimate arena of state activity, for although Christian Socialists like Noel and Headlam hoped the churches might reassert their influence over popular culture, they also suggested that the state should play a role. But when the state did eventually begin to develop its own cultural policies, they were often not of the sort that Christian Socialists had hoped for: as Headlam soon discovered, the state could be as puritanical as any religious body. Headlam thus found himself engaged in battle not only with a puritanical church, but also with puritanical municipal policies, especially those advanced by the LCC.

That certain socialists wanted to use the LCC and other municipal bodies to impose their own brand of puritanism on the populace cannot be disputed. Ernest E. Hunter, writing on the 'puritan peril' in 1908, opposed 'the joyless ascetics whose ultimate aim is prohibition'. But implicit in his plans to convince the state to elevate public houses and make them 'harmless' – in his hopes for rational recreation – their lurked an intense desire for moral sobriety, verging on the puritanical, that he believed the state should encourage.[63] Moreover, a number of other socialists shared Hunter's belief that the state should actively encourage the reform of popular culture. Even Blatchford, despite his opposition to Hardie and his alleged anti-puritanism, supported the Progressives on the LCC in hopes of securing the passage of measures aimed at the elevation of the masses.

In the 1890s Progressives in London were committed to purging the metropolis of moral corruption and vice, and they began to refuse licences to many of the smaller music halls. William Archer, an advocate of this particular LCC policy of regulation, claimed that while the Council was 'open to the influence of Puritan bigotry', it vested control of amusements in an elected body that served to regulate amusements in accordance with the wishes of the people. Puritanism was thus legitimated as the 'will of the people': 'Why', Archer continued, 'should we fear that a body which expresses the will of the people . . . thwart the will of the people in the matter of amusements?'[64] Municipal socialists also claimed to be voicing the will of the people. But at the same time they attempted to regulate the pleasures of the people, either by denying licences to certain popular haunts or by offering cultural facilities that might serve to elevate workers and remove them from temptation.

Progressives waxed lyrical about the cultural facilities bestowed by the LCC on Londoners. Frederick Dolman, Progressive candidate for Brixton in 1901, claimed that in providing opportunities for recreation the LCC had acted like a 'fairy godmother'.[65] But Dolman was one of many municipal puritans who refused to admit the element of control that accompanied the Council's 'gifts'. This led a number of critics to attack the LCC, motivated by the belief that the state was misusing its powers. Municipal socialists often hoped to influence the desire for pleasure by offering facilities for healthy recreation. But many Progressives hoped to use their power to regulate popular pleasures in a strict, moralistic manner. By 1907 the SDF was beginning to turn against

Progressivism, claiming that socialists should have little to do with the Council bureaucrat's 'smug Puritanism'.[66]

The conflict over LCC cultural policy culminated in Stewart Headlam's attack on the Council and his creation, along with other disgruntled individuals, of the Anti-Puritan League. Headlam's disagreements with Progressivism were made public in a lecture he delivered to the Fabian Society in 1904. There he called on the LCC, of which he was a member, to abandon its policy of revoking drink licences (Headlam wanted municipal public houses instead) and stop prohibiting games in parks on Sundays.[67] His arguments were elaborated the following year in a pamphlet, *On the Danger of Municipal Puritanism*. While the work reiterated ideas he had first put forward under the aegis of the Church and Stage Guild, Headlam now directed his energies against the state. He believed that a puritanical spirit had come to dominate the Progressive Alliance, one that ultimately damaged the cause of socialism by alienating workers. Headlam called for supervision – rather than suppression – of facilities for culture and recreation, but he claimed that mere supervision was not what the LCC was engaged in: 'This Puritan tyranny of the County Council', he wrote, may 'be carried much further and . . . a crude denunciation of Freedom which is popular in some socialist circles may be preparing the way for the evils which England . . . suffered under the Commonwealth.'[68]

The *Labour Leader* and *Justice* remained suspicious of Headlam's religiosity, although John Bruce Glasier, despite his own puritanical sentiments, supported the work of the League as an important step in the eradication of the worst aspects of the puritan menace: 'Let us lift our glasses now', he wrote, 'lest the law may forbid our lifting any glasses tomorrow, and drink to the new crusade of the Rev. Stewart Headlam and Conrad Noel.'[69]

The ideas of Stewart Headlam and the League have been interpreted in terms of an intellectual dispute between Headlam and the Fabian Society. Headlam's biographer claimed that there was a 'bleak austerity' in the Society which alienated the Christian Socialist. Sidney Webb fuelled such beliefs, although on many occasions he attempted to defend himself against Headlam's charges, claiming that Headlam believed him to be more sympathetic to the puritan cause than he actually was.[70] More recently, the charge of Fabian puritanism has been discredited and it has been quite rightly noted that even Headlam did not desire pleasure at any cost; that Headlam and the Webbs basically agreed about the need to avoid the extremes of asceticism and indulgence.[71] But

151

to see the work of Headlam simply in terms of a debate over puritanism is to miss its deeper significance, for Headlam was engaged in a broader quest to define the legitimate role of the state in the cultural arena. Despite the fact that the Webbs might have been less puritanical than their critics made them out to be, they were also less worried than Headlam about using the state to mastermind the pleasures of the new society they wanted to see brought about.

In 1907 Sidney Webb asserted that the LCC 'was the first public authority in England to make its deliberate policy the promotion of the pleasure and enjoyment of the people'.[72] It was also one of the first authorities to suppress and regulate pleasure in ways that not only alienated Headlam but also the SDF, which had originally hoped for much more from the LCC. Pleasure, a political issue throughout the nineteenth century, had become central to the debate about the legitimate role of the state in legislating social progress. By 1900 the state was potentially capable of enacting laws to encourage an endless number of rational recreations, selecting some pleasures for development while marginalising others. The financial objections raised by ratepayers may have prevented many hopes from being realised, but the idea had been established that the state could attempt to influence significantly the cultural preferences of its citizens.

In their enthusiasm for municipal reforms, socialists contributed unwittingly to enhancing the state's powers in the sphere of cultural regulation. In so doing, they also confused the desires of those they claimed to represent with their own cultural preferences. Some may have spoken out against municipal puritanism; others realised that forms of self-discipline encouraged by the puritan spirit were a necessary ingredient of socialist struggle. In one of the most eloquent defences of the labour movement's adoption of puritanism, James Ramsay MacDonald referred to it as 'an incident in the eternal process of perfection', a force that would encourage the development of those 'sterling qualities' of personal character that would prepare the ground for socialism.[73] But many workers were less concerned than MacDonald with 'sterling qualities'. One of them, condemning the attack on the Manchester Palace of Varieties, complained: 'We are in great danger of only being allowed such amusements as our self-constituted morality keepers think proper to give us.'[74] As David Howell has written with respect to puritanism, its preoccupations might have been 'shared by a sizeable proportion of working-class activists', but they had only 'a limited impact on the class as a whole'.[75]

Class culture and social citizenship

In 1949 T. H. Marshall argued that class conflict in Britain had in part been 'abated' by the development of new forms of social citizenship. He cited Alfred Marshall's claim, made more than fifty years earlier, that through state education workers were fast becoming 'gentlemen' and that the educational system fostered the growth of social citizenship by making available a common culture on which it depended. As Marshall wrote of the new cultural conditions: 'The claim of all to enjoy these conditions is a claim to be admitted to a share in the social heritage, which in turn means a claim to be accepted as full members of society, that is as citizens.' But full citizenship, for T. H. Marshall, could be realised only when society recognised the importance of a shared system of values and beliefs, of a culture that was 'an organic unity', based on a 'national heritage'. While the civilising process of which Marshall spoke had been institutionalised in the post-1945 welfare state – of which he both wrote and approved – its origins were to be found in the nineteenth century: 'The components of a civilised and cultured life, formerly the monopoly of the few, were brought progressively within the reach of the many, who were encouraged thereby to stretch out their hands towards those that still eluded their grasp.'[76]

It is worth taking stock of the argument advanced in this chapter in terms of Marshall's notions of citizenship. Ever since the threat of Chartism, the middle class had offered workers a 'civic ideology' as an alternative to a radical, class-conscious culture; they provided the working class with 'a way of understanding itself in terms of a version of citizenship rather than class'.[77] But the emergence of citizenship cannot be viewed simply in terms of the middle class offering the gift of culture and the promise of citizenship to workers. As this chapter has suggested, many socialists were party to the process. Just as Chartists had voiced their demands in the language of eighteenth-century radicalism, so socialists often voiced their cultural demands in the language of Matthew Arnold, of culture as a common heritage and necessary factor in citizenship. Moreover, while Chartists were aware of the repressive potential of the state, socialists viewed the state more benevolently, often attempting to make use of it, especially at the local level, in their struggle to bring culture to the people. In 'Culture for all', an address he delivered to the Gasworkers and General Labourers Union in 1909, the union's economist claimed: 'All that has been great and good in what has been said and written in the past . . . should be accessible . . . to every boy and girl of the nation.'[78] The state was the means by which this package of the 'great and good' was to be made widespread and accessible.

The belief in the importance of a general, shared culture coexisted with another set of beliefs about the importance of workers making their own culture. Blatchford was merely one of a number of socialists who moved uneasily from one set of beliefs to the other: in *Merrie England* he claimed in the same passage that he desired culture *for* the people, and that he would also have the people become their *own* artists, actors and musicians.[79] For individuals like Blatchford, municipal socialism provided a framework in which socialists could delude themselves that they could have it both ways. One of its advocates, for example, suggested that municipal socialism allowed the people to arrange its *own* pleasures: 'The municipality is ourselves, and all of us, and we therefore must see that it provides us with pleasures.' But he also viewed municipal socialism in paternalistic terms, of bringing culture *to* the people: 'The true Municipality should be as a father to its people.'[80]

Striving to develop quasi-autonomous and co-operative cultural forms, such as those that had been central in the Chartist movement, some socialists rejected policies they believed would both lead to the incorporation of the working class in the dominant culture and inhibit the development of a politics and culture of class. Even Blatchford had his doubts: while he often supported municipal socialism, he also worried that it might result in an all-powerful state – of the kind depicted by Edward Bellamy in *Looking Backward* – that would have little in common with Morris's vision of a decentralised Britain, a vision that had influenced his own thinking. Other socialists, often members of the SDF, adamantly condemned their comrades' statist enthusiasm: Harry Quelch believed that Progressivism was simply liberalism disguised, while H. M. Hyndman once claimed that municipal socialism was a mere palliative that 'stunts the revolutionary intelligence'. On one occasion John Trevor went further still. While admitting that, to 'the working man, the broader culture so easily open to the middle-class man is well nigh impossible', he also believed that by struggling for access to that culture workers were prevented from developing an alternative 'labour consciousness'.[81]

Despite the fears they expressed, voices like these were increasingly anachronistic in a world in which citizenship demanded civic responsibility rather than an alternative radical culture. Moreover, by 1918, when the Labour Party adopted its 'socialist' constitution, the belief that the state should develop the cultural prerequisites necessary for the development of social citizenship was firmly embedded in Party policy. The constitution called for the state to play a role in brightening 'the lives of those now condemned to almost ceaseless toil' by 'a great development of the means of recreation'. And it argued in favour of 'the promotion of music, literature, and fine art, which have been under Capitalism so greatly neglected, and upon which . . . any real development of civilisation fundamentally depends'.[82] It was their experience at the local level in the 1890s that led many socialists to call for the further development of such policies at the national level. But while state activity in the cultural arena appealed to so many socialists, it represented an experience of defeat for those, like Morris, who had wished to carve out a space for the development of an alternative to the dominant culture of Victorian society rather than witness its further extension.

CHAPTER SIX

Mass culture
and the decline of socialism

One of the goals of social reform in Victorian Britain was the creation of a cultural consensus that would transcend class barriers. From temperance advocates to settlement house workers, from organisers of people's palaces to supporters of working lads' clubs, reformers hoped the activities they offered would assist in breaking down class-specific cultural forms and encourage workers to feel part of a larger community rather than part of an excluded class. Paradoxically, this involved the erection of new barriers and the creation of new social divisions. The respectable were separated from the not so respectable; the young from the old; the girls from the lads; the teetotaller from the inebriate. By creating institutions for particular groups – mechanics' institutes for self-improving artisans, Bands of Hope for children, settlement houses for urban slum-dwellers – reformers encouraged forms of separatism that challenged the social co-operation they envisaged. In short, club life could offer 'positive opportunities for recognition of social position and achievement and the possibility of excluding the undesirable'.[1]

Socialists directed their own recreational efforts at groups of workers with well-defined cultural preferences. They established columns in their newspapers addressed to audiences for specific pursuits, such as the arts and crafts, drama, music and, increasingly, sports. Moreover, they published papers that appealed to special recreational appetites, such as the *King of the Road* and the *Clarion Cyclists Journal*, both aimed at socialists who were avid cyclists. And they developed quasi-political social groups, such as the Clarion Vocal Union, characterised by a unique style and presence that sharply demarcated enthusiasts from non-enthusiasts, members from non-members.

Such organisations offered a sense of belonging to those who chose to participate. But belonging was often accompanied by the cultivation of exclusivity and the rejection of those who failed to share members' aspirations. Moreover, as World War I approached, the social distance that existed between participants in socialist club life and non-participants increased. The further development of mass culture in these years alarmed those who feared their own loss of status in the community and encouraged them to define and maintain for themselves an elite position through the clubs they joined. As we shall see, participation in socialist cultural activities allowed the converted to distinguish themselves from others with whom they might not wish to associate.

Towards a political culture for the lonely

While Robert Blatchford and John Trevor hoped to generate a substantial working-class following for the cultural activities they offered, the type of person to whom Labour Church socials or *Clarion*-sponsored recreational clubs appealed shared interests that remained at odds with those of most workers. Men and women who did participate in socialist organisations often felt lonely and isolated, uncomfortable amidst the conviviality of pub-centred working-class culture and lacking the cultural capital or desire to participate in the world of middle-class culture. Most of them also felt alienated from the new, mass leisure pursuits that were developing, eager to turn their self-imposed exclusion from these pursuits into a mark of social distinction.

Blatchford often commented on his own separation from the emerging cultural configurations of the late nineteenth century. While his socialist convictions certainly distinguished him from the majority of workers, so did his background as an autodidact, which bred in him a sense of loneliness. Recalling his first visit to London, he wrote: 'I tramped the streets of modern Babylon, lonely and wandering in the crowd.'[2] In the 1890s Blatchford offered a fictional account of his marginality in what was perhaps his most widely read novel, *A Son of the Forge*. The novel's main character was born in the Black Country, his father an 'ignorant' man 'given to drink'. Immersing himself in books, he eventually moved to London, hopeful of meeting other 'thoughtful' people like himself. But in London, he wrote, 'a sense of utter loneliness came over me. All that vast city round me . . . and amidst it all I had not a friend, not one soul to speak to.'[3] After a brief spell in the army, where he finally discovered meaningful comradeship, he continued his search for fellowship in London, eventually finding peace of mind through study and the discovery of individuals who shared his interests.

A Son of the Forge appealed to *Clarion* readers who could identify with Blatchford's fictional self. Many of them sought comradeship, which some of them found by participating in socialist clubs. But many were overcome by a sense of insecurity, loneliness and intellectual aloofness, making it difficult for them to meet others like themselves. Some wrote letters to the *Clarion*, stressing their predicament: 'There are hundreds of young men today ... who, like myself, are interested in Socialism ... but ... are prevented from linking themselves to any organisation by one great failing, and that is – *shyness*.'[4] Intelligence and shyness: these are the traits individuals singled out as most responsible for their isolation. Hannah Mitchell, born on a farm in the Peak District, became active in the socialist and suffrage movements only after reading socialist literature and making an effort to overcome her isolation: 'Feeling very lonely at the time', she wrote, 'I began to hang around the socialist meetings in the public square.'[5] Edward Carpenter assumed that Tom Maguire experienced similar feelings:

> The mental and physical depression of large town life, the want of sociability ... the void of personal affection trying delusively to fill itself by the conviviality of the cup, the need which ... sensitive natures often experience under modern conditions ... all these things were to Tom Maguire, as they have been to many others, the kind of Hydra with which ... he had to battle.[6]

Socialists who shared this predicament wrote about how their cultural preferences separated them from their workmates. One worker writing in the *Labour Prophet* in 1894 claimed that his co-workers jeered at those who did not swear and lie and drink with them. As this individual's moral earnestness prevented him from participating fully in the culture of the workplace, he led an isolated existence, seeking comfort by reading Blatchford's columns and, eventually, by joining the local congregation of the Labour Church.[7] In a period when working-class patterns of leisure were often determined by the experience of work, and when friendships developed at work served as a basis for activities enjoyed after work, such individuals repudiated workplace sociability only to become isolated and lonely as a result. In many cases this served to intensify their already heightened introspective nature. Others lashed out, deprecating the culture from which they sought an escape. As George Meek wrote: 'When I was young I ... despised the drunkard. ... I have wearied of public-houses and public-house company. I have given up singing in public. There are few opportunities except in company for which I do not care.'[8]

There are many fictional equivalents of men like George Meek.

Take Frank Owen, for example, the main character in Robert Tressell's novel, *The Ragged Trousered Philanthropists*. Believing in the importance of 'the benefits of civilisation; the necessaries, comforts, pleasures and refinements of life, leisure, books, theatres, pictures, music [and] holidays', Owen was ostracised by his colleagues at work who regarded him as a 'crank' and claimed 'that there must be something wrong with a man who took no interest in racing or football and was always talking a lot about religion and politics'. In turn, Owen attacked the recreational passions of the working class and rejected the idea that the bulk of workers could ever be the agents of social change: like members of the SDF, he shared a 'multi-dimensional contempt for workers' attitudes and subcultures'.[9] While Owen could associate with individuals who shared his beliefs, other fictional autodidacts were more isolated. Robin, in Jack Common's autobiographical novel of working-class life in Newcastle, *Kiddar's Luck*, was a socialist, atheist, vegetarian, physical culturalist and bachelor whose life was 'obstinately different' from that of most workers, marked by isolation and 'frequent loneliness'.[10] Central to both novels are the problems faced by worker-intellectuals. Such individuals might, like Owen, attempt to rally their co-workers to the socialist cause. More often than not they were like Robin, seeking refuge in books or the company of other like-minded individuals, cut off from those experiences that were central in shaping working-class identity.

Just as some introspective workers with a penchant for learning rejected working-class culture for the camaraderie of socialist club life, some middle-class socialists rejected not only working-class culture but elements of their own culture as well. Eric Hobsbawm's account of the Fabians as exiles from the middle class suggests a similar search for a new community by the alienated.[11] Charles Marson, for example, Christian Socialist, folksong collector and Fabian lecturer, wrote of his own dilemma in a tone as condescending as George Meek's: 'We are only half-washed from bourgeois slush, and if we do not keep quite clear of the whole mud bath, we soon end up by wallowing again in dirty contentment.'[12] Deep-seated cultural alienation often served to link such disaffected middle-class intellectuals with working-class autodidacts. United by their ambivalent, if not at times overtly hostile, attitudes towards existing working-class culture, they searched for other individuals who shared their concerns, often finding them in the ranks of the socialist movement. This resulted in the gradual emergence of a culturally unified, albeit socially diverse, group of people, at times defensive of the new cultural arrangements and communitarian sentiments they were developing.

By examining the social background and particular interests of the individuals who participated in socialist clubs, we can begin to understand why the activities they cultivated failed to generate much enthusiasm in working-class circles. Just as Stephen Yeo has found it difficult to reduce the leaders of the 'religion of socialism' to any single class, sex or geographic region,[13] it is also difficult to find much homogeneity in the ranks of their supporters. Most, however, did not come from the lower echelons of the working class. Such workers seldom shared the value orientations espoused by members of socialist bodies. They were also excluded from many of those bodies by the cost of joining them. Membership in the Leeds branch of the Clarion Cycling Club, for example, cost two shillings, an additional shilling for a badge – and the price of the bicycle, itself prohibitive for most unskilled workers in the 1890s.[14] Workers who joined various Clarion clubs often held regular, well-paid jobs. Moreover, their expectations and motivations differentiated them from the unskilled.

In one of the most succinct analyses of the participants in the Clarion movement, Montague Blatchford stressed the importance of the lower middle class. He claimed that new recruits were often young men who were above average in intelligence. Usually they were clerks, shop assistants, school teachers and young professionals with some education and little money. Likewise, Leonard Hall suggested that only 'elite' workers joined the movement and that the 'really hopeful and likely' club members came from the ranks of the lower middle class.[15] *Clarion* readership patterns tend to substantiate these claims. Robert Blatchford believed that only half of those who read the paper were workers, most of whom were highly skilled. The other half consisted of clerks and shop assistants.[16] Members of the ILP shared similar backgrounds. Although workers contributed some 60 per cent of the Party's members, the majority were skilled. Clerks and supervisory workers were also attracted to the Party, while its upper echelons were filled by a considerable number of middle-class professionals.[17]

Individuals who read the *Clarion* or joined the ILP were often predisposed to the cultural assumptions which predominated in the columns and editorials of the socialist press. Earnest and sober, respectable and thoughtful, they were the backbone of the socialist movement. Moreover, they were actively sought by the leaders of the movement: 'The kind of working man that I wanted to associate myself with', John

161

Trevor once wrote, 'was not the Church goer, or the circus goer, or the music-hall goer, or the Public House goer. It was ... the "class-conscious working man" that I sought as a fellow worker.'[18]

The social background of socialist club members was not unlike that of the individuals who enjoyed the benefits of the philanthropic organisations discussed in Chapter three. Most workers could hardly afford the offerings of Leonard's Co-operative Holiday Association, and while Stanton Coit hoped that his Neighbourhood Guilds would benefit all workers he was candid in his admission that members of the Kentish Town branch were 'above the average of the community' in intelligence. While there were some unskilled members of the branch, they 'are not what is called "poor people" ', wrote Coit, 'but are typical of the average, honest working class – the class which the Guild believes will prove the saviors of the unemployed, the idle and the vicious'.[19]

Such individuals often joined voluntary organisations out of a desire for community with people like themselves. But once a sense of community had been generated, many were eager to erect barriers of exclusivity to prevent their status from being eroded by contact with those from whom they sought to distinguish themselves. One writer claimed that the appeal of the Co-operative Holiday Association to the respectable would diminish if the 'buoyancy of the gentleman' were to be contaminated by the 'rowdyism of the hooligan'.[20] Organisers of Labour Church socials shared similar attitudes and sought to distinguish the entertainment they offered from that of the commercial dance halls. In Bradford, for example, undesirable individuals were kept out of Labour Church gatherings by restricting entry to church members and their guests. And in Hyde, the congregation attributed the success of its dances to the fact that the reputation of those who attended them was strictly maintained.[21] If we accept George Meek's assertion that the lonely and cultured male worker was made fun of by his workmates, then we might assume that such individuals required a refuge from these attacks and a guarantee that such refuges could meet their needs for camaraderie. That this was indeed the case is attested to by Montague Blatchford, who suggested in 1898 that organisations like the CVU had to maintain a sense of exclusivity in order to offer the alienated a secure sense of belonging.[22]

It is hard to determine how many members of such bodies wished to erect rigid barriers between themselves and the bulk of the working class. But it appears that at least some of them did. When one journalist compared the individuals at an ILP dance in Liverpool with the 'habitués of the cheapest of cheap dancing rooms' he was roundly attacked by members of the ILP who asserted their own respectability and attempted to distinguish themselves from those who attended the commercial halls.[23] And yet, despite the social cohesion and pride generated by belonging, participation in socialist organisations was not always a panacea for personal feelings of loneliness and despair. Some individuals sensed that it was dangerous to seek well-being in socialist clubs because it might result in their dependence on the new forms of community they encountered, isolating them further from society. As one member of the Labour Church claimed: 'I am . . . afraid to think of what my life would be like without the Labour Church. . . . I wonder whether it is not more to me than it ought to be.'[24]

Although such individuals often worried about their dependence on the social activities of the movement, participation in socialist clubs allowed them temporarily to feel they belonged. In addition, it allowed some of them to carve out a space for the development of an alternative culture. But praise for the accomplishments of that culture should not obscure its limited appeal. Club life did offer socialists a sense of control over important spheres of activity, and this was of some consequence given the social isolation and corresponding lack of control that many of them felt before becoming involved in the movement at the branch level.[25] But, as we have seen, pride in belonging could be accompanied by the expression of condescending attitudes towards those who shared different aspirations, along with the assertion of exclusivity, bred of a desire to maintain social distance. As a result, the transformative potential of socialist club life was often blocked and its aspirations could not be generalised into a whole way of life with any widespread appeal.

Those at the margins of socialist branch life were well aware of the fact that participants in socialist organisations remained aloof from workers who shared other values. One correspondent to the *Clarion* in 1899, for example, complained about the evolution of a cultured elite within the ranks of the socialist movement and pointed out that individuals with less-developed interests were largely excluded from that movement.[26] The history of various Clarion clubs proves the validity of this assertion, for by 1900 they were increasingly developing a style of their own which served rigidly to demarcate members from non-members.

It is hard to understand the forms of exclusivity that increasingly characterised socialist branch life without invoking the concept of 'respectability' and without situating socialist activity within the broader

163

context of the transformation of late Victorian patterns of work and leisure. 'Respectability' is itself a tricky concept; in the nineteenth century it was more often a social role, adopted on grounds of its immediate utility, than it was a series of fixed attitudes, characteristic of a particular group or type of individual.[27] But the shifting occupational structure of the period, along with the decline of occupationally specific leisure cultures, formed the background against which many individuals gravitated towards socialist club life – as well as towards the activities of other voluntary organisations – as a means of asserting their own claims to respectability.

Earlier in the nineteenth century, working-class leisure patterns were closely related to the experiences and rhythms of work; not only did specific occupational subcultures exist (in mining and weaving, for example) but work more generally defined the parameters of play. But the late Victorian revolution in public transport, the advent of higher wages and shorter working hours for those in stable employment, and the proliferation of commercial leisure pursuits worked together to sever these connections. Moreover, the appearance of new forms of employment, without a history of occupationally specific cultural traditions, allowed many workers to feel less constrained in their leisure choices than their ancestors had been earlier in the century. This was particularly true of the new, lower middle-class 'blackcoated worker'. Some of them, like Leonard Bast, the fictional hero of E. M. Forster's *Howards End*, could in vain attempt to emulate the cultural life of their social superiors. Others could turn to the music halls, seeking entertainment and escape. Still others could join one or more of the many voluntary associations open to them and in so doing cultivate a sense of belonging that often eluded them at work.[28] Some, as we have seen, ended up in the ranks of the socialist movement.

Members of what has been termed the 'labour aristocracy' were also free of many of the traditional craft restraints that had shaped artisanal leisure patterns earlier in the century. While some opted to purchase their entertainment in the new market for mass leisure pursuits, others sought to differentiate themselves culturally and socially from the unskilled. In Kentish London and in Edinburgh, for example, labour aristocrats sometimes attempted to maintain their elite status by participating in voluntary associations with other individuals who shared their sentiments. Like members of the lower middle class, they sought to define themselves against those they considered socially inferior. Moreover, as their own privileged position in the workforce was never guaranteed and as they, like most unskilled workers, were also subject to periodic slumps and unemployment, their desire for status confirmation could manifest itself in the assertion of privilege in the cultural arena.[29]

Labour aristocrats and members of the new, lower middle class were abundantly represented in socialist organisations of all kinds. No doubt many of them devoted their free time to various pursuits and did not depend solely on the activities associated with socialist clubs. But it is clear that the search for belonging influenced a great number of them in their gravitation towards socialist club life. Obviously, the appeal of the movement cannot be explained simply in terms of various psychological phenomena, such as loneliness or the desire for community. While some skilled workers and members of the lower middle class were indeed attracted to the Labour Church and various Clarion organisations by their rhetoric of respectability and rationality, this is not to suggest that they were not also moved by a strong, political commitment to socialism or by a more general faith in the inevitability of the 'good time coming'. But the fact remains that the search for fellowship and belonging played a substantial role in the growth of the socialist movement. Moreover, that search reflected the existence of widespread cultural anxieties that were themselves a by-product of the extensive reordering of the links between work and leisure in late Victorian society.

No matter what their social background, most individuals who became active in socialist clubs were learned and articulate, sharing a faith with their leaders in the importance of rational recreation and self-discipline. In the face of very new ways of organising non-work time, they were attracted to a vision of order and respectability, of self-control, moderation and intellectual development. What passed as an emergent socialist culture in Britain can be viewed as the last gasp of an earlier nineteenth-century autodidact tradition, infused with a new political gospel. Overall, it was an activist culture, but because its rhetoric appealed narrowly to those who felt alienated from existing working-class culture, it remained limited in its appeal.

Women, socialism and the sexual divisions of leisure

Superficially, the experience of women who joined the socialist movement was not unlike that of their male comrades. Like men, they often became involved in local branch life in order to discover individuals who shared their interests. Annie Kenney, for example, who had entered the cotton industry as a full-time worker at the age of thirteen, became enamoured of the *Clarion* and soon sought the company of other 'Clarionettes'; her reason for joining the Oldham branch of the CVU, she claimed, 'was a desire for companionship among people whose ideas were in harmony with my own'.[30] The experience of Stella Davies was similar. The fourteenth child of a warehouse labourer, she was raised a strict Methodist, imbued with the values of thrift and moral sobriety. Her parents stressed the value of education and attempted to shield their daughter from the culture of the pub, dance hall and theatre. After reading Morris and Blatchford, Davies joined a Clarion group in Handforth, where she met her future husband.[31]

These personal histories should not obscure the fact that women's experiences of work and leisure were considerably different from men's. Such experiences played an important role in shaping gender-specific cultural norms within the socialist movement. While, for example, 'Saint Monday' had been a holiday for male artisans earlier in the century, women were compelled by necessity and tradition to use the day for various domestic tasks.[32] Moreover, as recreational opportunities available to working men grew towards the end of the century, long-term social and economic changes 'reached working class wives only after passing through the filter of the family's economy'.[33] On the whole, these new opportunities for leisure were shared unequally by men and women. In the ranks of the labour aristocracy, status was usually guaranteed by the work of women who, often freed from the necessities of paid employment, devoted their leisure to maintaining the respectability of the family unit. And in the ranks of the unskilled, domestic duties, accompanied by paid labour, allowed women little time to enjoy recreation outside of the home. Tom Mann recognised the dilemma and urged women to insist on 'freedom from the wash-tub'. Calling for communal kitchens, dining rooms and laundries Mann argued that such facilities would reduce the amount of domestic labour that was the fate of most working women and allow them more time for learning and recreation.[34]

Mann was one of the few male socialists to comment on the links between gender and leisure. On the whole, socialists – like other Victorian observers of popular culture – ignored women in their accounts of the phenomenon, making it difficult to place much emphasis on gender in this study. As Walter Besant once wrote, justifying his own silence on the subject, 'as regards the women . . . I have never been able to find out anything at all concerning their amusements'.[35] But while Besant seemed to exhibit little interest in the complex gendering of socio-cultural relationships, reformers had, none the less, always stressed the value of domestic pleasures and condemned a pub-based, male-centred world of public leisure pursuits. One observer wrote in 1912 that 'the first objection that can be levelled against the leisure occupations of the masses, is that they sever the man from his wife.'[36] The role of football in an emerging working-class culture was one of the many new 'leisure occupations of the masses' that served further to demarcate a male-dominated sphere of leisure. While the sport had attracted a number of women supporters in the 1880s, by the turn of the century it had become a bastion of working-class masculinity.[37]

If working-class women were often excluded from activities such as these, middle-class women, by contrast, were encouraged to become involved in the provision of 'improving' recreations for the working class as a whole. Here was one area of activity where the ideal virtues attributed to women – their penchant for caring, nurturing and motherhood – could be put to a good social use. An entire chapter of Alice Zimmern's *Unpaid Professions for Women* (1906) was devoted to recreational work, suggesting that opportunities were available to women in a number of organisations from the settlement houses to the Children's Country Holiday Fund and the Girls' Friendly Society.[38] Reformers argued that women could be particularly effective in guiding children's uses of leisure and they encouraged women to organise the play of working-class children in Board Schools and to bring their 'civilising influences' to bear on youth in a variety of ways.[39]

While middle-class women were urged to devote their leisure to the moral improvement of the poor, male socialists were often urged to pay greater attention to the recreational needs of their own wives. As Tom Mann wrote: 'Now that the eight-hour working day is within measurable distance, and the Saturday half-holiday is an accomplished fact . . . workmen's wives are naturally asking, "In what way are we to share in these better conditions?" ' Mann suggested that it was 'the duty of every workman to . . . enable the women to share in the advantages we are gradually acquiring.' But few socialists appeared to heed his call and male activists' wives were often excluded not only from their husbands' recreational activities but from their political work as well. The constraints on the time of women with families often made it easier for single women to reap the benefits of participation in the movement. But married women also struggled to impress upon their husbands their own equally important right to leisure and to join their husbands in socialist clubs.[40]

Married women could also grow alarmed at the sudden enthusiasm their husbands exhibited after their conversion to the cause – especially when they abandoned the home each evening in order to pursue their new interests:

> The politically minded woman, though present in the period, was not usual and many wives found themselves unable to enter into their husband's interests. This was particularly noticeable in the older women who had married before their husbands 'took to politics'. In their early married life, home and children had absorbed their attention. Now at forty or fifty, with a husband who scarcely talked the same language, they had a lost and bewildered expression and were fearful of how they would fit in, 'if he gets into the House, which he says he will, next go'.[41]

To prevent such estrangement from occurring, women often encouraged their husbands to be more considerate and share their political interests with them. One of them suggested that men who went to their own political meetings might say to their wives after the Sunday dinner: 'Now, Mary, it's your turn.' On Sunday evenings men would stay at home, 'minding the children' and 'fixing the tea', while their wives would attend their own meetings.[42]

Despite such pleas, men were usually reluctant to facilitate the participation of women in their own political affairs. They presumed that there were some 'fine socialist women', like Julia Dawson, editor of the women's column in the *Clarion*, but that most women were consumed by their 'trivial' domestic concerns. George Meek reiterated a belief of Thomas Wright, the journeyman engineer, when he claimed that women 'are supporters of the penny novelettes' and 'have no ideal beyond a fine frock or a new hat'.[43] Robert Blatchford expressed similar sentiments, arguing that women were basically uninterested in politics. The *Clarion* took its cue from these attitudes and emphasised women's roles as mothers, sisters and wives, best suited for a domestic occupation. Moreover, leaders of the SDF were particularly well known for their belief that political activity primarily concerned men.[44]

H. W. Hobart attacked such attitudes and urged male socialists to overcome the sexual division of leisure. Likewise, the Leeds *Labour Chronicle* berated its male readers for their selfishness in failing to pay attention to the political and social needs of their wives.[45] By the turn of the century many socialist newspapers, both at the national and local levels, had established women's columns, hoping they might serve to integrate the wives of male activists into the movement. But the demand for women's participation, sporadic as it was, failed to achieve the desired results, often because men underestimated the restraints placed on women by their domestic responsibilities. Early in 1892 the Labour Church held a conference on women's participation, reporting its findings in an article in the March number of the *Labour Prophet*, 'How can we reach the women?'. Despite the existence of such conferences, however, and despite the fact that a few women served as Labour Church lecturers and wrote for the *Prophet*, rank-and-file membership continued to be dominated by men.

The SDF thought it had the answer to the dilemma faced by the Labour Church:

> The only opportunity that a Socialist has of getting women to attend a socialist gathering is to paint a glowing picture of a tea night, of a concert, where certain celebrated artists will appear, of a soirée, and dance where there will be a possibility of witnessing new fashions.[46]

In the late nineteenth century women were increasingly positioned as central figures in an emerging world of mass consumption. In this context, the SDF was simply echoing beliefs that were becoming more and more widespread: namely, that if women had abandoned the penny novelette they had done so at the expense of becoming co-opted by a more glamorous and much larger world of consumer culture as a whole. The SDF believed that women might join the movement but that they should leave the important work to men and remain content with the narrower role of recreational provision. Women, as we have seen, could organise socialist bazaars and various socials in Halifax, but by encouraging this activity the SDF merely perpetuated the association of women with forms of philanthropy that had depended on their efforts throughout the nineteenth century.

While recognising that men and women enjoyed different leisure pursuits, most men in the socialist movement failed to conceive of ways of overcoming the division between them. They continued to urge their own wives to accept the kind of ancillary roles with which middle-class women were already quite familiar. Some of them wondered what was wrong, unable to comprehend why those women who joined the movement did not devote their leisure to political activity. And yet they were unwilling to admit that their own male comrades offered women little more than a subordinate role to play in socialist branch life. Keir Hardie, writing in the women's column of the *Labour Leader*, claimed that he always felt 'a bit disappointed' when he contrasted the 'number of women who turn out to socials and concerts . . . with those who attend lectures, and other social meetings . . . devoted to work'.[47] But women

169

knew why this was the case and they expressed their anger at men who claimed they wanted women in the movement but then failed to treat them as equals. Isabella Ford, for example, wrote to the editor of the *Clarion*'s women's column asking if socialism for women was 'to be nothing but tea parties and socials?'[48]

Of course, not all men succumbed to these widely held assumptions about the gendered nature of leisure. Tom Mann, H. W. Hobart and others made a genuine attempt to overcome popular prejudices. And recent work has suggested that at least amongst members of the ILP in the West Riding women were treated as equals and were not cast merely in a supportive role.[49] Moreover, if men often felt excluded from the conviviality of the workplace by their intellectual earnestness, cultural preferences and political convictions, it was possible for them to seek solace with their entire family in the context of socialist branch life; in such circumstances, club life could become 'a defence to bind members and their families together in the face of victimisation'.[50] Nevertheless, while men in the socialist movement attacked workers for succumbing to the appeals made by the leisure industry, most of them failed to recognise that they perpetuated a sexual division of leisure in their own lives that was central to the very industry they despised.

Towards a revolutionary use of joyfulness

For some women, as Isabella Ford claimed, socialism meant little more than 'tea parties and socials'. For some men, too, the sense of community available at the branch level was often as important – sometimes perhaps more important – than political work. This was, of course, less true for those who joined the SDF or the ILP. But for members of the various Clarion clubs or the Labour Church, social activities of all kinds contributed to the appeal of those organisations. When, in 1901, Julia Dawson surveyed *Clarion* readers in an attempt to ascertain their reasons for joining the movement, she discovered that direct political activity was low on their list of priorities. In descending order of importance, her respondents listed social evenings, literary study, music, attendance at socialist lectures, the distribution of literature, 'Cinderella' work (providing food and entertainment for children of the poor), arts and crafts activity, science clubs, athletics and, at the bottom of the list, political work.[51]

Socialist recreational activity remained the preserve of the converted and for every individual who engaged in political work there were large numbers of Clarion club members who did not. When Robert Blatchford claimed that he desired a 'sociable' socialism, that he wanted 'a family gathering, a brotherly – and sisterly, if you like – jollification, not a political conference', his followers often nodded in approval. Blatchford was attuned to the psychological needs of club members and claimed that the drudgery of work drove them to find fulfilment through their leisure. This, he suggested, was a major element in the appeal of the Clarion movement, while it differentiated that movement from the ILP and the SDF.[52] But even Blatchford believed that entertainment should not supplant political work: Clarion clubs, he argued, should blend leisure with politics. Blatchford, however, was unable to conceive of a satisfactory relationship between the two. One critic recognised the difficulty:

> Mr. Blatchford is troubled with a dual control. He is an artist who has fallen amongst politicians and economists, and who is not merely content to be their ally but desires to fight by their side. Not one man in a thousand can live the double life, and Mr. Blatchford is not the one.[53]

Tom Maguire also commented on the difficulties of reconciling the cultural activities of the converted with the necessary work of political organising. In addition, he complained that the social side of the movement was often stressed too much: 'Political progress is not made after the fashion of a Corydon-Phyllis dance, jigging along ... through pleasant places with the sun shining over us.'[54]

The problem was enormous. How could the enthusiasm of the converted for their 'new life' be harnessed to the struggle for socialism? Or, to paraphrase Blatchford, how could others be made to see the light as he saw it? Several members of the SDF addressed the issue. Ernest E. Williams, reiterating the ideas of Morris, explicitly linked the popular culture of the late Victorian worker with the experience of work itself and argued that all workers – not merely the converted – needed to discover the potential for joy in various realms of human activity. Once they had come to understand the poverty of their culture under capitalism, he claimed, they would realise that it was a whole system of commercial exploitation that led to their bondage and would join the movement dedicated to its destruction. Williams concluded that 'high spirits breed high courage and high aims' and that there was indeed a 'revolutionary use of joyfulness'.[55] For Williams, the purpose of socialist propaganda was to make this joyfulness infectious, thereby expanding the ranks of the converted.

171

In a similar vein, H. M. Hyndman suggested that 'well-managed pleasure gatherings' could benefit the cause: 'Socialists have learnt', he wrote in 1907, 'that there is no better way of attracting young people . . . to their organisations and keeping them when attracted than good entertainments of all sorts.'[56] But how many people accepted the 'joyfulness' offered at such 'pleasure gatherings' without considering its potentially 'revolutionary uses'? Many, as we have seen, were drawn to the movement and developed an identity around the social life they encountered in its ranks. But this did not necessarily lead them to share their enthusiasm widely, let alone convince others of the importance of the links that individuals like Williams were making between a politics of popular culture and the cause of socialism.

The converted sometimes did attempt to convert others, and this was what Hyndman had hoped for in advocating 'pleasure gatherings' in the first place. Take, for example, the activities of the Glasgow Socialist Rambling Club. According to an article in *Justice* on 'Propaganda and pleasure', members of that organisation blended their pleasure with the 'dull slogging work' of propaganda. Armed with socialist songbooks, banners and copies of *Justice*, they made their way to the Clyde singing 'When leisure and pleasure shall be free'. The paper claimed that the participants 'spent no more than a shilling' each and that their activities were meant to attract new recruits. But the club was most successful in offering its own members a sense of belonging, for the pleasures of the converted apparently failed to appeal to most of those with whom the ramblers came into contact.[57] Moreover, while the Glasgow ramblers saw their own pleasures as central to the work of political propaganda, others simply enjoyed their pleasures and let politics take care of itself. As George Meek wrote, linking his cultural preferences to a lack of interest in theory or politics, 'I take little part . . . in current politics. . . . I just bury myself in the books I am reading. . . . Some day, perhaps, justice will come by her own.'[58]

The socialist movement was not alone in witnessing its cultural endeavours appeal narrowly to a select group already attuned to their message. Earlier in the nineteenth century many Owenites concluded that the identity they gained through participating in the cultural life of the movement was more important than political work. As a result, they ceased to explore the means by which recreation might become part of an oppositional culture that could play a wider role in the process of social transformation. Later in the century, the Conservative Party's Primrose League also witnessed a divorce of pleasure from politics. As one observer wrote: 'Exhibitions of tame elephants, wild fireworks, conjuring performers, tightrope walkers, professional tumblers and many other entertainments, are all very well in their way; but where does the political argument come in?'[59]

Socialists' inability to sustain a widespread political culture can be seen most unequivocally in the history of the Clarion Handicraft Guild, a body indebted to the ideas of William Morris. For Morris, one channel for revolutionising the means of production while at the same time effectively propagating the socialist gospel was the arts and crafts movement. Small craft workshops, he believed, could provide the setting for men and women to develop greater pride in their work, reassert control over the work process and arrive at an understanding of capitalist exploitation. Morris's critique of the shoddiness and vulgarity of commercial production appealed to Montague Blatchford, who called for a social revolution that would allow the crafts to flourish once again: 'The true remedy', he wrote, 'is not to copy the old work, but to reproduce the conditions that called it forth.'[60] For Montague Blatchford, as for Morris, the arts and crafts seemed to be inseparable from widespread social change.

In 1901 Julia Dawson received a letter from Godfrey Blount, the tireless advocate of the arts and crafts movement, urging the readers of the *Clarion* to pay more attention to Morris's aesthetic theories. In response, Dawson helped launch the Clarion Handicraft Guild. 'Joy in work, and hope in leisure' became their motto as hundreds of *Clarion* readers enjoyed the social intercourse the Guild offered and discovered their talents in jewellery-making, book-binding, furniture construction and related activities. Such 'wholesome' pursuits were certainly in keeping with Blatchford's desire to prevent workers from straying towards less edifying pastimes. But the Guild did not reach those most likely to misuse their leisure. Members came either from the skilled ranks of the working class or from the lower middle class. Moreover, their participation in the Guild was diluted by the presence of many professional craftsmen who used the organisation as an agency through which they could market their own products.[61]

By the end of 1904 there were thirty branches of the Guild throughout Britain, displaying their wares at an annual exhibition. But, despite the enthusiasm of their participants, the exhibitions were rarely well received on aesthetic grounds. In 1902, for example, Montague Blatchford commented that much of the work he saw was 'amateurish, imitative, and not particularly useful'. In 1907, weekly Guild reports in the *Clarion* began to dwindle. The same year A. J. Penty, an enthusiastic supporter of the arts and crafts, found a good deal of 'rubbish' – the work of 'incompetent' amateurs – displayed at the annual exhibition.[62]

The Clarion Handicraft Guild was also plagued by a greater difficulty than the inability of Guild workers to live up to Morris's own high standards of craft work. In an article on the arts and crafts movement, A. R. Orage, editor of the *New Age*, complained that while the movement encouraged handicraft work its activities had become separated from the radical political critique with which they were initially associated. Culture and politics had, wrote Orage in 1907, gone their separate ways:

> on the one hand the Socialist movement may be said to have absorbed the political enthusiasm of the Arts and Crafts movement, and on the other hand the craftsmen were . . . too much engrossed in their work not to be willing . . . to resign the political propaganda, for which they felt themselves unfitted.[63]

Orage's observations can be applied not only to the Clarion Handicraft Guild but, more generally, to the work of socialists who attempted either to politicise cultural production or develop new forms of entertainment that could appeal to those who were not already members of the socialist movement. Few such individuals could generate a viable political culture in practice, despite the attempts of socialists like Ernest Williams to begin to conceive of such a culture in theory.

Mass culture and the politics of labourism

By 1914 socialists were on the whole less interested in the 'revolutionary uses of joyfulness' than they had been in the 1890s. They were also less interested in advancing an alternative culture of their own than they were in urging the state to combat those elements of an existing working-class culture they so disliked. The tension between the encouragement of a socialist culture for the converted and the use of the state to secure the benefits of 'culture' for the working class had existed in the ranks of the socialist movement since its earliest days. But with the establishment of the Labour Representation Committee (LRC) in 1900, a new emphasis on narrowly defined political activity tended to marginalise earlier conceptions of socialism as a whole way of life with a distinct culture of its own. In the process, the visionary appeal of a far-reaching reconstruction of society, central to the religion of socialism in the 1880s and early 1890s, began to lose its cutting edge.

E. M. Forster was one of many individuals who commented, with some regret, on the changes that were taking place. The labour movement, he argued in an appreciation of Edward Carpenter, 'advanced by committee meetings and statistics towards a State-owned factory attached to State-supervised recreation grounds. Edward's heart beat no warmer at such joys. He felt no enthusiasm over municipal baths and municipally provided bathing-drawers.'[64] Although it is difficult to date the changes that Forster noted with any precision, John Bruce Glasier spoke out against them as early as 1893:

> Instead of the complete ideal of Socialism involving . . . the exaltation of recreation and art above mere mechanical and industrial achievement, we have the prospect of an eight hour day, pensions for old age, and the Fabian elysium of an army of workers under the State receiving at least three pounds a week per adult male, held forth as the highest achievement of socialism possible.[65]

Glasier's was a voice in the wilderness in the 1890s. But in the new century other socialists shared his concerns. In 1900, Robert Blatchford suggested that the enthusiasm for the promises of municipal socialism was in part responsible for the decline of socialist branch activity. Moreover, the decline of branch life meant the demise of its vision of a 'new life' and its faith in widespread cultural transformation.[66] The missionary zeal of socialism at the branch level was indeed beginning to wane. In Halifax, for example, the ILP began to hold its political meetings on Sunday evenings in order to compete with Labour Church socials, believing that such activity was not 'practical' enough for the needs of the day. The Labour Church also came under attack from the clergy for its 'secularisation of the Lord's Day', finding it difficult to negotiate the shifting contours of culture and politics. Members of the church began to abandon that body or drift towards the ILP. The Halifax congregation of the Labour Church was finally dissolved in 1901.[67]

The politics of 'labourism' has often been blamed for this. As Sam Hobson wrote: 'In 1900 was begun a movement . . . in which conscious Socialism was absorbed into a vague, inchoate Labourism.'[68] The extraparliamentary left felt ambivalent at best about the changes that were taking place. Some socialists tentatively supported the new emphasis on parliamentary activity and hoped that the triumph of labourism would not necessarily mean the defeat of socialism as they knew it. But others felt lost, disillusioned or embittered. In the pamphlet *Let Us Reform the Labour Party* Leonard Hall argued that socialism had been bartered away in return for the promise of parliamentary seats, that the Party had caved

175

in to 'spiritless opportunism' and that the ILP should eschew parliamentary politics and revert to its earlier policy of making socialists. Support for Victor Grayson, the independent socialist who campaigned in the 1907 Colne Valley by-election, along with the eventual union of disgruntled members of the ILP, the SDF and various Clarion clubs in the British Socialist Party in 1911, suggests that there were many socialists who shared Hall's sentiments. These opponents of the Labour Party believed that the triumph of parliamentary politics fragmented the socialist movement and rendered it more difficult to conceive of a thorough socialist transformation of Britain.[69]

To what extent was the emphasis placed on parliamentary activity alone responsible for the decline of the religion of socialism? And to what extent might that decline have been the result of intellectual weaknesses within the ideology of socialism itself? Members of socialist clubs in the 1890s were often concerned with finding a refuge where they could cultivate their interests – both political and social – with like-minded individuals. But when they came into contact with what appeared to them to be a vast number of workers who failed to share their aspirations their faith in the power of conversion began to wane. The distinct style of life they cultivated was originally meant as a blueprint for the socialist transformation of popular culture and social relations in the nation at large. By 1900, however, it was little more than a preserve of the converted. Increasingly isolated from the realities of working-class culture, a culture they attacked with a vengeance from the sidelines, socialists berated workers even more vociferously for the poverty of their imagination in the new century than they had in the 1880s and 1890s. The new emphasis on winning parliamentary seats might well have absorbed a considerable amount of energy that earlier had been devoted to building a socialist culture at the branch level, but that culture had been marginal to working-class life, while its intellectual weaknesses were becoming ever more apparent.

Logie Barrow has attempted to make sense of these gradual changes by relating the rise of labourism to a rupture within the environmental determinist strands of socialist thought. In the 1880s and 1890s, according to Barrow, socialists believed that the environment shaped individual character. But they also believed that individuals could alter their environment and saw it as their task to effect changes both in the environment and in personal character. These two struggles became divorced from each other in the new century. Those who believed in 'educationalism', who held that the elevation of desire and the shaping of personal character were necessary aspects of socialist struggle, joined forces in the British Socialist Party. Those who believed in the necessity of legislative changes to transform the environment threw their support behind the Labour Party. The triumph of the legislative route to socialism had many causes, but in part it was the result of an erosion of the social basis of a politics of educationalism. A faith in moral elevation and intellectual development had been central to an earlier nineteenth-century autodidact culture. It was this culture, as the present chapter suggests, that became a source of values and members for the socialist movement. But the very existence of the social stratum which often provided that movement with its members was threatened by economic changes in the latter part of the century. While the rise of labourism tended to marginalise the politics of educationalism, the social base of educationalism was itself undermined in these years.[70]

Despite Barrow's convincing argument, educationalism as a component of socialist strategy declined also because those who had once cherished it became less optimistic about its viability in the new century. This was related to their declining faith in the working class as a whole. In the 1880s and early 1890s they had argued that socialism could be generalised as a whole way of life and they believed that workers could be made to see the importance of individual improvement and the necessity of their own cultural transformation. But in the early 1900s – and certainly by 1914 – this belief had largely evaporated. There are many reasons for this. But, more than anything else, the growing importance of commercial leisure pursuits in working-class life alarmed socialists and forced them to view an emerging culture of consumption, largely apolitical and hedonistic, as a challenge to their gospel of educationalism. While reformers had always viewed the public house as a threat to the growth of a self-conscious, working-class culture, based on the values of educationalism, the music hall, the football match and the popular press now tended to intensify that threat. In order to understand the triumph of labourism, then, we need to understand the shifting cultural configurations that undermined socialists' faith in educationalism.

That socialists held elements of an emerging mass culture to be responsible for the declining appeal of socialism is attested to by the bleak assessments they began to make of the relationship between consumerism, the leisure industry and the working class. As early as 1893 Sidney Dark had warned of the 'danger in choking ourselves with materialism',[71] a theme explored in Chapter one. By 1909 particular forms of materialism in the cultural arena were being related explicitly to the decline of socialist branch life. The *Halifax and District Labour News*, for example, quoted a speaker at a cycle union dinner that year who told the club's members that they 'seemed to have got into the age of counter-attractions'. These, he claimed, were not as good 'as the more solid entertainment' provided by the movement. An observer in Bradford thought likewise, blaming the growth of football and the music hall for the decline of the Labour Church.[72]

By 1900 more and more workers were turning to the products of the leisure industry for their recreational needs. Moreover, that industry was itself expanding rapidly. Music-hall syndicates had colonised the provinces with their halls, Saturday afternoons had been given over to football games and cinemas were soon to become a new rival for working-class uses of leisure: while there were only two cinemas in Bradford in 1908, for example, there were twelve in 1914. The prominence of such phenomena led one activist to conclude, shortly after World War I, that ILP dramatic groups were most likely to flourish in smaller towns that lacked an extensive commercial entertainment infrastructure.[73]

Socialist branch life had also flourished in towns where it could utilise the institutions and values that had been central in the history of liberalism. In such towns it could appeal to workers who desired to remain aloof from the new cultural apparatus of working-class life. In Burnley, for example, the local branch of the SDF drew its support from the ranks of skilled labour and contributed to the perpetuation of a culture that valued self-education and moral improvement. There were in fact two working-class cultures in Burnley: that of the skilled and that of the unskilled, separated by a wide chasm. By contrast, in Blackburn an autodidact culture failed to develop to the extent that it had in Burnley. Moreover, Blackburn liberalism was weak and the Conservative Party allied itself with workers and their culture against liberal and left puritanism. Thus, when the Independent Labour Party developed in Blackburn and inherited this Tory-supported working-class culture, its mouthpiece, the *Blackburn Labour Journal*, was wary of expressing the negative attitudes towards popular culture that were pervasive elsewhere in the movement. But in Burnley socialists roundly attacked the growth of cinemas and other popular entertainments. Nevertheless, the new mass culture drew its support both from the ranks of the skilled and the unskilled, undermining the enthusiasm for Burnley's self-improving institutions. Socialists became alarmed by the threat posed by the leisure industry to such institutions, for they had once served their own movement so well.[74]

Burnley was one of many towns that offered socialists a grim picture of a working class – even a skilled working class --slowly repudiating the values they cherished. As a result of such trends, socialists, settlement house workers and a number of other reformers became less optimistic about their ability to convert workers to the causes they championed, or to keep them once converted. Often disillusioned, socialists' enthusiasm for community and fellowship – central to their rhetoric in the 1890s – began to wane as more and more of them 'retreated into a particular form of bourgeois pessimism'.[75] As Percy Alden wrote:

> Much of the sanguine enthusiasm which animated workers among the poor fifteen or twenty years ago has given place to a dryer, more pedestrian, but probably more truthful view of the possible means for improving conditions of life. Many people believed that you had only to live amongst the poor, show them beautiful objects, and give them noble precepts of citizenship and morals and you would have created for them all the conditions which Plato would have created for an ideal Republic. That ardent belief has passed with experience.[76]

Not only had the faith soured, but the pessimism that came about in its wake was often manifested as a bitter attack on the working class itself. This can be seen in Blatchford's response to the lack of enthusiasm workers seemed to show for his own brand of socialism. In 1900 he wrote: 'I have now come to the belief that the great mass of workers are too apathetic and selfish to be moved.' And in 1910: 'Are the people sufficiently educated and intelligent to desire Socialism?'[77] James Leatham explicitly attributed the working-class apathy Blatchford noted to the emergence of new forms of mass entertainment. The enemy, for Leatham, was not labourism, but rather sports and the music hall. In an article he wrote in 1913 he argued that the working class devoted more time and money to sport than to advancing its 'most solid interests'. In the nineteenth century, he claimed, working men took life 'seriously' and attended mechanics' institutes. But today, he continued, the 'cinema palace following the football match' had taken the place of self-improvement.[78] Leatham was soon to abandon the working class and place his faith in middle-class intellectuals for the reforms he desired.

Socialists often despaired of the new leisure pursuits although, like other reformers who had attempted to provide rational recreations for the working class, they could seldom muster the resources to compete successfully with a whole new industry.[79] More important, they despaired of the ethos that seemed to them to accompany the products of that industry. For individuals like Blatchford and Leatham, leisure was to be more than a frivolous form of escape, more than mere empty time to be filled, more than a quest for immediate gratification. While shunning the puritanism of Sabbatarians and strict temperance advocates – or even of the more stern-minded of their comrades on the LCC – they believed that individuals had a moral responsibility to use their leisure in order to improve themselves and the society in which they lived. Attendance at football games or visits to music halls not only usurped the time that could be devoted to more edifying pursuits but challenged the very premises on which socialists based their definition of leisure. No doubt there were numerous individuals who both attended football matches and committed a considerable amount of energy to the socialist movement. But for Blatchford, and for those who shared his aspirations, this combination of roles was wholly incompatible with the definition of socialism as a whole way of life with a unique culture of its own.

It was easy for socialists to condemn working-class uses of leisure. But it was more difficult for them to decide upon a policy to guide their actions in a world of mass entertainment. This became particularly apparent in the debates that took place about whether or not the labour and socialist press should cater to workers' recreational interests when those interests were perceived as a menace to socialism. On the one hand, the press wished to maintain its ideological purity and stand aloof from working-class materialism. On the other, socialist newspapers also needed to reach as many workers as possible, increasingly, as the new century opened, to boost circulation figures and thus attract advertising revenue. Robert Blatchford once claimed that the *Clarion* would have been ruined in three months if it had devoted its columns solely to labour issues.[80] Well-known for its explicit rejection of narrow, political coverage, the *Clarion* continued to enjoy a circulation of some 50,000 copies or more throughout the first decade of the century. But the cultural and recreational coverage it offered was directed to the converted and the paper only tended to capitulate to more popular tastes on the eve of World War I.

But what of those papers that desired to reach an even broader audience? They were increasingly forced to take into consideration the recreational interests of workers far removed from the experiences of official branch life. In Bradford, for example, the first local socialist newspapers, the Labour Church's *Bradford Labour Echo* (1849–99) and the ILP's *Forward* (1904–07), refused to cater to working-class interests and never published a sports column. But when the *Bradford Pioneer* was established in 1913, it included such a column. While papers like these flourished (the *Pioneer* did not collapse until 1935), those refusing to bow to the new trends were, as Blatchford anticipated, endangered. A flyer once praised the *Labour Leader* for keeping aloof from sporting interests, while John Bruce Glasier, editor of the *Leader* after Hardie's retirement, was proud of maintaining the paper's rather puritanical reputation. But there was a price to be paid for such policies and the *Leader*'s circulation figures declined.[81]

Debates over the future of the socialist press culminated in the battle over the proposed contents of labour's first daily newspaper. When it was decided to launch a daily in 1911, arguments took place about the degree to which the paper should appeal to workers' recreational interests. During the initial planning stages, one of the paper's supporters claimed that 'if you attempt to . . . specialise on Labour politics, I am strongly of the opinion that you would fail. . . . Racing and sport has such a hold upon the public that you could not with success ignore them.' Likewise, a report from the advertising subcommittee claimed that 'if the *Citizen* is to compete on equal terms with other papers as a medium for advertisers, similar matter [to that in the Northcliffe Press] will have to be included.'[82] When the *Daily Citizen* appeared on 8 October 1912, it had been agreed that the paper should devote some space to sport and recreation but that it should not offer betting or gambling tips.

Despite the caution, the paper still proceeded to flatter the new consumer of leisure. The first issue eagerly catered to women as domestic consumers, instituting a women's column virtually indistinguishable from those in the *Mail* and *Express*. The next day the paper began its 'Special Page of Sporting News'. Here it capitulated to existing working-class taste and jettisoned the beliefs that had once characterised the educationalist strands of socialist thought. In 'The fascination of football', for example, it praised the Saturday match for bringing affordable entertainment to the masses: 'As a spectacle', the paper wrote, football 'is unrivalled for the thrilling interest it provides.'[83] The following year, the directors decided by a vote of five to three to add betting tips to the sports coverage. As Glasier recorded in his diary: 'The editor, manager and circulation agent have declared that without betting news the paper cannot go. All the directors are personally against betting, but several have for some time been insisting that it is necessary to yield to this foible of the working class.' Glasier voted against the decision, regarding betting 'as a more degrading slavery than landlordism and capitalism'. While Glasier remained on the board, other members, like Arthur Henderson, resigned immediately.[84]

The position taken by Glasier and Henderson represents one of the last gasps of a nineteenth-century emphasis on the values of self-improvement, moral restraint and 'self-culture' in the face of a massive challenge to them. The lack of success experienced by Glasier in convincing the *Citizen* to stay clear of the working-class interests of which he did not approve is indicative of the limited appeal of those values in the new century. But even in the 1880s and 1890s such values had undermined the potential strength of socialism by elevating gambling over capitalism as the main enemy of the movement. In so doing they had also weakened the appeal of socialism to workers who repudiated such attempts to interfere with their leisure.

Like Glasier, there were other socialists who continued to place their faith in self-culture, attempting to keep the flame of educationalism alive. In 1909, for example, Arthur Ransom argued in the *Socialist Review* that the greatest obstacle to the realisation of socialism was the 'untrained and degraded condition of a large part of our British proletariat'. Believing that 'true socialism' was merely 'the highest morality realised in practice', Ransom called on the state to develop an effective system of 'moral instruction'.[85] By 1909, however, most socialists had tired of the struggle. Either, like Blatchford and Trevor, they lashed out at workers for being seduced by consumerism, or, like the *Daily Citizen*, they simply accepted the new trends. Little attempt was made to probe any deeper, to understand why educationalist strategies had failed or how the leisure industry was more capable than they were of appealing to particular working-class needs.

In the 1880s and 1890s, socialists had made the call for rational recreation central to their battle against popular taste. But in so doing they had judged that taste according to their own code of moral absolutes and found it wanting. Rational recreation was an admirable tool when wielded by socialist converts in their attempts to prepare themselves for the new life that socialism promised. But as a particular discourse of cultural criticism it could not offer socialists the intellectual means to develop a more wide-ranging critique of consumer capitalism. Moreover, individuals like Glasier, in holding to beliefs that predominated in the movement in the 1890s, were never able to remove the blame for the cultural ills they dissected from the individual worker. If some of them still called for a return to the virtues they had upheld in the past it was largely because they were uncertain of what else they could do.

In this they were not alone. In the 1880s and 1890s a vast array of articles poured forth suggesting how workers might best use the leisure they were gaining. Reformers hoped it would be devoted to self-improvement or to participation in morally edifying voluntary organisations. Many socialists believed that it should be devoted to the development of a complete socialist identity. Leisure was debated endlessly because there were many who believed that its use by the working class was in a state of flux and could thus still be influenced. Such was not the case by 1914. No longer was it a question of how workers might use the leisure they were gaining; according to those who still wrote about the subject, one had only to look around in order to see how it was being used. Few were encouraged by what they saw, although the widespread concern about popular culture that was evident in the late nineteenth century seemed to have become much more muted.

By 1914 reformers were less interested in popular culture than they had been a generation earlier. This can be measured by charting the decline in the number of articles devoted to a discussion of the matter in the more important of the monthlies and quarterlies. Articles on 'amusement' and 'recreation', along with more specialised articles on the use of music, literature and other edifying pursuits in the attempted moral elevation of the working class, declined in proportion to the growth of new recreational pursuits in working-class life. Between 1878 and 1889, for example, the *Nineteenth Century* carried fourteen articles on some aspect of popular culture and social reform; between 1902 and 1913 the number had fallen to five, all of which appeared before 1908. Likewise, while there were ten such articles in the *Contemporary Review* between 1890 and 1901, there were only two between 1902 and 1913.

Writers for the socialist press also seemed to discuss popular culture on fewer occasions in the new century. In the 1880s and 1890s even the SDF's *Justice* published a considerable number of articles and editorials by Hobart and Williams, and to a lesser extent by Quelch, Hyndman and Bax, on questions of socialism and the politics of pleasure. Taken together, these writers attempted to develop a radical critique of popular culture and link the fortunes of socialism with the reconstruction of pleasure in working-class life. At times they were unable to transcend the platitudes of rational recreation, although the desire to develop a 'revolutionary use of joyfulness' was always on the agenda. But after the Boer War, *Justice*, too, gave up these efforts and rarely discussed popular culture, except to suggest that the provision of entertainments might be of some use in drawing workers into the movement. Whether they liked it or not, critics now realised that the entertainment industry was there to stay.

Preparing a new soil for socialist culture

In 1909 C. F. G. Masterman suggested that most workers wanted 'to be left alone'. He added that while the awareness of this fact was widespread, there were many individuals who were 'not convinced that they ought to be left alone'.[86] Socialists, like settlement house workers and philanthropists with their gifts of 'culture for the people', had been engaged in a great crusade to transform working-class culture. And yet the majority of them were perceived as outsiders, against whom defences were required. The style of life developed by converts to the cause of socialism was radically different from that of the working class as a whole. Moreover, it largely failed to develop any widespread appeal. As a result, the culture of socialism and the culture of everyday working-class life expressed themselves in different languages. As Masterman wrote:

> In Mr. Grayson . . . a certain type has become articulate; the 'Clarionette' with red tie, flannel shirt, and bicycle . . . Such men see the world transfigured in the light of a great crusade. They are convinced that by demonstration and violence . . . 'the people' will rise in their millions and their might . . . and inaugurate the golden age of the Socialistic millennium. But meantime the 'people' are thinking of almost everything but the Socialistic millennium. They are thinking how to get steady work . . . which horse is going to win in some particular race, or which football eleven will attain supremacy in some particular league. They are thinking . . . of entertainment.[87]

Socialists recognised that they were increasingly unable to bridge the gap between these two worlds. As John Bruce Glasier wrote in his diary in 1905: 'I now see that we must change our socialist appeal or our movement will fail.'[88] But how could that appeal be changed? Few seemed to know the answer. On the eve of World War I, the late Fenner Brockway wrote an article on 'The religion of socialism', offering 'a vision that will save the people'. Brockway stressed the importance of cultivating once again the rhetoric and imagery that had been central to the religion of socialism in its early years. 'Unless', he wrote, 'the Socialist movement can bring the necessary vision to the people, unless it can instill, also, that dynamic force which compels people to realise the vision when their eyes have been opened to it, the Socialist Movement must fail.'[89] That vision is not to be disparaged. But if it had failed to move a great number of people in 1894 or 1904, how could it be effective in 1914, given the prevalence of new ways of organising leisure that undermined its aspirations? The religion of socialism had always offered a radical vision of a new society, but it appealed narrowly to individuals already quite receptive to it. Moreover, it could not offer an analysis of those very real obstacles that blocked its own widespread acceptance. The religion of socialism was concerned with generating a new life, but increasingly it could do so only in the limited space it could carve out in a corner of an emerging consumer society.

Four years after Brockway attempted to breathe new life into 'new life socialism', George Bernard Shaw argued that carving out a space for the development of a limited, alternative socialist culture would be the best that socialists could achieve if they failed to challenge the 'universal environment' their opponents controlled. 'Socialism', he continued, 'will not take root and grow in the soil cultivated by our present educational system, nor flourish in the artificial climate such cultivation produces.' Shaw recognised that most workers would not become socialists while they remained embedded in a whole culture that socialists failed to understand. Rather than suffer their own despair in isolation, as did Leatham and Trevor in the new century, or lash out at the working class for falling prey to the blandishments of capitalism – Blatchford's response – socialists had to think about changing the environment.

Educationalism alone, according to Shaw, would not suffice in the struggle to effect the changes he desired; it would have to be linked once again to environmentalist strategies. At this point in his argument Shaw lapsed into the chicken-and-egg dilemma faced by an earlier generation of environmental determinists: 'We cannot induce men to accept a socialist environment before they are Socialists', he wrote, 'And they cannot become Socialists . . . without a socialist environment.' But Shaw also recognised the importance of 'saturating' the educational and cultural institutions of society with socialist principles.[90] And he recognised that appealing to individual character was alone inadequate for the task at hand. Few of his contemporaries seemed to see the need for what Shaw was suggesting; few were as precise as Shaw in dissecting the weaknesses of the religion of socialism in an age of labourism and mass culture.

CONCLUSION

It would be an exaggeration to claim that popular culture was first and foremost among the concerns of socialists in Britain prior to 1914. Nevertheless, until the early 1900s, at least, socialists were as concerned with ethics as they were with narrowly conceived municipal or parliamentary politics, as interested in the moral reform of the individual as in effecting widespread economic changes. They believed that the advent of a socialist society would require more than a legislative revolution: it would require converts who shared a collective faith in the values of self-improvement, self-culture and self-discipline. Those values, they argued, had to be cultivated diligently, for the socialist movement depended on them. But when they looked around them, socialists saw workers who seemed to be developing recreational tastes of which they did not approve, uninterested in cultivating the values that were important in their own lives and, they argued, central to the struggle for socialism. Their critique of popular culture at the end of the century was implicitly a critique of ways of using leisure time that appeared, then, to undermine the growth of the very cause to which they were so committed.

It has not been my intention in this study simply to rescue obscure socialist attacks on the values of an emerging working-class culture and claim for them an undue significance. Rather, I have attempted to link widespread socialist beliefs about the importance of individual responsibility and morality, and more generally about the relationship between individual character and the environment, to broader intellectual and political currents of thought. I have focused on the response of the socialist movement to existing working-class culture, on socialist hopes for the uses of leisure in a future socialist society and on the contours of a new socialist culture that emerged in the 1890s at the branch level. In so doing, I have suggested that the attitudes that directed socialist thinking in all of these areas were shaped by a number of beliefs and assumptions about 'culture' that had their origins earlier in the century, outside the ranks of the socialist movement itself.

In and of themselves, these attitudes may seem insignificant. But they are important for two reasons. First, they severely handicapped socialists in their discussion of popular culture. While the relationship between workers and an emerging mass culture was being redrawn in the late nineteenth century – often precipitating a sense of despair among socialists and more traditional critics of popular culture alike – these individuals were unable to develop the intellectual tools that might have allowed them to offer an analysis of the appeal of that culture in working-class life. The attitudes they shared were predicated on a series of moral categories through which popular culture had been judged and found wanting throughout the nineteenth century and they directed socialists to focus less on the industry that flattered the new consumer of leisure than on the moral failings of the individuals who were themselves being flattered. In other words, although socialists were fuelled by a desire both to transform the individual and to change the environment, the intellectual baggage they inherited meant that when they turned their attention to workers' recreational pursuits, more often than not they simply blamed individuals for the poverty of their cultural preferences, tastes and desires. Put more bluntly, I have tried to suggest that socialists were prisoners of a cultural discourse that provided them with the only possible language for discussing popular culture at the end of the nineteenth century. Given the prevalence of this discourse throughout late Victorian society, it is not clear that socialists could have thought – or acted – differently. Thus, my purpose in this study has not been to condemn socialists for any paucity of imagination, but rather to suggest the existence of discursive constraints on that imagination.

Secondly, and perhaps more important, the attitudes socialists shared – and the cultural critique to which they gave rise – often led members of the socialist movement to be impatient, condescending and contemptuous of workers themselves. Recall Rutland Boughton's exasperation at those who rejected the choral music he offered them: 'You won't have it because you have long ago renounced all jolly, lively, meaty tunes, and taken to yourself the dull, dry bones of music they serve up to you in those cathedrals of yours – the music halls.'[1] Given such tirades – and there were many of them – one can understand why workers often repudiated the moral sermons preached by socialists. As C. F. G. Masterman once reminded those who had their own ideas about how workers should live, workers 'don't want to be cleaned, enlightened, inspected, drained. They don't want regulation of the hours of their drinking. . . . They don't want compulsory thrift, elevation to remote standards of virtue . . ., irritation into intellectual or moral progress.'[2] Such attitudes, then, served to consolidate the division that already existed between those who shared a faith in the moral vision of socialism and those who did not. In so doing, they contributed to the failure of socialism in Britain to become a genuinely popular and widespread movement.

Since the 1970s, and especially since the consolidation of Thatcherism, there has been a tendency on the left to romanticise an earlier 'golden age' of British socialism, a period that supposedly existed before the movement was 'captured' by labourism. Searching for alternatives to contemporary, bankrupt Labour Party strategies, committed socialists in the recent past have paid tribute to a more 'heroic' past. Often they have focused their attention on the vanished solidarities of the late nineteenth century.[3] For Stephen Yeo, for example, the 'period from the mid-1880s to the mid-1890s was no backwater in the history of British socialism. Nor was it a mere tributary feeding into a supposed mainstream – "the origins of the Labour Party" '. On the contrary, this period 'had its own special dynamism' which only ceased to operate when socialism became 'the prisoner of a particular, elaborate party machine'.[4] Before the development of the Labour Party, Yeo convincingly suggests, socialists did not merely put forward a narrow, political programme; instead they offered a series of guidelines for a whole new way of life.

We have encountered elements of the 'new life' that socialists both anticipated and devoted their energies to bringing about throughout this study. Central to that 'new life', for example, was a socialist musical culture that stressed the importance of communal participation and offered a unique blend of songs written for the movement and works appropriated from other cultural and political traditions. In general, socialists attempted to inspire enthusiasm for new forms of association and new cultural practices, and they hoped the activities they promoted would offer workers a foretaste of life under socialism and would thus become widely accepted. Those who participated in socialist branch life, enthusiastically embracing the values it stressed, often recalled the significance of the 'new life' long after socialists' faith in their ability to bring about the transformation of society had waned. Take, for example, the following reminiscence, offered by a member of the Bristol Socialist Society:

> It still lingers in my memory as some Enchanted Hall of Dreams. There was music and song and dance. Enid [Stacy]'s sisters were wonderful dancers. How proud she was of their beauty! The Guild of St. Matthew was working hard under the Rev. Stewart Headlam to release Britain from its Puritan ban on dancing and the stage generally. . . . Night after night bands of socialists, young and old, would meet for study and debate, and terribly practical work, too, for the unemployed and unskilled workers. . . . Never did our meetings break up without our singing one of Morris's

songs to a crooning Irish melody – I think 'The Message of the March Wind' to the tune of 'Teddy O'Neill' was the favourite.[5]

These social, recreational and political activities, central to socialist branch life in the 1880s and 1890s, emerged at a unique moment in the history of popular culture. Traditional uses of leisure, often circumscribed by specific occupational and community structures, were in decline, while a modern leisure industry was only beginning to impose its own restraints on the uses of leisure. There was still space available for individuals to develop alternative cultures of their own. But those who were most attracted to such cultures were, as we have seen, a relatively small number of men and women who felt 'vulnerable to the disrupting effects of economic change, to the anxieties resulting from social mobility, and to the uncertainties produced by a deepening religious and cultural crisis'.[6] Often attempting to keep alive the values of an older autodidact tradition within the confines of newer voluntary associations – and not merely those associated with the socialist movement – such individuals remained aloof from workers who led a very different kind of existence. The aspirations of Alice Foley or George Meek or Hannah Mitchell, or indeed of most of those who rallied to the Labour Church or to the Clarion clubs, were not shared widely in the working class.

Association for learning and self-improvement could serve as a model for social advance, while forms of self-discipline, generated in the enjoyment of rational recreations, could strengthen the resolve and marshall the energies of those who devoted themselves to the cause of socialism.[7] Moreover, the values of co-operation, intellectual endeavour, mutual self-help and association in the pursuit of social justice had been central to many working-class movements in the nineteenth century,[8] and they flourished once again in socialist organisations during the 1880s and 1890s. These values have largely been lost, and only now can we regret that loss. But it has not been my primary intention in this work to rehearse the arguments in favour of such important forms of association, nor to reconstruct the lives of those members of socialist clubs who cherished them. Rather, my aim has been to consider the experiences of such individuals in a wider context and in so doing to suggest that while they had always been marginal to working-class life in Britain they became even more marginal towards the end of the century.

One of the problems, then, with the values cultivated by 'new life' socialists was their limited currency in working-class circles and the tendency of those who already held them to denigrate those who did not.

It has been suggested that in the 1880s and early 1890s socialism had 'not yet become confused with superior understanding by experts of what the working class "needed" '.[9] And yet there were many converts to the cause who set themselves up as 'experts' and who, while deploying the rhetoric of self-activity, nevertheless continued to lecture workers about the need for their moral elevation. In short, socialists never escaped that great Victorian mission to make workers 'moral' beings. As Julia Dawson once claimed, the leaders of the socialist movement had attempted to make 'gentlemen out of the multitude of hogs and clods' and that Blatchford had 'instilled into them a love of culture'.[10] Of course, there were a few socialists, like William Morris, who objected to the idea of workers being robbed of culture in their daily lives only to have it offered back to them again by well-meaning reformers, no matter what their political persuasion. But Morris's thinking, despite the lip-service often paid to it, failed to exert much influence on socialists like Blatchford, individuals who all too often despised many workers' cultural preferences and set out to change them.

It was easy for socialists to condemn working-class culture in the late nineteenth century. But it was harder for them to envisage successful ways of redirecting its energies, other than through an attempt to bring 'culture' to the 'hogs and clods' of the nation. Thomas Wright had pointed this out as early as 1881, noting the failure of reformers to generate a more progressive culture, detached from traditional working-class pursuits. Wright argued that most of the leaders of the working-class movement saw a simple solution to a 'great social problem' – the absence of culture in working-class life – in the 'elevation of the masses'. But, he continued, those leaders failed to consider 'the causes from which this absence of culture results'.[11] This was an astute observation. Few socialists at the end of the century were capable of appreciating the complexities of the culture they so often desired to transform; even fewer could come to grips with the appeal of sport, the music hall and the popular press in that culture.

The socialist press was not wholeheartedly opposed to actually existing working-class culture. On the eve of World War I, for example, the *Sheffield Guardian* claimed that the 'holiday spirit' embodied a revolt not only against the conditions of urban life but 'against mother Grundy and the nastiness concealed in the folds of her skirt'. But, the paper continued, asserting its readers' own superiority: 'We are out for wholesomeness.'[12] Caution and suspicion were the norm, even in editorials like this one in the *Sheffield Guardian* that tacitly supported popular recreational pursuits. Moreover, it remained much easier for converts to the cause to stress the virtues of their own cultural experiences over and against those of most workers. In so doing, however, they contributed to the consolidation of a narrow, corporate, defensive and marginal culture, quite distinct from working-class life. Socialists succeeded in carving out a space where they could cultivate an alternative culture. But they were less successful in challenging the increasing determination of working-class uses of leisure by the new leisure industry. In addition, by retreating more and more into their own, narrow world, they failed to engage with the very forces that made their retreat so appealing in the first place. As Raymond Williams has noted:

> The idea of an alternative culture is radical but limited. It can very easily become a marginal culture; even, at worst, a tolerated play area. It is certainly always insufficient unless it is linked with effective opposition to the dominant system, under which the majority of people are living.[13]

Socialists never intended to create a culture that would remain the narrow preserve of the converted. In fact, they had hoped that the potential growth of leisure that was promised by the advent of the eight-hour day would result in a significant portion of it being devoted to personal improvement or to the cause of socialism. But workers turned in increasing numbers not to socialism but to the leisure industry to meet their needs. In response, a number of socialists began to lose their faith in the working class and turned to the state to help bring about the changes in popular culture they desired. This new strategy was not merely imposed on 'new life' socialism by the Fabians and their sympathisers; nor did it simply accompany the rise of labourism. Rather, the belief that the state, both at the national and local levels, could work to disseminate new values in working-class communities was widespread, and had been expressed in the 1880s and 1890s by socialists who already despaired of working-class uses of leisure and wished to see them reformed.

The idea that the state should encourage working-class access to the cultural inheritance of the nation – often to counter the perceived effects of a popular culture viewed to be harmful – proliferated in the socialist movement between the wars. As we have seen, the Labour Party's constitution had called for greater state intervention in the cultural arena as early as 1918. Eight years later, in a pamphlet entitled *Art and Culture in Relation to Socialism*, Arthur Bourchier called specifically for municipal theatres, and more generally for the state to make 'good' culture available to all. This, he claimed, was necessary to counter 'inane, vulgar and disappointingly trashy' Hollywood films and 'crude, savage, cacophonous' American jazz.[14] Stephen Jones has offered a detailed analysis of the labour movement's response to working-class culture in these years, suggesting that left intellectuals seldom came to terms with tastes considerably different from their own and failed to take workers seriously for what they were rather than what socialists wanted them to be.[15] They continued to stress the importance of rational recreation, much as they had in the 1890s, and at a Clarion Vocal Union concert held in Halifax in 1934 the programme was still dominated by the works of Eaton Faning and Dudley Buck, those proverbial favourites at earlier CVU gatherings.[16]

In terms of drink, the labour movement in the 1930s did become more sensitive to the texture and character of working-class life, appreciative of the fact that the pub was deeply embedded in working-class culture and hence difficult to challenge.[17] Moreover, the *Daily Herald* was more successful than the *Citizen* had ever been in offering a blend of entertainment, political analysis and news of the movement that stayed clear both of the didacticism of many socialist newspapers in the 1890s and of the sensationalism of tabloid journalism. But while the *Herald* was a genuinely popular paper, and while organisations like the Plebs League and the Labour College Movement kept alive an earlier emphasis on educationalism in an age of mass culture, socialists continued to express their despair at the trajectories of that culture, both between the wars and in the 1950s.[18] When, for example, Tony Crosland once spoke of new forms of automation that were leading to a twenty- or thirty-hour working week, his ideas echoed many of those that had, at the end of the nineteenth century, accompanied the struggle for the eight-hour day. He argued that Britain needed more open air cafés, pleasure gardens and local repertory theatres, and he suggested that the nation required 'determined government planning' in the 'field of cultural values' in order to counterbalance the appeal of newer forms of mass culture like television.[19] In 1959 the Labour Party's election manifesto, *Leisure for Living*, also emphasised the role of the state in guiding the uses of leisure in a society that was witnessing a reduction in working hours and the emergence of unparalleled affluence. As Lord Bridges put it: 'It is the duty of the state to provide something of the best in the arts as an example or inspiration to the whole of the country.'[20]

Such calls for the state to offer 'the best' of the national culture to 'the people' have been characteristic of socialist thinking throughout the history of the movement and cannot simply be associated with the

193

Labour Party. In addition, the more general demand for the cultivation of 'correct' leisure pursuits by workers, a product of the belief that existing uses of leisure are somehow flawed, continues to be made on the left today by individuals who are still eager to stress the superiority of their own wisdom. Nevertheless, as an astute critic of one such individual, Jeremy Seabrook, has noted, Seabrook's antipathy towards consumerism in post-war working-class culture has led to a 'view of the working class which is lacking in compassion and borders on contempt'.[21] The political ramifications of attitudes such as these are obvious. As Stuart Hall has suggested: 'The approach which takes a rather patronising tone to where ordinary people are at, and addresses them as if "we" know better, only seems to marginalise the left from the parameters and circumstances of everyday life which ordinary people inhabit as a fact of daily modern existence.'[22]

These forms of elitism are as old as the socialist movement in Britain itself. In part they can be attributed to the pervasiveness of ways of thinking about culture and society – emanating from the 'culture and civilisation' tradition as it has been called[23] – largely derived from the work of Matthew Arnold and given a new lease on life in the twentieth century by F. R. Leavis. From the earliest days of the socialist movement, socialists' thinking about popular culture has been framed by particular cultural discourses that have prevented them from approaching the working class with the degree of candour, honesty and understanding necessary for socialism to become a genuinely popular movement. As a result, socialists have been unable significantly to influence the course of popular culture in Britain. Two recent cultural theorists have put their fingers on the problem: 'Popular culture and puritanism . . . have been in almost perpetual conflict since the sixteenth century. It is an expensive irony of our history that the party of the people inherited only the puritan tradition, leaving to entrepreneurial capitalism the lucrative pastures of popular culture.'[24]

Despite the enormous influence of nineteenth-century patterns of cultural thought on the socialist movement throughout the first half of the twentieth century, the dominant paradigm for understanding popular culture in Britain has shifted dramatically in the last two or three decades. Indeed, it is the very existence of new forms of radical cultural politics in contemporary Britain that permits us to see more clearly the theoretical unity of an earlier cultural discourse, shared by many British socialists prior to World War I. In its final years, for example, the Greater London Council (GLC) challenged the assumption that culture is to be 'administered by experts and . . . enjoyed by all'. And it strove to place workers, women, gay men and lesbians, and members of ethnic minorities in a situation where genuine choice would again be possible; where the leisure industry would no longer be viewed as natural and unassailable; and where such individuals could play an active role in developing their own cultures, free from the interference of didactic 'experts' telling them what they should enjoy.[25]

While the policies developed by the GLC may point to a radical departure from the thinking of many socialists we have been concerned with in this study, they serve merely to bring us back to William Morris. While Morris on occasion admitted that he was out of touch with the realities of working-class life, seldom was his condescension to working-class culture as great as that of many of his contemporaries. Moreover, Morris, along with a large number of his comrades at the end of the century, cherished a vision of a new social order, a vision that is as appealing today as it was in the 1890s. As Miles Malleson, the advocate of ILP drama societies between the wars, put it: 'We have to imagine another [society] sufficiently vividly and widely, or go down in the general wreckage.'[26] Socialists in the late nineteenth century exercised their imagination in an attempt to see the contours of that new society. It was not their imagination that was flawed; rather, the problems began when they noted the existence of a vast number of workers who failed to share their aspirations, and when they proceeded to condemn such individuals accordingly. The SDF's weekly, *Justice*, claimed in an editorial on utopianism in 1899 that socialists 'began by expecting too much, and have finished by hoping too little'.[27] It is time to develop more realistic expectations, divorced from those moral values that so disfigured the hopes cherished by British socialists in the late nineteenth and early twentieth centuries.

NOTES

The place of publication is London, unless otherwise stated.

Introduction

1 Susan Pennybacker, ' "It was not what she said, but the way in which she said it": the London County Council and the music halls', in Peter Bailey, ed., *Music Hall: The Business of Pleasure*, Milton Keynes, 1986, p. 118; Tony Mason, *Association Football and English Society 1863–1915*, Brighton, 1980, p. 141. On working-class culture in the late nineteenth century, see Gareth Stedman Jones, *Languages of Class*, Cambridge, 1983, ch. 4; E. J. Hobsbawm, *Worlds of Labour*, 1984, chs 10–11.

2 Geoff Mulgan and Ken Worpole, *Saturday Night or Sunday Morning? From Arts to Industry – New Forms of Cultural Policy*, 1986, p. 99. See also Tony Bennett, 'The politics of "the popular" and popular culture', in Bennett, *et al.*, eds, *Popular Culture and Social Relations*, Milton Keynes, 1986.

3 Vernon Lidtke, *The Alternative Culture*, New York, 1985.

4 Martin Pugh, *The Tories and the People 1880–1935*, Oxford, 1985, p. 2.

5 Ross McKibbin, 'Why was there no marxism in Great Britain?', *English Historical Review*, XLIX, 1984, p. 307.

6 Hugh Cunningham, *Leisure in the Industrial Revolution*, 1980, p. 141; Peter Bailey, *Leisure and Class in Victorian England*, 1987 ed., esp. chs 2 and 4.

7 Robert Blatchford, *Merrie England*, 1976 ed., p. 21.

8 It appeared in *Justice* on 13 and 20 February 1886, 13 March 1886, 22 May 1886 and 24 July 1886. For Lafargue, see Leszek Kolakowski, *Main Currents of Marxism*, Oxford, 1978, II, pp. 141–8; Yvonne Kapp, *Eleanor Marx*, 2 vols, New York, 1972 and 1976, *passim*. Both Kolakowski and Kapp seem to be unaware of these English editions of Lafargue's work.

9 Paul Lafargue, *'The Right to be Lazy' and Other Studies*, Chicago, 1907, p. 40.

10 *Justice*, 31 July 1886, p. 4.

11 *Justice*, 14 August 1886, p. 4. For a similar defence of Lafargue as a satirist, see the *Northern Democrat*, June 1912, p. 2. Karl Marx also commented on the satirical nature of Lafargue's work. See his 1882 letter to Laura Lafargue, quoted in Ernst Benz, *Das Recht auf Faulheit, oder die friedliche Beendigung des Klassenkampfes*, Stuttgart, 1974, p. 111.

12 Lafargue, *Right to be Lazy*, pp. 22, 57.

13 *Justice*, 14 August 1886, p. 4 (emphasis added).

14 For Sparling, see *Commonweal*, 30 October 1886, pp. 244–5; *Labour Journal* (Bradford), 28 October 1892, p. 2. For Carnie, see the *Woman Worker*, 14 April 1909, p. 342.

15 M. A. Bienefeld, *Working Hours in British Industry*, 1972.

16 E. P. Thompson, 'Time, work-discipline, and industrial capitalism', *Past and Present*, XXXVIII, 1967, p. 86. See also John Myerscough, 'The recent history of the use of leisure time', in Ian Appleton, ed., *Leisure Research and Policy*, Edinburgh, 1974, pp. 9–10.

17 Lynn Hollen Lees, 'Getting and spending: the family budgets of English industrial

workers in 1890', in John M. Merriman, ed., *Consciousness and Class Experience in Nineteenth Century Europe*, New York, 1979, pp. 182–4.

18 *Justice*, 18 May 1895, p. 2. For a brief biography of Hobart, see the *Labour Annual*, 1896.

19 Talbot S. Peppin, *Club-Land of the Toiler*, 1895, p. 9.

20 See, for example, the *Labour Prophet*, December 1892, p. 96.

21 Sidney Webb and Harold Cox, *The Eight Hours Day*, 1891, p. 2. Sidney Webb, *A Plea for an Eight Hours Bill*, Fabian Tract no. 16, 1892, p. 1. These themes are explored by Ian Britain, *Fabianism and Culture*, Cambridge, 1982, pt 3.

22 Philip Snowden, *The Living Wage*, 1912, p. 166. See also Tom Mann, *What a Compulsory Eight Hour Day Means to the Workers*, n.d.; Mann, *The Regulation of Working Hours*, 1891.

23 *Justice*, 5 July 1884, p. 4; 15 May 1886, p. 4. For the complexity of the relationship between leisure and politics, see the *Cotton Factory Times*, 7 March 1913, p. 5.

24 James Leatham, *An Eight Hours' Day, with Ten Hours' Pay*, Aberdeen, 1890, pp. 2, 7. For Leatham, see Bob Duncan, *James Leatham, 1865–1945*, Aberdeen, 1978.

25 Raymond Williams, *Keywords*, 1976, pp. 198–9.

26 John Morley, 'On popular culture', in Morley, *Critical Miscellanies*, 1886, III, pp. 1–36; T. H. S. Escott, *Social Transformations of the Victorian Age*, 1897, ch. 26.

27 Thomas Wright, 'On a possible popular culture', *Contemporary Review*, XXXX, 1881, p. 36. For Wright's analysis of working-class life, see Alastair Reid, 'Intelligent artisans and aristocrats of labour: the essays of Thomas Wright', in Jay Winter, ed., *The Working Class in Modern British History*, Cambridge, 1983.

28 Cunningham, *Leisure in the Industrial Revolution*, pp. 12–13.

29 James Paget, 'Recreation', *Nineteenth Century*, XIV, 1883, p. 977.

30 Walter Besant, 'The people's palace', *Contemporary Review*, LI, 1887, p. 227.

31 Joseph Gutteridge, *Lights and Shadows in the Life of an Artisan*, Coventry, 1893, p. 23.

32 Vernon Lee [Violet Paget], 'A patron of leisure', *Contemporary Review*, LXX, 1896, pp. 854–5. See also Laurence Gronlund, 'Leisure', *Labour Leader*, 4 August 1894, p. 14. Writers also began to discuss the 'leisure classes': see Alex Wylie, *Labour, Leisure and Luxury*, 1884, p. 42.

33 *Report of the Committee to Inquire into the Condition of the Bristol Poor*, Bristol, 1885, pp. 109–10. For the subtle shifts in late Victorian discussions of popular culture, see Hugh Cunningham, 'Leisure', in John Benson, ed., *The Working Class in England 1875–1914*, 1985; J. M. Golby and A. W. Purdue, *The Civilisation of the Crowd*, New York, 1985, esp. ch. 8.

34 William Haig Miller, *The Culture of Pleasure; or, the Enjoyment of Life in its Social and Religious Aspects*, 1872, p. ix. I have touched upon such taxonomies of pleasure in ' "All sorts and any quantity of outlandish recreations": history, sociology and the study of leisure in England, 1820 to 1870', *Historical Papers/Communications Historiques*, 1981, pp. 30–1.

35 Karl M. Groos, *The Play of Man*, New York, 1901, p. 398; see also pp. 1–5, 334–60, 379–406; *The Play of Animals*, 1898, esp. pp. 1–81, 287–328. For the development of parallel ideas in Britain, see Charles Roberts, 'The physiology of recreation', *Contemporary Review*, LXVIII, 1895, pp. 103–13. Anthony Giddens has examined the theories of Groos in his 'Notes on the concept of play and leisure', *Sociological Review*, XII, 1964, pp. 73–89.

36 Samuel Barnett, 'The recreation of the people', *Living Age*, 3 August 1907, p. 276; A.

M. Thompson, in the *Woman Worker*, 7 April 1909, p. 316. See also Lady Cook's articles in *Justice*, 6 November 1897, p. 6; 18 June 1898, p. 2.

37 *Women Folk*, 22 June 1910, p. 1081. See also Margaret McMillan, writing in the *Labour Leader*, 17 June 1904, p. 114; Barclay Baron, *The Growing Generation*, 1911, esp. pp. 78–83. For the Band of Hope, see Lilian Shiman, 'The Band of Hope movement: respectable recreation for working-class children', *Victorian Studies*, XVII, 1973, pp. 49–74.

38 Mary L. Pendered, 'The psychology of amusement in its relation to temperance reform', *Socialist Review*, III, 1909, pp. 284–6.

39 Stephen Yeo, 'A new life: the religion of socialism in Britain, 1883–1896', *History Workshop Journal*, IV, 1977, p. 7.

40 William Morris, 'The socialist ideal. I, art', *New Review*, IV, 1891, p. 1.

41 Philip H. Wicksteed, *What Does the Labour Church Stand For?*, Labour Prophet Tracts, second series, no. 1, n.d., p. 11. See also 'Studies in the religion of socialism', *Labour Prophet*, May 1897, pp. 66–7; June 1897, pp. 81–2; October 1897, p. 122; February 1898, pp. 153–4. For more recent discussions, see Sheila Rowbotham and Jeffrey Weeks, *Socialism and the New Life*, 1977, pp. 42–75; Stanley Pierson, *Marxism and the Origins of British Socialism*, Ithaca, NY, 1973, esp. pp. 140–73.

42 Edward Carpenter, *England's Ideal, and Other Papers on Social Subjects*, 1887, p. 132.

43 Quoted in E. P. Thompson, 'Homage to Tom Maguire', in Asa Briggs and John Saville, eds, *Essays in Labour History*, 1967 ed., p. 313.

44 See Philip Frankford, writing in the *Worker* (Huddersfield), 7 March 1908, p. 2. Hyndman also praised the work of the Clarion movement, a movement usually seen at odds with the 'scientific marxism' of the SDF. See the letter, Blatchford to A. M. Thompson, 14 May 1908 (Blatchford papers); H. M. Hyndman, *Further Reminiscences*, 1912, pp. 246, 360–3, 365.

45 Duncan, *Leatham*, *passim*; Judith A. Fincher, 'The Clarion Movement', MA thesis, Manchester, 1971, pp. 70, 81–2.

46 See Britain, *Fabianism and Culture*, esp. ch. 1; D. D. Wilson, 'The search for fellowship and sentiment in British socialism, 1880–1914', MA thesis, Warwick, 1971, *passim*.

47 The term comes from Eileen and Stephen Yeo, 'Ways of seeing: control and leisure versus class and struggle', in Yeo, ed., *Popular Culture and Class Conflict 1590–1914*, Hassocks, 1981, p. 135. For an elaboration of the argument, see Stephen Yeo, 'Towards "making form of more movement than spirit": further thoughts on labour, socialism and the new life from the late 1890s to the present', in J. A. Jowitt and R. K. S. Taylor, eds, *Bradford 1890–1914*, Bradford Centre Occasional Papers, no. 2, 1980.

48 For socialist attitudes towards the working class in general, see John F. Whelan, 'The working class in British socialist thought, 1880–1914', M.Phil. thesis, Leeds, 1974.

49 Stuart Hall, 'Notes on deconstructing "the popular" ', in Raphael Samuel, ed., *People's History and Socialist Theory*, 1981, p. 229.

Chapter one

1 Patrick Joyce, *Work, Society and Politics*, Hassocks, 1980, p. 338.

2 'Pastime and business', *Chambers's Journal*, LXXII, 1895, p. 801. See also 'Leisure thoughts', *All the Year Round*, LXVII, 1890, pp. 228–30.

3 Leo Lowenthal, *Literature, Popular Culture and Society*, Palo Alto, 1961, p. 52.

4 J. H. Plumb, *The Commercialisation of Leisure in Eighteenth Century England*, Reading, 1974. For commercial leisure activity in the 1700s, see also Ian Watt, *The Rise of the Novel*, Berkeley, 1957, ch. 2; Pat Rogers, *Literature and Popular Culture in Eighteenth Century England*, Brighton, 1985.

5. Guy Chapman, *Culture and Survival*, 1940, p. 100. See also J. L. and Barbara Hammond, *The Age of the Chartists 1832–1854*, Hamden, Conn., 1962, pp. 331, 351.

6 Geoffrey Best, *Mid-Victorian Britain 1851–75*, New York, 1972, pp. 201ff; James Walvin, *Leisure and Society 1830–1950*, 1978, ch. 2.

7 Cunningham, *Leisure in the Industrial Revolution*, p. 37. For the role of the publican, see Brian Harrison, *Drink and the Victorians*, 1971, ch. 2.

8 Thomas Wright, *Some Habits and Customs of the Working Classes*, 1867, p. 175; Edmund Yates, *The Business of Pleasure*, 1865, I, p. 2.

9 John Lowerson and John Myerscough, *Time to Spare in Victorian England*, Brighton, 1977; Stephen Yeo, *Religion and Voluntary Organisations in Crisis*, 1976, p. 314; Asa Briggs, *Mass Entertainment*, Adelaide, 1960; Michael Marrus, *The Rise of Leisure in Industrial Society*, St Louis, 1974, p. 10; Gareth Stedman Jones, 'Working-class politics and working-class culture in London, 1870–1900', *Journal of Social History*, VII, 1974, p. 478.

10 T. H. S. Escott, *England: Its People, Polity and Pursuits*, 1885, p. 536.

11 *Parl. Papers*, 1892, vol. 18, 'Report from the select committee on theatres and places of entertainment', p. 79; Samuel Barnett, 'The recreation of the people', *Living Age*, CCLIV, 1907, p. 273.

12 Kathleen Barker, *Entertainment in the Nineties*, Bristol, 1973, p. 1; H. E. Meller, *Leisure and the Changing City 1870–1914*, 1976, pp. 210–12; Paul Wild, 'Recreation in Rochdale, 1900–1940', in John Clarke, *et al.*, eds, *Working-Class Culture*, 1979, p. 140; Trevor Lumis, 'The historical dimension of fatherhood: a case study 1890–1914', in Margaret O'Brien and Lorna McKee, eds, *The Father Figure*, 1982, pp. 52–3.

13 See Peter Bailey, 'Custom, capital and culture in the Victorian music hall', in Robert Storch, ed., *Change and Continuity in Victorian Popular Culture*, 1981, esp. p. 187; David Mayall, 'Places for entertainment and instruction: a study of early cinema in Birmingham, 1908–1918', *Midland History*, X, 1985, pp. 94–109.

14 Records of the Halifax Royal Skating Rink Co. Ltd (Calderdale Borough Archives).

15 William H. Sewell, *Work and Revolution in France*, Cambridge, 1980, p. 9. For the language of Chartism, see Stedman Jones, *Languages of Class*, ch. 3.

16 James Norris, *et al.*, *Artizans' Prize Essays. 'On the Influence of Rational and Elevating Amusements Upon the Working Classes'*, Liverpool, 1849, p. 25.

17 Discussed by Bruce Haley, *The Healthy Body and Victorian Culture*, Cambridge, Mass., 1978, pp. 124–5.

18 Norris, *Artizans' Prize Essays, passim*.

19 Hugh Cunningham, 'The metropolitan fairs: a case study in the social control of leisure', in A. P. Donajgrodzki, ed., *Social Control in Nineteenth Century Britain*, 1977, pp. 163–4, 179–80.

20 *Labour Leader*, 2 June 1894, p. 15.

21 *Labour Leader*, 3 December 1909, p. 774. For recreational entrepreneurs and the language of rational recreation, see also Bernard Waites, 'The music hall', in the Open University's course U-203, *Popular Culture*, Milton Keynes, 1981, unit 5, pp. 46–7, 54.

22 Alfred Butt, 'Free trade in amusement', *Reynolds's Newspaper*, 27 September 1908, p. 2.

23 Hugh Shimmin, *Liverpool Life: Its Pleasures, Practices and Pastimes*, Liverpool, 1857,

pp. 14, 17–18.

24 Ernest Ensor, 'The football madness', *Contemporary Review*, LXXIV, 1898, p. 760.

25 *Justice*, 19 January 1884, p. 2; 16 February 1889, p. 2. See also Daisy Halling and Charles Lister, 'A minimum wage for actors', *Socialist Review*, I, 1908, pp. 441–51.

26 Cunningham, *Leisure in the Industrial Revolution*, p. 175.

27 *Clarion*, 14 July 1900, p. 219. See also 21 July 1900, p. 227; 28 July 1900, p. 235.

28 Thomas Cooper, *The Life of Thomas Cooper*, 1886, pp. 392–4.

29 Ross McKibbin, 'Working-class gambling in Britain, 1880–1939', *Past and Present*, LXXXII, 1979, pp. 157, 165, 175–6.

30 *Commonweal*, 9 March 1889, p. 74. See also Martha Vicinus, *The Industrial Muse*, New York, 1974, pp. 239, 280.

31 E. Belfort Bax, 'Socialism and the Sunday question', in Bax, *The Religion of Socialism*, 1887, pp. 54–5. These beliefs were shared by German Social Democrats who felt that commercial pamphlet fiction encouraged passivity, robbing workers of the desire to shape their own culture. See Ronald A. Fullerton, 'Toward a commercial popular culture in Germany: the development of pamphlet fiction, 1871–1914', *Journal of Social History*, XII, 1979, pp. 500, 503.

32 'Leisure thoughts', *All the Year Round*, LXVII, 1890, p. 228.

33 William Morris, *Collected Works*, XXIII, p. 210; May Morris, *William Morris: Artist, Writer, Socialist*, Oxford, 1936, II, pp. 471–3. For similar beliefs, see Carpenter, *England's Ideal*, pp. 3–4; A. P. Hazell, 'The intellectual barrenness of capitalism', *Justice*, 2 April 1892, p. 2.

34 James Leatham, *Shows and Showfolk I Have Known*, Turriff, 1936, pp. 13ff., 51.

35 *Labour Leader*, 2 December 1904, p. 420.

36 *New Age*, 21 May 1896, pp. 120–1; 28 May 1896, p. 129; 'Report from the select committee', p. 327.

37 Escott, *England*, p. 540. See also C. E. B. Russell and E. T. Campagnac, 'Poor people's music halls in Lancashire', *Economic Review*, X, 1900, pp. 307–8.

38 Charles E. B. Russell and Lilian M. Rigby, *Working Lads' Clubs*, 1908, p. 277.

39 Quoted in Waites, 'Music hall', p. 70.

40 Will Thorne, *My Life's Battles*, 1925, pp. 28–9. For recent attempts to understand the content of music-hall entertainment, see J. S. Bratton, ed., *Music Hall: Performance and Style*, Milton Keynes, 1986.

41 John Burns, *Music and Musicians*, Manchester, n.d.

42 James Burnley, *Phases of Bradford Life*, 1871, p. 54. For an overview of popular culture in Bradford, see David Russell, 'The pursuit of leisure', in D. G. Wright and J. A. Jowitt, eds, *Victorian Bradford*, Bradford, 1981, pp. 199–221.

43 *Bradford Labour Echo*, 28 January 1899, p. 3. Likewise, Captain Footlight's 'Amusement' column in the socialist *Aberdeen Standard* (1893–94) seldom criticised music-hall entertainment.

44 Palace Theatre, *Souvenir 1913*, Manchester, 1913, pp. 3–5. For an elaboration of the argument put forward here, see Chris Waters, 'Manchester morality and London capital: the battle over the Palace of Varieties', in Bailey, ed., *Music Hall*, 1986.

45 Manchester Palace of Varieties, 'Minute book of director's meetings, 1889–1893' (Manchester Central Library, archives).

46 For Blatchford and his colleagues on the Palace and other halls in Manchester, see *Sunday Chronicle*, 8 March 1891, p. 2; 15 March 1891, p. 2; 29 March 1891, p. 3; *Clarion*, 27 August 1892, p. 8; 3 September 1892, p. 2.

47 John Burns, *Labour and Drink*, 1904, pp. 1–5, 36; Burns, *Music and Musicians*, pp. 1–2.

48 Diary, 3 June 1896 and 2 May 1910 (Glasier papers). See also David Howell, *British Workers and the Independent Labour Party 1888–1906*, Manchester, 1983, pp. 335–6, 358.

49 *Labour Prophet*, February 1893, p. 11; March 1893, pp. 22–3; April 1893, p. 31; May 1893, pp. 34–5. See also H. Gifford Oyston, *Socialism and the Drink Evil*, 1909, p. 60.

50 Charles E. Muse, *Poverty and Drunkenness*, Manchester, 1895.

51 H. M. Hyndman, *The Social Reconstruction of England*, 1884, p. 20. See also H. Russell Smart, *Socialism and Drink*, Manchester, 1890, pp. 3–4; Geo. S. Reaney, 'Socialism and national sobriety', *To-Day*, III, 1885, p. 121. For an overview, see Guy Hayler, 'Labour and temperance: a brief historical survey of Labour's attitudes to the drink problem', *Alliance Year Book and Temperance Reformers' Yearbook*, 1928.

52 Edward Carpenter, *My Days and Dreams*, 1916, pp. 298–300. On the tied house, see David M. Fahey, 'Brewers, publicans, and working-class drinkers: pressure group politics in late Victorian and Edwardian England', *Histoire sociale/Social History*, XIII, 1980, pp. 85–103.

53 For an elaboration, see Harrison, *Drink and the Victorians*, pp. 395–405.

54 'Professionals in English sports', *Saturday Review*, LXV, 1888, pp. 437–8. See also 'Football: the game and the business', *The World's Work*, I, 1902, pp. 77–9; Mason, *Association Football*, esp. pp. 69–81, 230.

55 John Burns, *Brains Better than Bets or Beer*, Clarion Pamphlet no. 36, 1902, p. 12.

56 Edward Carpenter, *Angel's Wings*, 1898, pp. 213–14. See also 'Gavroche' [Willie Stewart], 'Is football anti-social?', *Labour Leader*, 19 March 1904, p. 96; John Bruce Glasier, *The Meaning of Socialism*, Manchester, 1919, p. 95; Mason, *Association Football*, pp. 235, 263–7.

57 *Northern Democrat*, March 1908, p. 1.

58 Robert Blatchford, 'A socialist's answer to Dr Crozier's challenge', *Fortnightly Review*, LXXXIX, 1908, p. 233.

59 *Labour Leader*, 21 July 1894, p. 13; 15 September 1894, p. 12.

60 *Sheffield Guardian*, 23 April 1909, p. 2.

61 'Socialism and sport', *Justice*, 26 December 1891, p. 4.

62 John Lubbock, *The Uses of Life*, 1894, p. 68.

63 *Woman Worker*, 28 July 1909, p. 85.

64 Tony Bennett, 'Hegemony, ideology, pleasure: Blackpool', in Bennett, *et al.*, *Popular Culture*, p. 140.

65 Letter, Blatchford to Palmer, n.d. (Blatchford papers). For Roberts, see *The Classic Slum*, Harmondsworth, 1971, p. 49. For the *Clarion* on Blackpool, see 27 August 1892, p. 8; 20 May 1893, p. 3; 26 May 1900, p. 168. See also John K. Walton, *The Blackpool Landlady*, Manchester, 1978, esp. pp. 27–40, 137–44.

66 Robert Blatchford, *Saki's Bowl*, 1928, p. 87.

67 'A study by the seashore', *Labour Leader*, 2 September 1904, p. 253. Glasier, *Workman's Times*, 17 June 1893, p. 1.

68 *Forward*, 11 August 1906, pp. 5–6.

69 'A study by the seashore', p. 253.

70 Snowden, *Living Wage*, p. 66.

71 Thorstein Veblen, *The Theory of the Leisure Class*, New York, 1953 ed.

72 J. A. Hobson, 'The theory of the leisure class', *The Reformer*, VIII, 1904, p. 615. See also E. J. Urwick, *Luxury and Waste of Life*, 1908, p. 41.

73 J. Ramsay MacDonald, 'Gambling and citizenship', in B. Seebohm Rowntree, ed., *Betting and Gambling*, 1905, p. 122.

74 MacDonald, 'Gambling and citizenship', pp. 118–19.

75 MacDonald, 'Gambling and citizenship', p. 133.

76 *Labour Leader*, 12 May 1900, p. 146.

77 Charles Charrington, 'Communal recreation', *Contemporary Review*, LXXIX, 1901, p. 851.

78 Mason, *Association Football*, p. 237.

79 H. W. Hobart, 'Pleasure', *Justice*, 29 December 1894, p. 3.

Chapter two

1 Bailey, *Leisure and Class*, p. 169.

2 George Kateb, 'Utopia and the good life', in Frank E. Manuel, ed., *Utopias and Utopian Thought*, Boston, 1966, pp. 242–9. See also Zygmunt Bauman, *Socialism: The Active Utopia*, 1976, ch. 7.

3 William Morris, 'Art and socialism', *Collected Works*, XXIII, p. 195.

4 William Thompson, *A Prospectus of Socialism*, n.d.; Robert Blatchford, *The Sorcery Shop*, 1907. Frankford's novel, *The Coming Day*, was serialised in Huddersfield's *Worker* between February and June 1908.

5 Edward Herbert, *Newaera*, 1910; Ernest Bramah, *The Secret of the League*, 1909.

6 A. L. Morton, *The English Utopia*, 1952, p. 11.

7 *Justice*, 22 February 1890, p. 2.

8 Discussed in E. P. Thompson, *William Morris*, New York, 1976 ed., p. 791.

9 Thompson, *Morris*, p. 806. See also Raymond Williams, 'Utopia and science fiction', in Williams, *Problems in Materialism and Culture*, 1980, pp. 202–3.

10 Perry Anderson, *Arguments within English Marxism*, 1980, pp. 157–75.

11 Clapperton, *A Vision of the Future*, 1904, pp. 15, 44, 66. Dora B. Montefiore, socialist, feminist and writer of women's columns for *The New Age* and *Justice*, praised her work: Montefiore, *From a Victorian to a Modern*, 1927, p. 115; 'Women's Interests', *New Age*, 4 May 1905, p. 282. *The Labour Leader* (27 May 1904, p. 87) also reacted favourably to her work. For biographical information, see the *Labour Annual*, 1898, p. 195.

12 Webb and Cox, *Eight Hours Day*, p. 148; Webb, *Plea for an Eight Hours Bill*, p. 1.

13 John C. Kenworthy, 'Culture and socialism', *Commonweal*, 31 May 1890, p. 173.

14 William Morris, *News from Nowhere; or, an Epoch of Rest*, 1970 ed., pp. 60, 67, 114.

15 Morris, *News from Nowhere*, p. 110.

16 See also Annie Besant in the *Practical Socialist*, August 1886, p. 135; Jack C. Squire, *Socialism and Art*, 1907, p. 12.

17 Quoted in Britain, *Fabianism and Culture*, p. 79.

18 Morris, *News from Nowhere*, p. 111; Morris, 'Communism', *Collected Works*, XXIII, p. 270.

19 Quoted in Colin Mercer, 'A poverty of desire: pleasure and popular politics', in Formations Collective, ed., *Formations of Pleasure*, 1983, p. 84. Earlier in the nineteenth century John Stuart Mill also seemed unclear about whether the 'capacity for the nobler feelings' was innate or acquired. See Mill, *Utilitarianism*, Indianapolis, 1957 ed., pp. 14, 39–40, 50–1.

20 Robert Blatchford, *The New Religion*, 1897, p. 1; Burns, *Brains Better than Bets*, p. 13.

21 William Tuckwell, 'How can a love and appreciation of art be best developed among the masses of the people?', in Tuckwell, *et al.*, *Art and Hand Work for the People*, 1885, p. 7.

22 E. Harcourt Burrage, *J. Passmore Edwards, Philanthropist*, 1902, p. 6.

23 *ILP Journal*, 25 April 1896, p. 4.

24 Dora Walford, 'Socialist Sunday schools', *Worker*, 29 February 1908, p. 7. See also F. Reid, 'Socialist Sunday schools in Great Britain 1892–1939', *International Review of Social History*, XI, 1966, pp. 18–47.

25 *ILP Journal*, 3 February 1895, pp. 2–3.

26 Ben Tillett, 'The Labour platform: new style', *New Review*, VI, 1892, p. 178. Hird's speech, 'The building of character', was reported in Huddersfield's *Worker*, 30 April 1910, p. 2.

27 Morris, *News from Nowhere*, p. 88.

28 *ILP Journal*, 3 February 1895, pp. 2–3.

29 Ben Tillett, *An Address on Character and Environment*, Manchester, n.d., p. 12. My discussion here owes much to Logie Barrow, 'Determinism and environmentalism in socialist thought', in Raphael Samuel and Gareth Stedman Jones, eds, *Culture, Ideology and Politics*, 1982. For Tillett, see Jonathan Schneer, *Ben Tillett*, 1982.

30 James Leatham, *Socialism and Character*, 1897.

31 *Clarion*, 15 December 1900, pp. 40–1.

32 William Morris, 'The worker's share of art', *Commonweal*, April 1885, p. 19.

33 *Clarion*, 22 March 1907, p. 1.

34 *Clarion*, 2 August 1907, p. 2.

35 John Burns, *Address Given by the Rt Hon. John Burns, P.C., at the Opening of the Tudor Barn and Art Gallery*, 1936, p. 2; 'Jacobus' [Leatham], 'Face to Face', *Worker*, 26 March 1910, p. 4; Duncan, *Leatham*, p. 32.

36 *Woman Worker*, 25 September 1908, p. 431; *Clarion*, 21 May 1909, p. 4.

37 Charles Charrington, 'Communal recreation', *Contemporary Review*, LXXIX, 1901, p. 850.

38 Changes in the work process are discussed by James Hinton, *The First Shop Stewards Movement*, 1973, ch. 2. On the confusion caused by the new leisure options for workers, see Peter N. Stearns, 'The effort at continuity in working-class culture', *Journal of Modern History*, LII, 1980, pp. 647–50.

39 See Charles More, *Skill and the English Working Class 1870–1914*, 1980.

40 See C. E. B. Russell and E. T. Campagnac, 'Gambling and aids to gambling', *Economic Review*, X, 1900, p. 482; Robert Halstead, 'The stress of competition from the workman's point of view', *Economic Review*, IV, 1894, p. 45.

41 Thomas Wright, 'Our craftsmen', *Nineteenth Century*, XX, 1886, pp. 530–52.

42 'A nation at play: the peril of games', *Blackwood's Edinburgh Magazine*, CLXXV, 1904, p. 24.

43 Barnett, in the preface to Peppin, *Club-Land*, p. vii; Barnett, 'The recreation of the people', *Living Age*, 3 August 1907, pp. 272, 276. See also F. J. Marquis and S. E. F. Ogden, 'The recreation of the poorest', *Town Planning Review*, III, 1913, p. 244.

44 The literature is extensive. The examples discussed here are drawn from: James Paget, 'Recreation', *Nineteenth Century*, XIV, 1883, pp. 977–88; 'Dunraven' [W. T. W. Quin], 'Opening national institutions on Sundays', *Nineteenth Century*, XV, 1884, pp. 416–34; Charles Roberts, 'The physiology of recreation', *Contemporary Review*, LXVIII, 1895, pp. 103–13; Vernon Lee, 'Wasted pleasures', *Contemporary Review*,

XCIV, 1908, pp. 679–92; [H. Highet], 'The psychology of golf', *Blackwood's Edinburgh Magazine*, CXLIII, 1888, pp. 683–9; John Lubbock, 'Free libraries', *New Review*, IV, 1891, pp. 60–6; Janetta Rutland [Manners], 'How intemperance has been successfully combated', *New Review*, VI, 1892, pp. 76–88, 460–71. For an excellent analysis of the effects of mass production on leisure, see Robert Goldman and John Wilson, 'The rationalization of leisure', *Politics and Society*, VII, 1977, pp. 157–87.

45 'Our national dulness', *Progressive Review*, II, 1897, p. 113.
46 Harry Lowerison, 'On "organised games" ', *Daily Herald*, 1 June 1912, p. 4; W. Diack, *The Moral Effects of Socialism*, Aberdeen, 1893, p. 14.
47 *Labour Leader*, 12 March 1904, p. 6.
48 Edward Carpenter, *Towards Industrial Freedom*, 1917, pp. 50–4; Glasier, *Meaning of Socialism*, pp. 94–7.
49 Morris, 'Art of the people', *Collected Works*, XXII, p. 33. See also 'Art and labour', in Eugene D. Lemire, *The Unpublished Lectures of William Morris*, Detroit, 1969, p. 113. On Morris and work, see Alasdair Clayre, *Work and Play*, 1974, pp. 69–78; Thompson, *Morris*, pp. 641–54; Nicholas Pearson, 'Art, socialism and the division of labour', *Journal of the William Morris Society*, IV, 1981, pp. 7–25.
50 'Attractive labour', *Commonweal*, June 1885, pp. 49–50; 'Useful work *versus* useless toil', *Collected Works*, XXIII; 'A factory as it might be', *Artist, Writer, Socialist*, II.
51 'Useful work *versus* useless toil', p. 99.
52 'The revival of handicraft', *Fortnightly Review*, XLIV, 1888, p. 609. See also 'How we live and how we might live', *Collected Works*, XXIII, pp. 19–20; 'How shall we live then?', in Paul Meier, 'An unpublished lecture of William Morris', *International Review of Social History*, XVI, 1971, pp. 230–2. Meier offers the most thorough analysis of Morris's utopian vision in his *William Morris*, Hassocks, 1978, vol. II.
53 Edward Bellamy, *Looking Backward 2000–1887*, New York, 1960 ed., pp. 136–7, 165.
54 Morris, 'Looking backward', *Artist, Writer, Socialist*, vol. II.
55 Morris, *News from Nowhere*, p. 78.
56 'The aims of art', *Collected Works*, XXIII, pp. 93–4; 'Why I am a communist', *Liberty*, I, 1894, p. 14.
57 'How we live', p. 19. For a discussion of these themes, see Patrick Brantlinger, ' "News from Nowhere": Morris's anti-novel', *Victorian Studies*, XIX, 1975, pp. 35–49.
58 The celebration in *News from Nowhere* is discussed on p. 56. For Morris and medievalism, see Michael Naslas, 'Medievalism in Morris's aesthetic theory', *Journal of the William Morris Society*, V, 1982, pp. 16–24.
59 Fred L. Polak, *The Image of the Future*, Leyden, 1961, I, pp. 360–1.
60 Karl Marx, *Capital, vol. III*, ed. by Frederick Engels, New York, 1967 ed., p. 820.
61 Blatchford, *Sorcery Shop*, p. 28. There is little secondary literature on Blatchford's novel, but see V. Dupont, *L'utopie et le roman utopique dans la littérature anglaise*, Cahors, 1941, pp. 558–69; David Smith, *Socialist Propaganda in the Twentieth-Century British Novel*, 1978, pp. 17–20.
62 Blatchford, *Sorcery Shop*, p. 189.
63 Edward Bulwer-Lytton, *The Coming Race*, Edinburgh, 1871, p. 115.
64 Blatchford, *Sorcery Shop*, pp. 104–5.
65 Blatchford, *Sorcery Shop*, pp. 61, 86, 99.
66 Blatchford, *Sorcery Shop*, pp. 94, 137.
67 Bellamy, *Looking Backward*, pp. 138, 165.
68 *Worker*, 18 April 1908, p. 4. See also 22 February 1908, p. 7; 29 February 1908, p. 2; 21

March 1908, p. 2.

69 Thompson, *A Prospectus of Socialism*, p. 223.

70 E. Belfort Bax, *Outlooks from the New Standpoint*, 1891, pp. viii–ix.

71 [Fairfield], *The Socialist Revolution of 1888, by an Eye-Witness*, 1884, pp. 20–1, 32, 35. See also Innominatus [Edward Heneage Dering], *In the Light of the Twentieth Century*, 1886.

72 Eugene Richter, *Pictures of the Socialist Future*, 1907 ed., pp. vi–ix. The *Aberdeen Standard* (2 November 1893, p. 2) urged socialists to read and discuss Richter's novel.

73 Bramah, *Secret of the League*, p. 87.

74 *Secret of the League*, pp. 82–3.

75 Herbert, *Newaera*, esp. pp. 75–8, 201, 208–11.

76 *Socialist Revolution of 1888*, p. 26 (emphasis in original).

77 Glasier, *Meaning of Socialism*, pp. 95–6.

Chapter three

1 Isabella O. Ford, *On the Threshold*, 1895, p. 177.

2 Beatrice Webb, *My Apprenticeship*, 1926, pp. 207–8, 211, 214, 250.

3 Tillett, *Address on Character*, pp. 10, 15.

4 Gareth Stedman Jones, *Outcast London*, Harmondsworth, 1976, chs 13 and 18. On these shifts, see Michael E. Rose, 'Culture, philanthropy and the Manchester middle classes', in Alan J. Kidd and K. W. Roberts, eds, *City, Class and Culture*, Manchester, 1985, pp. 103–17.

5 B. Kirkman Gray, *Philanthropy and the State, or Social Politics*, 1908, p. 315. Clementina Black wrote of Gray: 'From being a philanthropist he had become a sociologist, and was . . . a socialist of the progressive type' (Henry Bryan Bins, *A Modern Humanist: Miscellaneous Papers of B. Kirkman Gray*, 1910, p. 63).

6 Charles Roberts, 'The physiology of recreation', *Contemporary Review*, LXVIII, 1895, p. 111; also, Octavia Hill, 'Our dealings with the poor', *Nineteenth Century*, XXX, 1891, pp. 162, 168.

7 Russell and Rigby, *Working Lads' Clubs*, p. 279; Violet Greville, 'Social reforms for the London poor. I – the need for recreation', *Fortnightly Review*, XXXV, 1884, pp. 21–30; Maude Stanley, 'Clubs for working girls', *Nineteenth Century*, XXV, 1889, pp. 73–83; Harry Jones, 'Amusements of the people', *Good Words*, XXXII, 1891, pp. 163–6; M. E. Jersey, 'Children's happy evenings', *Nineteenth Century*, LVIII, 1905, pp. 942–50.

8 M. Jeune, 'Amusements of the poor', *National Review*, XXI, 1893, pp. 306, 312.

9 Samuel Barnett, *Worship and Work*, Letchworth, 1913, pp. 90, 103, 124.

10 Henrietta Barnett, 'Principles of recreation', in Samuel and Henrietta Barnett, *Towards Social Reform*, 1909, pp. 289–90. See also Henrietta Barnett, *Canon Barnett*, 1918, I, pp. 152, 158; Samuel Barnett, 'The mission of music', *International Journal of Ethics*, IX, 1898, pp. 494–504; Henrietta Barnett, 'Passionless reformers', in Henrietta and Samuel Barnett, *Practicable Socialism*, 1888, pp. 55–9. On the cultural activities of Toynbee Hall, see J. A. R. Pimlot, *Toynbee Hall*, 1935; Seth Koven, 'Culture and poverty: the London settlement house movement 1870 to 1914', Ph.D. thesis, Harvard, 1987.

11 See, for example, Florence A. Marshall, 'Music and the people', *Nineteenth Century*, VIII, 1880, pp. 925–6.

12 *Report of the [Bristol] Committee*, p. 112; Russell and Rigby, *Working Lads' Clubs*, pp. 22–3; Arnold Freeman, *Boy Life and Labour*, 1914, pp. 129–31.

13 Francis Hitchman, 'The penny press', *Macmillan's Magazine*, XLIII, 1881, p. 398.

14 Freeman, *Boy Life*, p. 128.

15 Quoted in Michael Macmillan, *The Promotion of General Happiness*, 1890, p. 84.

16 For Blatchford on the Manchester slums, see the *Sunday Chronicle*, 1889, *passim*; for Nevinson, see P. J. Keating, *The Working Classes in Victorian Fiction*, New York, 1971, p. 104.

17 *Labour Prophet*, January 1893, p. 5.

18 C. Stella Davies, *North Country Bred*, 1963, p. 19.

19 *Clarion*, 10 October 1896, p. 328; 31 October 1896, p. 352; 28 November 1896, p. 384.

20 *Forward*, 17 March 1906, p. 9. On the Guild, see Michael Cahill and Tony Jowitt, 'The new philanthropy: the emergence of the Bradford City Guild of Help', *Journal of Social Policy*, IX, 1980, pp. 359–82.

21 *Socialist*, November 1894, p. 4.

22 J. Keir Hardie, *From Serfdom to Socialism*, 1907, p. 26; Fred Reid, *Keir Hardie*, 1978, pp. 146–50, 180–4; Kenneth O. Morgan, *Keir Hardie*, 1975, pp. 201–17.

23 See *Justice*, 12 June 1893, p. 1; 1 July 1893, p. 4; 22 July 1893, pp. 2–3.

24 Morris, 'How I became a socialist', *Collected Works*, XXIII, pp. 277–81.

25 Morris, 'Philanthropy', *Artist, Writer, Socialist*, II, pp. 122–4. See also 'Art and socialism', *Collected Works*, XXIII, p. 211; 'Communism', *Collected Works*, XXIII, pp. 264–5.

26 Morris, 'At a picture show', *Artist, Writer, Socialist*, II, pp. 412–3. See also 'Art and the people: a socialist's protest', *Artist, Writer, Socialist*, II, pp. 382–406; 'Art or no art . . .?', *Justice*, 15 March 1884, p. 2.

27 *Clarion*, 12 March 1898, p. 84; Edward Carpenter, 'An open-air gymnasium', *Sandow's Magazine of Physical Culture*, IV, 1900, p. 80; 'High art in lowly homes', *Sheffield Guardian*, 20 July 1906, p. 2; Arthur Ransom, 'Substitutes for the public house', *Worker*, 7 March 1908, p. 2.

28 Diack, *Moral Effects of Socialism*, pp. 15, 19; Leatham, *Socialism and Character*, p. 152.

29 *Clarion*, 28 May 1892, p. 7; 18 June 1892, p. 5; 16 July 1892, p. 5; 25 February 1893, p. 5; 24 June 1893, p. 5; 2 September 1893, p. 5; 29 February 1896, p. 72; 25 April 1896, p. 135; 2 May 1896, p. 144; 3 November 1898, p. 373; 3 December 1898, p. 387.

30 *Clarion*, 27 November 1903, p. 3; 14 March 1896, p. 85.

31 *Clarion*, 11 September 1897, p. 293.

32 For Blatchford on Smiles, see the *Clarion*, 21 August 1897, p. 268; 28 August 1897, p. 277; 4 September 1897, p. 285. His series on 'Self culture' ran from 5 February to 25 March 1904.

33 *Clarion*, 8 June 1895, p. 183. See also T. A. Leonard, *Adventure in Holiday Making*, n.d.

34 William Booth, *In Darkest England and the Way Out*, 1890, pp. 237–40.

35 *Labour Prophet*, July 1895, p. 102.

36 *Rochdale Labour News*, June 1899, p. 4.

37 *Clarion*, 9 June 1894, p. 8; *Labour Prophet*, July 1895, p. 104. See also Jill Liddington, *The Life and Times of a Respectable Radical: Selina Cooper*, 1984, pp. 80–8.

38 Stanton Coit, 'The dynamics of democracy', in Coit, *Ethical Democracy*, 1900, pp. 342–3. See also I. D. Mackillop, *The British Ethical Societies*, Cambridge, 1986, pp. 99–137.

39 'Neighbourhood Guilds: an interview with Dr Stanton Coit', *London: A Journal of Civil*

and Social Progress, 8 June 1893, p. 295. See also Coit, *Neighbourhood Guilds*, 1891; Coit, *The Ethical Movement Defined*, 1898?

40 Coit, *Neighbourhood Guilds*, pp. 108–16.

41 Coit, *Neighbourhood Guilds*, p. 150.

42 *Fabian News*, September 1891, p. 28; *Labour Prophet*, March 1893, p. 18; D. F. Summers, 'The Labour Church and allied movements of the late 19th and early 20th centuries', Ph.D. thesis, Edinburgh, 1958, p. 35.

43 Rowley, *Social Politics*, Manchester, 1885, p. 16.

44 Rowley, *Fifty Years of Work Without Wages*, 1912, pp. 211, 213, 247. See also Rowley, *A Workshop Paradise and Other Papers*, 1905, pp. 59–60, 130–2; *Labour Record and Review*, December 1905, p. 318; J. I. Rushton, 'Charles Rowley and the Ancoats recreation movement', M.Ed. thesis, Manchester, 1959.

45 Ancoats Recreation Committee, *Programmes of the Autumn and Winter Work of the ARC*, Manchester, 1893.

46 Reginald Groves, *The Mystery of Victor Grayson*, 1946, p. 17.

47 G. B. Shaw, 'The climate and soil for Labour culture', in Louis Crompton, ed., *Bernard Shaw, The Road to Equality*, Boston, 1971, p. 327.

48 *Labour Annual*, 1897, pp. 98, 234; Rowley, *Workshop Paradise*, pp. 183–8; Summers, 'Labour Church', pp. 12, 519; Fincher, 'Clarion movement', pp. 37–8, 147–8.

49 *Labour Prophet*, January 1896, pp. 4–5.

50 *New Moral World*, 20 July 1839; 25 August 1838.

51 Walter Besant, 'The amusements of the people', *Contemporary Review*, XLV, 1884, p. 344.

52 Besant, 'Amusements', pp. 347–8.

53 Besant, *Autobiography of Sir Walter Besant*, 1902, pp. 260–1.

54 Keating, *Working Classes in Victorian Fiction*, p. 100.

55 Elizabeth Bisland, 'The People's Palace in London', *Cosmopolitan*, X, 1891, p. 261. See also Besant, 'The People's Palace', *Contemporary Review*, LI, 1887, pp. 226–33; Andrew Chapman, 'The People's Palace for East London: a study of Victorian philanthropy', M.Phil. thesis, Hull, 1979.

56 H. T. Smart, 'The recreations of the people', *Wesleyan Methodist Magazine*, XIV, 1890, pp. 666–7; George Haw, *Today's Work*, 1901, pp. 228–9.

57 *Justice*, 21 May 1887, p. 2.

58 *Clarion*, 19 February 1898, p. 61. See also John Williams, 'Sunday at the People's Palace', *Lend a Hand*, III, 1888, p. 322; Besant, 'People's Palace', *North American Review*, CXLVII, 1888, p. 59.

59 H. A. Barker, 'A People's Palace', *Commonweal*, 17 July 1886, pp. 121–2.

60 *Commonweal*, 13 November 1886, p. 257.

61 Besant, 'People's Palace', *Contemporary Review*, p. 233.

62 *Palace Journal*, 16 January 1889, p. 850.

63 Quoted in Laurence Thompson, *Robert Blatchford*, 1951, pp. 54–5.

64 Coit, *Neighbourhood Guilds*, pp. 114–15. See also Annie Besant, writing in the *Link*, 11 August 1888, p. 1.

65 George Lansbury, *My Life*, 1928, p. 130.

66 Percy Alden, 'The amusements of the London poor', *The World To-Day*, IX, 1905, p. 1071.

67 Will Reason, 'Settlements and recreations', in Reason, ed., *University and Social Settlements*, 1898, p. 86; Percy Alden, 'The ideal church for East London', in Richard

Mudie-Smith, ed., *The Religious Life of London*, 1904, pp. 43–4.

68 *Bradford Labour Echo*, 7 December 1895, p. 3. On Alden and Hardie, see Morgan, *Keir Hardie*, p. 76; on Alden and labour politics, see Paul Thompson, *Socialists, Liberals and Labour*, 1967, pp. 24, 110; see also Koven, 'Culture and poverty', pp. 528–51.

69 F. W. Pethick-Lawrence, *Fate Has Been Kind*, 1942, pp. 35–6, 48–51, 63.

70 Helena Born, *Whitman's Ideal Democracy, and Other Writings*, Boston, 1902, pp. xiv–xv.

71 'What attitudes should Christian churches take in relation to amusements?', *Congregationalist*, VIII, 1879, p. 556.

72 Robert Currie, *Methodism Divided*, 1968, p. 138. On religion and leisure, see esp. J. H. S. Kent, 'The role of religion in the cultural structure of the later Victorian city', *Transactions of the Royal Historical Society*, XXIII, 1973, pp. 153–73.

73 John Trevor, *My Quest for God*, 1897, p. 194.

74 Trevor, *My Quest*, p. 260.

75 Trevor, *Our First Principle*, Labour Prophet Tract no. 3, n.d., p. 37. See also Wicksteed, *What Does the Labour Church Stand For?*, p. 13.

76 *Labour Prophet*, May 1893, p. 41. On the Cinderella clubs, see Summers, 'Labour Church', pp. 133–44; Logie Barrow, 'The socialism of Robert Blatchford and the Clarion newspaper', Ph.D. thesis, London, 1975, pp. 133–44; Fincher, 'Clarion Movement', pp. 149–54.

77 *Sheffield Guardian*, 28 September 1906, p. 1.

78 The Cinderella Club, *Souvenir, 1913*, Manchester, 1913; Summers, 'Labour Church', p. 340.

79 Henry Pelling, *The Origins of the Labour Party*, 1965, ch. 7; Hobsbawm, *Primitive Rebels*, pp. 142, 144. See also K. S. Inglis, 'The Labour Church movement', *International Review of Social History*, III, 1958, pp. 445–60; Stanley Pierson, 'John Trevor and the Labour Church movement in England, 1891–1900', *Church History*, XXIX, 1960, pp. 463–78.

80 Edward G. Salmon, 'What girls read', *Nineteenth Century*, XX, 1886, p. 526. See also F. K. Prochaska, *Women and Philanthropy in Nineteenth Century England*, Oxford, 1980, ch. 2.

81 She owned 600 of the 1114 shares in the press (shareholders lists, Twentieth Century Press Ltd, Public Record Office BT31/15187/35009).

82 *Bolton and District ILP Pioneer*, March 1895, p. 3.

83 *Merrie England Fayre, Liverpool, May 1895. Programme.*

84 Annual reports and balance sheets of the Halifax branch of the ILP exist for 1897, 1898 and 1900 (Lister papers, SH:7/JN). Two ILP ledgers also exist: account book of the ILP (Halifax) and socialist hall, 1895–1904 (TU93/2); Halifax ILP account book, 1904ff (TU73/1/1). For the socialist movement in Halifax, see Hugh J. O'H. Drake, 'John Lister of Shibden Hall (1847–1933): a portrait of an individual in late Victorian provincial society', Ph.D. thesis, Bradford, 1973; John Lister, 'Early history of the ILP in Halifax', unpublished ms (Lister papers, SH:7/JN/B/37); E. P. Thompson, 'Homage to Tom Maguire', in Briggs and Saville, eds, *Essays in Labour History*, pp. 276–316.

85 *Clarion*, 13 October 1894, p. 7.

86 *Labour Leader*, 9 June 1894, p. 4; 13 October 1894, p. 7; 6 April 1895, p. 4.

87 *Clarion*, 13 October 1894, p. 7.

88 *Clarion*, 26 March 1898, p. 100; 21 April 1894, p. 4.

89 *Clarion*, 16 November 1901, p. 3.

90 *New Age*, 13 April 1905, p. 234.
91 On the class-specific emphases hidden *within* the more general demands for rational recreation, see Anthony Delves, 'Popular recreation and social conflict in Derby, 1800–1850', in Yeo and Yeo, eds, *Popular Culture and Class Conflict*, esp. pp. 105–7.
92 Michael Walzer, 'Socialism and the gift relationship', *Dissent*, XXIX, 1982, p. 433.
93 *Labour Record and Review*, August 1905, p. 90.

Chapter four

1 *Keighley Labour Journal*, 19 December 1898, quoted in David Russell, 'The popular musical societies of the Yorkshire textile district, 1850–1914', Ph.D. thesis, York, 1979, p. 291.
2 *Justice*, 25 June 1910, p. 3.
3 Yeo, 'A new life', p. 103.
4 *Clarion*, 7 July 1905, p. 3.
5 Carpenter papers, MSS 14; *Clarion*, 20 November 1903, p. 8.
6 H. R. Haweis, *My Musical Life*, 1886, pp. 116–18.
7 Haweis, *Music and Morals*, 1871, book I; Stephen Banfield, 'Aesthetics and criticism', in Nicholas Temperley, ed., *Music in Britain: The Romantic Age*, 1981, p. 460.
8 Bernarr Rainbow, *The Land Without Music*, 1967, pp. 111–23; E. D. Mackerness, *A Social History of English Music*, 1964, pp. 154–5.
9 Florence A. Marshall, 'The People's Concert Society', *Macmillan's Magazine*, XLIII, 1881, p. 437; Marshall, 'Music and the people', *Nineteenth Century*, VIII, 1880, pp. 922–4.
10 Cunningham, *Leisure in the Industrial Revolution*, pp. 102–4.
11 S. Midgley, *Music and the Municipality*, Bradford, 1912. See also Midgley, *My 70 Years' Memories*, 1934, esp. ch. 5; M. E. Robinson, 'Music as a social discipline', *Sociological Review*, II, 1909, pp. 152–8.
12 Samuel Barnett, 'The mission of music', *International Journal of Ethics*, IX, 1898, pp. 500–2.
13 *Clarion*, 19 March 1892, p. 3; 4 March 1893, p. 5; Clement Templeton, 'Musical evenings for children', *Labour Prophet*, June 1893, pp. 55–6.
14 *New Moral World*, 20 January 1838, pp. 162–3.
15 Robert Blatchford, 'A plea for pleasure', *Labour Prophet*, July 1894, pp. 84–5; *Labour Prophet*, June 1893, p. 50.
16 B. Hope, 'Music for the Labour Church', *Bolton and District ILP Pioneer*, June 1895, pp. 4–6.
17 Dan H. Laurence, ed., *Shaw's Music*, 1981, I, pp. 198, 625–8, 651; III, pp. 733–9.
18 Robert Blatchford, *Julie*, 1900(?), p. 40. The novel was first serialised in the *Clarion*, May to September 1900.
19 See T. Thomas, 'Representations of the Manchester working class in fiction 1850–1910', in Kidd and Roberts, eds, *City, Class and Culture*, pp. 193–216.
20 *Clarion*, 22 September 1900, p. 304; 12 January 1901, pp. 9–10.
21 Boughton, 'Music and the people', *Musical Standard*, 9 December 1905, pp. 369–70; 16 December 1905, pp. 385–7; 13 January 1906, pp. 21–2.
22 Boughton, 'Signs of the times. IV, socialism', *Musical Standard*, 6 August 1904, p. 85. For biographical information, see Michael Hurd, *Immortal Hour*, 1962.

23 Edgar L. Bainton, *Music and Socialism*, Manchester, 1910(?). For a review, see *Northern Democrat*, April 1910, p. 14. On Bainton, see Helen Bainton, *Remembered on Waking*, Sydney, 1960. For similar ideas, see Granville Bantock, 'Music and the working man', *Daily Citizen*, 27 November 1913, p. 4.

24 Dave Harker, 'May Cecil Sharp be praised?', *History Workshop Journal*, XIV, 1982, pp. 49–50.

25 *Clarion*, 15 March 1907, p. 3. For a discussion of musical genres and working-class taste, see Richard Middleton, 'Popular music of the lower classes', in Temperley, ed., *Music in Britain*, pp. 63–91.

26 Templeton, 'Musical evenings for children', p. 55.

27 *Labour Prophet*, June 1895, pp. 83–5.

28 Britain, *Fabianism and Culture*, pp. 259–61.

29 Rutland Boughton, 'Socialist musical festivals', *Clarion*, 16 February 1912, p. 4. On the 'manufacture' of folksong, see Dave Harker, *Fakesong*, 1985.

30 *Clarion*, 6 January 1905, p. 2; 29 December 1905, p. 1; 5 April 1907, p. 3; 22 November 1907, p. 3; 12 March 1909, p. 2; 19 March 1909, p. 2.

31 *Clarion*, 22 May 1908, p. 2; see also 2 June 1905, p. 3.

32 *Daily Herald*, 26 August 1912, p. 4.

33 Publishing committee minutes, Fabian Society, 3 November 1911, 3 May 1912. Prior to its publication of a specifically 'Fabian' songbook, the Society had published Edith Nesbit's *Ballads and Lyrics of Socialism 1883–1908*.

34 J. Bruce Glasier, *Socialism in Song*, Manchester, 1919, p. 8. On the songs and their publication history, see Thompson, *Morris*, pp. 667–9; Eugene D. LeMire, 'The Socialist League leaflets and manifestos: an annotated checklist', *International Review of Social History*, XXII, 1977, pp. 26–7; Chris Waters, 'Morris's "Chants" and the problems of socialist culture', in Florence Boos and Carole Silver, eds, *Socialism and the Literary Artistry of William Morris*, Columbia, Mo., 1989.

35 H. S. Salt, *Songs of Freedom*, 1893, pp. xix–xx, xxii.

36 For Jones and the charge that he was merely a bourgeois idealist, see Horst Rössler and Ian Watson, 'In defence of Ernest Jones', *Gulliver: Deutsch-Englische Jahrbücher*, XXII, 1983, pp. 134–9. On Chartist poetry and its links with the romantic and socialist movements, see Watson, *Song and Democratic Culture in Britain*, 1983; John Miller, 'Songs of the Labour movement', in Lionel N. Munby, *The Luddites and Other Essays*, 1971, pp. 115–42.

37 Letter, Glasier to Carpenter, 17 June 1903 (Carpenter papers, MSS 386–110).

38 *Justice*, 26 October 1895, p. 2.

39 J. Bruce Glasier, *Socialist Songs*, Glasgow, 1893.

40 Isabella Ford, ed., *Tom Maguire, a Remembrance*, Manchester, 1895, pp. 21–2.

41 *The Labour Church Hymnbook*, Manchester, 1892, preface.

42 Hobsbawm, *Primitive Rebels*, pp. 142–5.

43 David Cox, 'The Labour Party in Leicester: a study of branch development', *International Review of Social History*, VI, 1961, pp. 204–5. On socialism and working-class religion, see the illuminating article by A. J. Ainsworth, 'Religion in the working-class community, and the evolution of socialism in late nineteenth century Lancashire: a case of working-class consciousness', *Histoire Sociale/Social History*, X, 1977, pp. 354–80.

44 For music in the settlements, see *The Mansfield House Songbook*, 1906, pp. v–vi.

45 *The Sunday Afternoon Songbook for 'Pleasant Sunday Afternoons' and Other Gatherings*,

1892, p. 3. Trevor's collection also shares twelve titles with the *Hymns and Anthems for the Use of the South Place Ethical Society*, 1889.

46 Malcolm Quin, *Memoirs of a Positivist*, 1924, p. 52.

47 *Methodist Free Church Hymns*, 1889 (see hymns 42 and 315).

48 Haweis, *Music and Morals*, p. 48.

49 Socialist League (Aberdeen Branch), ed., *Socialist Songs*, preface.

50 A. L. Lloyd, *Folk Song in England*, 1967, pp. 378–9; Watson, *Song and Democratic Culture*, p. 28, n. 30.

51 'Socialism in song', *Justice*, 19 May 1888, p. 2.

52 Glasier, *Socialist Songs*, preface.

53 *Justice*, 19 January 1907, p. 10; 17 August 1907, p. 6.

54 Samson Bryher, *An Account of the Labour and Socialist Movement in Bristol*, Bristol, 1931, I, pp. 18–19, 24–5, 37.

55 Montague Blatchford praised the tunes in Pearce's anthology in the *Clarion*, 7 December 1906, p. 8. For Pearce on Carpenter's *Chants*, see the *Clarion*, 20 October 1905, p. 3.

56 *Justice*, 19 May 1888, p. 2.

57 For Meek, see his autobiography, *George Meek, Bath Chair-Man*, 1910, pp. 35, 243, 283. Henderson is discussed in Pierson, *Marxism*, p. 148. For John Gregory, see his *My Garden and Other Voices*, Bristol, 1907; Bryher, *Bristol*, I, pp. 12, 32–3.

58 *Labour Leader*, 9 April 1904, p. 2.

59 Lloyd, *Folk Song*, p. 318.

60 'William Wilson: poet, blacksmith, trade unionist', *ASE Journal*, April 1906, pp. 22–3.

61 *Church Reformer*, October 1895, pp. 227–8.

62 E. P. Thompson, 'Tom Maguire', p. 314.

63 See 'Francis Adams: a poet of socialism', *Progressive Review*, II, 1897, pp. 233–41. Similar problems arose with the work of John Barlas: see David Lowe, *John Barlas, Sweet Singer and Socialist*, Cupar, Fife, 1915.

64 Davies, *North Country Bred*, pp. 117–18; Bryher, *Bristol*, II, p. 68.

65 *Halifax and District Labour News*, 3 April 1909, p. 1. See also Montague Blatchford's obituary in Huddersfield's *Worker*, 23 April 1910, p. 2.

66 Montague Blatchford, 'The CVU. What it is and what it might be', *Clarion*, 14 September 1901, p. 297. Branches or affiliated choirs were established in Armley, Ashton-under-Lyne, Attercliffe, Barrow-in-Furness, Birmingham, Bolton, Bradford, Brighouse, Brighton, Burnley, Coven (30), Darwen and Blackburn, Dunfermline (46), Eccles, Glasgow (60), Halifax (148), Huddersfield, Hull (40), Hyde, Keighley (40), Kentish Town, Leeds, Leicester, Liverpool, Manchester (various affiliated choirs, 272), Nottingham (60), Oldham (59), Openshaw, Preston, Ramsbottom, Rochdale (36), Salford West (40), Sheffield (48), Slaithwaite, Staffordshire North, Stockport, Stockton, West Ham and York (15). Figures refer to membership in 1896. Source: *Scout*, February 1896.

67 *Clarion*, 1 September 1894, p. 5; 15 September 1894, p. 5. On the 'Tudor Revival', see Frank Howes, *The English Musical Renaissance*, 1966, pp. 68–84.

68 Herbert Antcliffe, 'The Home Music Study Union', *Comradeship*, December 1913, pp. 22–3; *Clarion*, 1 September 1894, p. 5

69 Peter J. Pirie, *The English Musical Renaissance*, 1979, p. 20.

70 *Yorkshire Musical Record*, January 1900, pp. 253–4.

71 *Yorkshire Musical Record*, May 1900, p. 54. On the similarity between the CVU and

other choral groups, see Dave Russell, *Popular Music in England 1840–1914*, Manchester, 1987, pp. 50–9.

72 *Clarion*, 19 March 1898, p. 93.

73 Clarion Vocal Union, 'Programme of the 1899 Competition, Free Trade Hall, Manchester, 13 May 1899', back cover.

74 'Socialism and music', *Sheffield Guardian*, 22 March 1907, p. 3. For Rutland Boughton's praise of the festivals, see the *Clarion*, 16 February 1912, p. 4; *Daily Citizen*, 8 October 1912, p. 5; 25 October 1912, p. 4.

75 'The Clarion musical festival at Sheffield', *Clarion*, 3 May 1907, p. 3; Laurence, *Shaw's Music*, I, p. 19; II, pp. 869–70.

76 *Clarion*, 19 September 1902.

77 *Clarion*, 27 May 1899 (emphasis in original).

78 *Scout*, June 1895, pp. 53–4; *Clarion*, 29 September 1894, p. 5.

79 See his obituary in the *Keighley News*, 1 January 1938.

80 *Clarion*, 9 December 1910, p. 8.

81 Rutland Boughton, *The Self-Advertisement of Rutland Boughton*, n.d., p. 5. See also the letters from Boughton to Carpenter, 15 and 30 September 1912 (Carpenter papers MSS 386, 204–5).

82 *Clarion*, 24 November 1911, p. 3. On Boughton's Stockport audience, see Summers, 'Labour Church', p. 678.

83 Dave Russell, 'Popular musical culture and popular politics in the Yorkshire textile districts, 1880–1914', in John K. Walton and James Walvin, eds, *Leisure in Britain 1780–1939*, Manchester, 1983, p. 107.

84 *Clarion*, 3 February 1905, p. 7; 23 June 1905, p. 3.

85 *Clarion*, 14 September 1901, p. 297. For a testimonial, see Annie Kenney, *Memories of a Militant*, 1924, p. 24.

86 *Sheffield Guardian*, 8 March 1907, p. 3. See also the *Glasgow Commonweal*, April 1896, p. 13.

87 Watson, *Song and Democratic Culture*, p. 47.

88 D. C. Parker, 'Music and socialism', *Socialist Review*, II, 1909, p. 923.

89 Duncan, *James Leatham*, p. 78.

90 Vernon L. Lidtke, 'Songs and politics: an exploratory essay on *Arbeiterlieder* in the Weimar Republic', *Archiv für Sozialgeschichte*, XIV, 1974, pp. 257–9. See also Lidtke, *Alternative Culture*, ch. 5; Dieter Dowe, 'The workingmen's choral movement in Germany before the First World War', *Journal of Contemporary History*, XIII, 1978, pp. 285–90.

91 Carmen Claudin-Urondo, *Lenin and the Cultural Revolution*, Hassocks 1977. See also Frank Trommler, 'Working-class culture and modern mass culture before World War I', *New German Critique*, XXIX, 1983, p. 61; Dieter Langwiesche, 'The impact of the German labour movement on workers' culture', *Journal of Modern History*, LIX, 1987, pp. 506–23.

Chapter five

1 Philip Poirier, *The Advent of the British Labour Party*, 1958, p. 59.

2 'A collective holiday', *Municipal Reformer*, XLVI, 1902, pp. 78–9. On municipal socialism, see J. R. Kellett, 'Municipal socialism, enterprise and trading in the

Victorian city', *Urban History Yearbook*, 1978, pp. 36–45.

3 F. W. Jowett, *The Socialist and the City*, 1907, p. 2.

4 Leon Faucher, *Manchester in 1844*, 1969 ed., p. 56.

5 Gladstone, quoted in Janet Minihan, *The Nationalisation of Culture*, New York, 1977, p. 32; Thomas Greenwood, *Museums and Art Galleries*, 1888, esp. ch. 2.

6 'Report from the select committee', q. 5144. For the state and popular culture, see John Clarke and Chas Critcher, *The Devil Makes Work: Leisure in Capitalist Britain*, 1985, pp. 122–43.

7 H. G. Gibbons, 'The opposition to municipal socialism in England', *Journal of Political Economy*, IX, 1901, pp. 245–7; 'The gospel of amusement', *Spectator*, 26 October 1889, p. 548.

8 See Frederick Dolman, *Municipalities at Work*, 1895.

9 Godfrey Turner, 'Amusements of the English people', *Nineteenth Century*, II, 1877, p. 821. See also *Transactions of the National Association for the Promotion of Social Science*, 1878, pp. 702, 708; letters to the *Daily Telegraph*, 18–22 July 1891.

10 Charles Rowley, *Fifty Years of Ancoats, Loss and Gain*, 1899, pp. 8–9; Alden, editorial, *Echo*, 30 August 1902, p. 2.

11 Gray, *Philanthropy and the State*, pp. 70–1. For a discussion of these issues, see David Owen, *English Philanthropy 1660–1960*, Cambridge, Mass., 1964, ch. 18; Brian Harrison, 'State intervention and moral reform', in Patricia Hollis, ed., *Pressure from Without in Early Victorian England*, 1974, esp. pp. 298–9, 305; Stuart Hall, 'Popular culture and the state', in Bennett *et al.*, eds, *Popular Culture and Social Relations*, pp. 22–49.

12 See M. Cahill, 'Socialism and the city', in Jowitt and Taylor, eds, *Bradford 1890–1914*, pp. 43, 48–9.

13 H. M. Hyndman, *The Social Reconstruction of England*, 1884, p. 13; Hyndman, *A Commune for London*, 1887, pp. 1, 6, 14–15.

14 Drake, 'John Lister', pp. 382–3. For James Parker, a labour councillor in Halifax, and his plans for municipalisation, see the *ILP Journal* (Keighley), 20 January 1895, p. 3.

15 *Fabian News*, December 1891, p. 37.

16 Sidney and Beatrice Webb, *A Constitution for the Socialist Commonwealth of Great Britain*, Cambridge, 1975 ed., pp. 238, 321, 323.

17 *Clarion*, 1 June 1901, p. 170. See also 'Mr Fred Brocklehurst, B.A.', *Municipal Reformer*, I, 1899, pp. 177–8; *Clarion*, 22 October 1898, p. 344.

18 *Clarion*, 8 June 1901, p. 181.

19 See 'Should amusements be municipalised?', *Labour Leader*, 2 December 1904, p. 420; 'Municipalities and leisure', *Labour Leader*, 12 March 1904, p. 6.

20 Langdon Everard, 'Socialism and the theatre', *Labour Leader*, 30 October 1908, p. 689.

21 Dan Irving, *The Municipality, from a Worker's Point of View*, 1906(?), p. 9. For Charrington, see *Fabian News*, February 1897, p. 47; *Labour Leader*, 19 February 1898, p. 60; 'The municipal theatre', *Contemporary Review*, LXXXII, 1902, pp. 411–28. See also 'The drama as a social force', *Sheffield Guardian*, 17 January 1908, p. 3; 'Municipal theatres', *Clarion*, 12 March 1898, pp. 84–5.

22 Midgley, *Music and the Municipality*, pp. 9–10. See also 'Municipal Music', *Sheffield Guardian*, 24 January 1908, p. 2. For Bournemouth, see Richard Roberts, 'The corporation as impresario: the municipal provision of entertainment in Victorian and Edwardian Bournemouth', in Walton and Walvin, eds, *Leisure in Britain*, pp. 136–57.

23 *Glasgow Commonweal*, July 1896, p. iii; August 1896, p. 6. See also Elspeth King, 'Popular culture in Glasgow', in R. A. Cage, ed., *The Working Class in Glasgow*

1750–1914, 1987, pp. 174–8; Joan Smith, 'Labour tradition in Glasgow and Liverpool', *History Workshop Journal*, XVII, 1984, pp. 32–56. For the municipalisation of music, see J. C. B. Tirbutt, in the *Municipal Journal*, 28 April 1905, pp. 421–2; 5 May 1905, p. 452.

24 *Labour Leader*, 22 October 1898, p. 348; P. P. Howe, 'The municipalisation of music halls', *Socialist Review*, V, 1910, pp. 424–32.

25 Geo. S. Reaney, 'Socialism and national sobriety', *To-Day*, III, 1885, p. 122.

26 See Tom Maguire, 'Teetotalist economics', *Commonweal*, 28 April 1888, pp. 132–3.

27 J. Spargo, 'Municipalisation of the drink traffic', *Social Democrat*, II, 1898, pp. 266–70; Thomas M. Wilson, 'How they control the drink trade in Norway', *Labour Prophet*, June to September 1893.

28 Pease, *The Case for Municipal Drink Trade*, 1904, p. 8.

29 *Rochdale Labour News*, May 1898, p. 2. See also Hardie's proposals in the *Workman's Times*, 3 March 1894, p. 3.

30 *Labour Leader*, 3 June 1904, p. 100. See also Mary L. Pendered, 'The psychology of amusement in its relation to temperance reform', *Socialist Review*, III, 1909, pp. 290–1.

31 See P. F. Clarke, 'The Progressive Movement in England', *Transactions of the Royal Historical Society*, XXIV, 1974, pp. 159–81.

32 Thompson, *Socialists, Liberals and Labour*, *passim*; John Davis, 'Progressivism and the early LCC', in Andrew Saint, ed., *Politics and the People of London*, 1989.

33 For an elaboration, see Chris Waters, 'Progressives, puritans and the cultural politics of the early LCC', in Saint, ed., *Politics and the People*.

34 George Haw, *From Workhouse to Westminster: The Life Story of Will Crooks, M.P.*, 1907, p. 92.

35 Thompson, *Socialists, Liberals and Labour*, pp. 116, 118, 185; Chris Wrigley, 'Liberals and the desire for working-class representatives in Battersea, 1886–1922', in Kenneth D. Brown, ed., *Essays in Anti-Labour History*, 1974, pp. 126–58.

36 John Burns, *Address*, pp. 5–6.

37 *The Times*, 26 September 1902 (cited from 'Newspaper cuttings, 1901–1911', Battersea Public Library, Q072; hereafter 'cuttings'); Burns, *Music and Musicians*.

38 *Clarion*, 8 June 1901, p. 184.

39 'Minutes of the proceedings', Battersea council, 24 July 1901, p. 168; *Morning Leader*, 29 March 1902; *Daily Chronicle*, 28 March 1902 ('cuttings'); *Municipal Journal*, 27 September 1901, p. 748; John Burns, 'Municipal socialism', in R. C. K. Ensor, ed., *Modern Socialism*, 1904, esp. pp. 275–7.

40 Thorne, *My Life's Battles*, p. 177; Thompson, *Socialists, Liberals and Labour*, pp. 130–2.

41 Edward G. Howarth and Mona Wilson, *West Ham*, 1907; J. J. Terrett, *Municipal Socialism in West Ham*, 1902; Hugh Legge, 'Socialism in West Ham', *Economic Review*, IX, 1899, pp. 489–502; F. H. Billows, 'Socialism in West Ham', *Economic Review*, X, 1900, pp. 52–61.

42 Percy Alden, *Democratic England*, New York, 1912, p. 192. See also the *Clarion*, 3 December 1898, p. 385.

43 Percy Alden, 'Settlements in relation to local administration', in Reason, *University and Social Settlements*, p. 27.

44 Thorne, *Battles*, p. 56; Kapp, *Eleanor Marx*, II, esp. pp. 325, 360.

45 Will Crooks, *Percy Alden M.A.*, 1903, p. 6.

46 Alden, 'Settlements', pp. 32–3, 37; Crooks, *Alden*, pp. 6–7; Alden, *Democratic England*, p. 214; *Mansfield House Magazine*, IV, 1897, pp. 231–2.

47 Billows, 'West Ham', pp. 58, 60. See also the *Clarion*, 6 April 1901, p. 109; 20 July 1901, p. 232.
48 Howell, *British Workers*, pp. 199–203.
49 'Municipal music', *Forward* (Bradford), August 1907, p. 5. For the dispute, see 'Bradford city council minutes', 8 and 22 October 1907 (book no. 20, pp. 177–9, 183–5, 193–4).
50 *Sheffield Guardian*, 22 February 1907, p. 3. The debate resonated in the pages of the *Guardian* for the next year.
51 E. B. Bax, 'Luxury, ease and vice', in Bax, *Outspoken Essays on Social Subjects*, 1897, pp. 125–6. See also 'Socialism and the Sunday question', in Bax, *Religion of Socialism*, p. 57.
52 'W', *The Anti-Puritan; or, An Effort to Drive the Puritans from Paradise*, Lichfield, 1828, pp. 5, 22.
53 W. Diack, 'May Day – Old and New', *Justice*, 27 April 1895, pp. 6–7. See also Glasier, in the *Labour Leader*, 21 August 1908, p. 529; 28 August 1908, p. 545.
54 See Davies, *North Country Bred*, p. 83. For Pearce and Hall, see the *Clarion*, 2 June 1905, p. 3; 11 August 1900, p. 260.
55 Quoted in Fincher, 'Clarion Movement', p. 347.
56 Howell, *British Workers*, pp. 207–9, 375, 380.
57 A. Neil Lyons, *Robert Blatchford*, 1910, p. 83; Shaw, in the *Clarion*, 13 February 1897, p. 49.
58 Lyons, *Blatchford*, p. 117; Blatchford, *The Sorcery Shop*, p. 27. For Blatchford's puritanical revolt against 'the animal craving for enjoyment', see J. M. Ludlow, 'Two books on socialism by "Nunquam" and "Nemo" ', *Economic Review*, V, 1895, p. 539.
59 'JG', 'Workers and sport', *Daily Citizen*, 31 December 1912, p. 6.
60 Glasgow Working Men's Sabbath Protection Association, *Report of the Public Meeting Against the Opening of Museums, Art Galleries, &c, on the Sabbath*, Glasgow, 1881, p. 15. For Broadhurst, see W. T. W. Quin, 'Opening national institutions on Sundays', *Nineteenth Century*, XV, 1884, pp. 418–19. For an elaboration of these themes, see Brian Harrison, 'Religion and respectability in nineteenth-century England', in Harrison, *Peaceable Kingdom*, Oxford, 1982, pp. 123–56.
61 *Labour Leader*, June 1893, p. 1; *Justice*, 18 November 1899, p. 4. On West Ham, see the letter to the *Daily Citizen*, 18 October 1912, p. 3. See also John Wigley, *The Rise and Fall of the Victorian Sunday*, Manchester, 1980, pp. 151–5.
62 Conrad Noel, *The Day of the Sun*, 1901, p. 12. See also his arguments in the *Bradford Labour Echo*, 5 September 1896, p. 3. For Noel, see R. Woodifield, 'Conrad Noel, 1869–1942, Catholic crusader', in M. B. Reckitt, ed., *For Christ and the People*, 1968, pp. 135–79; Noel, *Autobiography*, 1945.
63 *Justice*, 21 March 1908, p. 6. For the SDF on puritanism, see *Justice*, 19 December 1903, p. 1; 7 May 1904, p. 4.
64 William Archer, 'The County Council and the music halls', *Contemporary Review*, LXVII, 1895, p. 322. For further discussion, see Penelope Summerfield, 'The Effingham Arms and the empire: deliberate selection in the evolution of music hall in London', in Yeo and Yeo, eds, *Popular Culture and Class Conflict*, pp. 209–40; Susan Pennybacker, ' "It was not what she said . . ." ', in Bailey, ed., *Music Hall*, pp. 118–40.
65 *Echo*, 22 February 1901, p. 1.
66 *Justice*, 12 January 1907, p. 5; 23 February 1907, p. 7.
67 *Fabian News*, November 1904, pp. 41–2.
68 Headlam, *On the Danger of Municipal Puritanism*, 1905, p. 12. See also John R. Orens,

'The Mass, the masses, and the music hall: Stewart Headlam's radical Anglicanism', *A Jubilee Paper*, 1979.

69 *Labour Leader*, 1 June 1906, p. 20.

70 Bettany, *Headlam*, pp. 133, 161.

71 Britain, *Fabianism and Culture*, pp. 151, 160–1.

72 *Fabian News*, March 1907, p. 28.

73 J. Ramsay MacDonald, 'A plea for puritanism', *Socialist Review*, VIII, 1912, pp. 422–30. See also Rodney Barker, 'Socialism and Progressivism in the political thought of Ramsay MacDonald', in A. J. A. Morris, ed., *Edwardian Radicalism*, 1974, pp. 114–30.

74 *Manchester Examiner and Times*, 19 February 1891.

75 Howell, *British Workers*, p. 375.

76 T. H. Marshall, 'Citizenship and social class', in Marshall, *Class, Citizenship and Social Development*, Chicago, 1963, pp. 76, 90, 101, 106. For a discussion of liberalism, socialism and citizenship, see Mary Langan and Bill Schwarz, eds, *Crises in the British State 1880–1930*, 1985, chs 1, 3, 6.

77 Eileen Yeo, 'Culture and constraint in working-class movements', in Yeo and Yeo, eds, *Popular Culture and Class Conflict*, p. 178. See also A. J. Ainsworth, 'Aspects of socialism at the branch level, 1890–1900: some notes towards analysis', *Northwest Labour History Society Bulletin*, IV, 1977, pp. 17–18.

78 *Forward* (Glasgow), 19 June 1909, p. 5.

79 Blatchford, *Merrie England*, p. 18.

80 Haw, *Today's Work*, pp. 94, 230.

81 Blatchford, in the *Clarion*, 17 July 1908, p. 7; Quelch, 'Socialism and progressivism', *Clarion*, 22 March 1907, p. 7; Hyndman, 'Municipalism and socialism', *Justice*, 30 November 1895, p. 4; Trevor, *My Quest for God*, pp. 234, 259–60. For a further discussion, see Whelan, 'The working class in British socialist thought', esp. pp. 161–76.

82 *Labour and the New Social Order*, 1918, p. 19. For a discussion, see Ross McKibbin, *The Evolution of the Labour Party 1910–1924*, 1974, pp. 91–106. For socialism and the turn to statism, see Stephen Yeo, 'Notes on three socialisms . . .', in Carl Levy, ed., *Socialism and the Intelligentsia 1880–1914*, 1987.

Chapter six

1 See John Lowerison, 'Joint stock companies, capital formation and suburban leisure in England, 1880–1914', in Wray Vamplew, ed., 'The economic history of leisure', papers presented at the Eighth International Economic History Congress, pp. 61–71.

2 Robert Blatchford, *My Eighty Years*, 1931, p. 15.

3 Robert Blatchford, *A Son of the Forge*, 1894, p. 37.

4 *Clarion*, 7 October 1899, p. 317 (emphasis in original).

5 Hannah Mitchell, *The Hard Way Up*, 1968, p. 86.

6 Quoted in Ford, *Tom Maguire*, p. xiii.

7 *Labour Prophet*, May 1894, p. 53.

8 Meek, *George Meek*, pp. 208, 251.

9 James D. Young, 'Militancy, English socialism and the ragged trousered philanthropists', *Journal of Contemporary History*, XX, 1985, p. 294; Robert Tressell, *The Ragged Trousered Philanthropists*, New York, 1962 ed., pp. 16, 28.

10 Jack Common, *Kiddar's Luck*, Glasgow, 1951, pp. 174–8. See also Michael Pickering and Kevin Robins, ' "A revolutionary materialist with a leg free": the autobiographical novels of Jack Common', in Jeremy Hawthorn, ed., *The British Working-Class Novel in the Twentieth Century*, 1984, pp. 76–92.

11 E. J. Hobsbawm, 'The Fabians reconsidered', in Hobsbawm, *Labouring Men*, esp. pp. 255–9.

12 Quoted in Britain, *Fabianism and Culture*, p. 261.

13 Yeo, 'A new life', pp. 26–7.

14 *Scout*, May 1895, p. 19; June 1895, pp. 66–7. See also David Rubinstein, 'Cycling in the 1890s', *Victorian Studies*, XXI, 1977, pp. 47–71.

15 *Clarion*, 8 February 1896, p. 46; 30 April 1898, p. 140. See also Fincher, 'The Clarion movement', pp. 180–93.

16 *Clarion*, 11 June 1892, p. 7; 26 August 1899, p. 265. See also Barrow, 'Socialism of Robert Blatchford', pp. 53–7.

17 Deian Hopkin, 'The membership of the Independent Labour Party, 1904–10: a spatial and occupational analysis', *International Review of Social History*, XX, 1975, pp. 175–97; T. G. Ashplant, 'The Working Men's Club and Institute Union and the Independent Labour Party: working-class organisation, politics and culture c.1880–1914', D.Phil. thesis, Sussex, 1983, esp. pp. 245–63.

18 Trevor, *My Quest for God*, p. 235.

19 Coit, *Neighbourhood Guilds*, p. 138.

20 'The CHA: a criticism', *Comradeship*, VI, 1912, pp. 35–6.

21 Summers, 'Labour Church', pp. 112–13.

22 *Clarion*, 30 April 1898, p. 140.

23 *Liverpool Review*, 25 November 1899, p. 7; 9 December 1899, p. 13.

24 *Labour Church Record*, January 1899, p. 3.

25 See Alice Foley, *A Bolton Childhood*, Manchester, 1973, pp. 65–73.

26 Carl Levy, 'Education and self-education: staffing the early ILP', in Levy, ed., *Socialism and the Intelligentsia*, p. 148.

27 See Peter Bailey, ' "Will the real Bill Banks please stand up?" Towards a role analysis of mid-Victorian working-class respectability', *Journal of Social History*, XII, 1979, pp. 336–53; Brian Harrison, 'Traditions of respectability in British labour history', in Harrison, *Peaceable Kingdom*, pp. 157–216.

28 See G. L. Anderson, 'Victorian clerks and voluntary associations in Liverpool and Manchester', *Northern History*, XII, 1976, pp. 202–19; Geoffrey Crossick, ed., *The Lower Middle Class in Britain 1870–1914*, 1977.

29 Robert Q. Gray, *The Labour Aristocracy in Victorian Edinburgh*, Oxford, 1976, p. 4; Geoffrey Crossick, *An Artisan Elite in Victorian Society*, 1978, pp. 60, 119, 244; Alastair Reid, 'Politics and economics in the formation of the British working class: a response to H. F. Moorhouse', *Social History*, III, 1978, pp. 357–8.

30 Kenney, *Memories of a Militant*, p. 27.

31 Davies, *North Country Bred*, pp. 82–5, 121.

32 Ivy Pinchbeck, *Women Workers and the Industrial Revolution*, 1930, pp. 279–80.

33 Laura Oren, 'The welfare of women in labouring families: England, 1860–1950', in Mary S. Hartman and Lois Banner, eds, *Clio's Consciousness Raised*, New York, 1974, p. 226.

34 Tom Mann, 'Leisure for workmen's wives', *Halfpenny Short Cuts*, 28 June 1890, p. 163. On women's roles in the maintenance of working-class respectability, see Ellen Ross,

' "Not the sort that would sit on the doorstep": respectability in pre-World War I London neighborhoods', *International Labor and Working Class History*, XXVII, 1985, pp. 39–59.

35 Walter Besant, 'The amusements of the people', *Contemporary Review*, XLV, 1884, p. 346.

36 John Garrett Leigh, 'Amusements', *Economic Review*, XXII, 1912, p. 250.

37 Mason, *Association Football*, pp. 152–3. See also Peter N. Stearns, 'Working-class women in Britain, 1890–1914', in Martha Vicinus, ed., *Suffer and Be Still*, Bloomington, 1972, pp. 117–18.

38 Alice Zimmern, *Unpaid Professions for Women*, 1906, pp. 71–85. On the Girls' Friendly Society, see Brian Harrison, 'For church, queen and family: the Girls' Friendly Society 1874–1920', *Past and Present*, LXI, 1973, pp. 107–38. On middle-class women and leisure in general, see David Rubinstein, *Before the Suffragettes*, Brighton, 1986, ch. 12.

39 Bernard Holland, 'London playgrounds', *Macmillan's Magazine*, XLVI, 1882, pp. 321, 324; E. L. Jebb, 'Recreative learning and voluntary teaching', *Contemporary Review*, XLVIII, 1885, p. 533; F. M. Foster, 'Women as social reformers', *National Review*, XIII, 1889, p. 221. See also John Gillis, *Youth and History*, New York, 1981 ed., pp. 166–7.

40 Tom Mann, 'The workman's wife', *Labour Prophet*, February 1892, pp. 9–10; 'The workman's wife – by one of them', *Labour Prophet*, March 1892, pp. 23–4.

41 Davies, *North Country Bred*, p. 196.

42 Dorothy Scott, 'The wife's Sunday out', *Labour Prophet*, February 1892, p. 15.

43 Meek, *George Meek*, p. 27; Wright, *Some Habits and Customs*, p. 190.

44 See Jill Liddington and Jill Norris, *One Hand Tied Behind Us*, 1978, pp. 119–22; Judith S. Lohman, 'Sex or class? English socialists and the woman question, 1884–1914', Ph.D. thesis, Syracuse, 1979, pp. 188–91; Karen Hunt, 'Women and the Social Democratic Federation: some notes on Lancashire', *North West Labour History Society Bulletin*, VII, 1980–1, pp. 51–2.

45 H. W. Hobart, 'Leisure', *Justice*, 18 May 1895, p. 2; 'Notes on women's life and labour', *Labour Chronicle*, May 1893, pp. 4–5.

46 Quoted in Hunt, 'Women and the SDF', pp. 56–7.

47 *Labour Leader*, 11 January 1896, p. 11.

48 *Clarion*, 5 June 1897, p. 194.

49 June Hannam, ' "In the comradeship of the sexes lies the hope of progress and social regeneration": women in the West Riding ILP, *c*.1890–1914', in Jane Rendall, ed., *Equal or Different*, Oxford, 1987, pp. 214–38.

50 Hunt, 'Women and the SDF', p. 53.

51 *Clarion*, 23 November 1901, p. 2.

52 *Clarion*, 25 May 1895, p. 168.

53 'Art, life, and Robert Blatchford', *New Age*, 24 June 1897, p. 197.

54 Quoted in Ford, *Tom Maguire*, p. vi.

55 'The economics of joy', *Justice*, 6 May 1893, p. 6.

56 'A festive evening at Burnley', *Justice*, 19 January 1907, p. 2.

57 *Justice*, 1 July 1893, pp. 2–3. See also 22 July 1893, pp. 2–3.

58 Meek, *George Meek*, p. 294.

59 'The Primrose League', *Westminster Review*, CXXXV, 1891, p. 479. For the Owenites, see Eileen Yeo, 'Robert Owen and radical culture', in Sidney Pollard and John Salt, eds, *Robert Owen*, 1971, pp. 98–9.

60 *Clarion*, 21 September 1901, p. 6.

61 Blount's letter appeared in the *Clarion* on 1 June 1901, p. 170; the first lengthy discussion of the Guild appeared on 21 September 1901, p. 6; Blatchford focused on its work on 11 October 1907, p. 7; Dawson emphasised the debt to Morris on 30 March 1901, p. 98 and 23 October 1903, p. 2.

62 Blatchford, in the *Clarion*, 4 April 1902, p. 10; A. J. Penty, 'The Clarion Guild of Handicraft', *New Age*, XXVI, 1907, p. 349. See also Stewart Dick, 'Handicraft exhibition at Manchester', *The Craftsman*, VIII, 1905, pp. 195–204.

63 A. R. Orage, 'Politics for craftsmen', *Contemporary Review*, XCI, 1907, p. 783. In a recent assessment, Christopher Frayling and Helen Snowdon suggest that what 'had seemed at the outset to be "a great social movement" . . . had rapidly turned into a branch of *haute culture*' ('Perspectives on craft', *Craft*, LVII, 1982, p. 15.) See also Peter Stansky, *Redesigning the World*, Princeton, 1984.

64 Quoted in Gilbert Beith, ed., *Edward Carpenter*, 1931, p. 78.

65 *Labour Prophet*, August 1893, pp. 69–70.

66 *Clarion*, 5 May 1900, p. 1. See also Fenner Brockway, *Socialism Over Sixty Years*, 1946, p. 99.

67 Summers, 'Labour Church', p. 401.

68 Hobson, *Pilgrim to the Left*, p. 69.

69 Leonard Hall, *et al.*, *Let Us Reform the Labour Party*, Manchester, 1910, p. 14. See also Howell, *British Workers*, pp. 129, 327–42. The classic work on labourism is Ralph Miliband, *Parliamentary Socialism*, New York, 1972.

70 Barrow, 'Determinism and environmentalism in socialist thought', in Samuel and Stedman Jones, eds, *Culture, Ideology and Politics*, pp. 194–214.

71 Sidney Dark, 'Poetry for the people', *Workman's Times*, 25 March 1893, p. 2.

72 'Waning popularity of glee-singing', *Halifax and District Labour News*, 27 March 1909, p. 1; Michael Harris, 'The decline of the Labour Church movement', dissertation in the Bradford Central Library, p. 14.

73 Miles Malleson, *The ILP Arts Guild*, 1925.

74 Most of this argument is derived from Geoffrey Trodd, 'Political change and the working class in Blackburn and Burnley, 1880–1914', Ph.D. thesis, Lancaster, 1978, and from a perusal of the *Blackburn Labour Journal*.

75 Wilson, 'The search for fellowship and sentiment in British socialism', p. 74.

76 *Echo* (editorial), 25 August 1902, p. 2.

77 *Clarion*, 5 May 1900, p. 141; 21 March 1910, p. 1.

78 James Leatham, 'The Victorian era', *The Gateway*, I, 1910, pp. 14–15. See also Duncan, *James Leatham*, p. 71.

79 For the phenomenon in Germany, see Trommler, 'Working-class culture and modern mass culture', esp. p. 66.

80 Deian Hopkin, 'The socialist press in Britain, 1890–1910', in George Boyce, *et al.*, eds, *Newspaper History*, 1978, p. 299.

81 Flyer in the John Johnson Collection, Bodleian Library. For Glasier, see his diary, 18 September 1905 (Glasier papers). See also Morgan, *Keir Hardie*, pp. 234–7.

82 Letter, Roberts to Pease, 17 June 1911; Report of the advertising subcommittee, n.d. (*Daily Citizen* file, British Library of Political and Economic Science).

83 *Daily Citizen*, 9 October 1912, p. 6. See also R. J. Holton, 'Daily Herald v. Daily Citizen, 1912–15: the struggle for a labour daily in relation to the "Labour Unrest" ', *International Review of Social History*, XIX, 1974, pp. 347–76.

84 Glasier, diary, 18 June 1913 (Glasier papers). See also Laurence Thompson, *The Enthusiasts*, 1971, pp. 181, 186.
85 Arthur Ransom, 'Socialism and the moral instruction movement', *Socialist Review*, III, 1909, pp. 435–41.
86 C. F. G. Masterman, *The Condition of England*, 1909, p. 117.
87 Masterman, *Condition*, pp. 143–4. For an elaboration, see Roberts, *Classic Slum*, ch. 8.
88 Glasier, diary, 4 December 1905 (Glasier papers).
89 *Labour Leader*, 30 April 1914, p. 4.
90 Shaw, 'The climate and soil for labour culture', pp. 299, 322, 324–5.

Conclusion

1 *Clarion*, 24 November 1911, p. 3.
2 Masterman, *Condition of England*, p. 116. For a more recent confirmation of Masterman's beliefs, see Stedman Jones, *Outcast London*, pp. 344, 349.
3 For the impact of the contemporary political crisis on the research agenda of left historians, see the editorial in *History Workshop Journal*, XII, 1981, pp. 1–7.
4 Yeo, 'A new life', pp. 7, 31.
5 Bryher, *Bristol*, p. 22.
6 Pierson, *British Socialists*, p. 345; see also pp. 1, 128, 347.
7 See Jonathan Reé, *Proletarian Philosophers*, Oxford, 1984, esp. pp. 8–9.
8 See Stephen Yeo, 'Socialism, the state, and some oppositional Englishness', in Robert Colls and Philip Dodd, eds, *Englishness*, 1986, pp. 308–69.
9 Yeo, 'A new life', p. 31. See also Royden Harrison's critique of Yeo and Yeo's reply, *History Workshop Journal*, V, 1978, pp. 214–17; VII, 1979, pp. 215–19.
10 Quoted in Barrow, 'Socialism of Blatchford', p. 242.
11 Thomas Wright, 'On a possible popular culture', *Contemporary Review*, XXXX, 1881, p. 25.
12 'Holidays', *Sheffield Guardian*, 1 August 1913, p. 4.
13 Raymond Williams, *Communications*, Harmondsworth, 1976 ed., pp. 186–7.
14 Arthur Bourchier, *Art and Culture in Relation to Socialism*, 1926, pp. 10–11.
15 Stephen G. Jones, *Workers at Play*, 1986, esp. ch. 6; Jones, *The British Labour Movement and Film, 1918–1939*, 1987.
16 'Programme of the [CVU] concert at West End Methodist Church, Halifax, 21 April 1934' (Clarion Vocal Union collection, Calderdale Central Library). Socialist songbooks also remained unchanged. See, for example, the ILP's *Labour's Songbook*, 1931.
17 Stephen G. Jones, 'Labour, society and the drink question in Britain, 1918–1939', *The Historical Journal*, XXX, 1987, pp. 120–1.
18 Stuart MacIntyre, 'British labour, marxism and working-class apathy in the nineteen twenties', *The Historical Journal*, XX, 1977, pp. 480–9. On the Plebs League and the Labour College Movement, see Reé, *Proletarian Philosophers*.
19 C. A. R. Crosland, *The Future of Socialism*, 1956, pp. 520–4. See also Herbert Samuel, *Leisure in a Democracy*, 1949.
20 Labour Party, *Leisure for Living*, 1959, p. 26.
21 Huw Beynon, 'Jeremy Seabrook and the British working class', *The Socialist Register*, 1982, p. 291.

22 Stuart Hall, 'The culture gap', *Marxism Today*, XXVIII, 1984, p. 22.
23 For a discussion, see Tony Bennett, 'Popular culture: history and theory', in the Open University's course, U-203, *Popular Culture*, Milton Keynes, 1981, unit 3.
24 Mulgan and Worpole, *Saturday Night*, p. 13.
25 Alan Tomkins, 'The state and public cultural policies', *Another Standard*, spring 1984, p. 22. See also the Greater London Council, *Campaign for a Popular Culture*, 1986; Franco Bianchini, 'GLC R. I. P. Cultural policies in London 1981–1986', *New Formations*, I, 1987, pp. 103–17. For the outline of a new cultural politics, see Another Standard, *Culture and Democracy: The Manifesto*, 1986.
26 Malleson, *The ILP Arts Guild*, p. 6.
27 'Utopianism', *Justice*, 15 April 1899, p. 4.

BIBLIOGRAPHY

The bibliography lists all the works used in preparing this study. Articles cited from turn-of-the-century periodicals are referred to in full in the notes; here only the title of the periodical is given. Articles in books, both primary and secondary, are not listed separately in the bibliography.

I. Primary works

(A) manuscript collections

Battersea Public Library:
> Council of the Metropolitan Borough of Battersea, minutes of the proceedings, 10 April 1901 to 26 March 1902
> Newspaper cuttings, 1901–1911

Bodleian Library:
> John Johnson collection

Bradford Public Library:
> Bradford City Council, minutes, 1907 and 1914

British Library of Political and Economic Science (LSE):
> *Daily Citizen* file
> Labour News Ltd, minutes of directors' meetings
> Fabian Society, publishing committee, minutes

Calderdale Central Library (Halifax):
> Clarion Vocal Union collection
> Halifax ILP, account book
> Halifax Royal Skating Rink Co. Ltd, papers
> ILP (Halifax) and socialist hall, account book
> John Lister, 'Early history of the ILP in Halifax', unpublished manuscript
> John Lister papers

Manchester Central Library:
> Clarion Vocal Union, programme of the 1899 competition in the Free Trade Hall
> Manchester Palace of Varieties Ltd., minute book of directors' meetings, 1889–1893
> Robert Blatchford correspondence

Public Record Office:
> Twentieth Century Press Ltd, shareholders' lists

Sheffield Central Library:
> Edward Carpenter papers

Sydney Jones Library (University of Liverpool):
> John and Katharine Bruce Glasier papers

(B) labour and socialist periodicals

> *The ASE Journal*
> *The Aberdeen Standard*
> *The Blackburn Labour Journal*

BIBLIOGRAPHY

The Bolton and District ILP Pioneer
The Bradford Labour Echo
The Bradford Pioneer
The Clarion
The Clarion Cyclists' Journal
The Commonweal
The Cotton Factory Times
The Daily Citizen
The Daily Herald
The Fabian News
Forward (Bradford)
Forward (Glasgow)
The Glasgow Commonweal
Halifax and District Labour News
The Hammersmith Socialist Record
The ILP Journal (Keighley)
The ILP News
Justice
The Keighley Labour Journal
The King of the Road
The Labour Annual
The Labour Chronicle (Edinburgh)
The Labour Chronicle (Leeds)
The Labour Church Record
The Labour Journal (Bradford)
The Labour Leader
The Labour Prophet
The Labour Record and Review
Liberty
The New Moral World
The Northern Democrat
The Practical Socialist
The Reformers' Year Book
Rochdale Labour News
The Scout
The Sheffield Guardian
The Social Democrat
The Socialist (Sunderland)
The Socialist Review
To-Day
The Woman Worker
Women Folk
The Worker (Huddersfield)
The Workman's Times

(C) newspapers, reviews and other periodicals

All the Year Round

Blackwood's Edinburgh Magazine
The Catholic World
Chambers's Journal
The Church Reformer
Comradeship
The Congregationalist
The Contemporary Review
Cosmopolitan
The Craftsman
The Daily Telegraph
The Echo
The Economic Review
The Ethical World
Ethics: An Organ of the Ethical Movement
The Fortnightly Review
The Gateway
Good Words
Halfpenny Short Cuts
The Independent Review
International Journal of Ethics
The Journal of Political Economy
Keighley News
Lend a Hand
The Link: A Journal for the Servants of Man
The Liverpool Review
The Living Age
London: A Journal of Civic and Social Progress
Macmillan's Magazine
The Manchester Examiner and Times
The Manchester Guardian
The Mansfield House Magazine
The Municipal Reformer
The Musical Standard
The National Review
The New Age
The New Review
The Nineteenth Century
The North American Review
The Palace Journal
The Progressive Review
The Reformer
Reynolds's Newspaper
Sandow's Magazine of Physical Culture
The Saturday Review
The Sociological Review
The Spectator
The Sunday Chronicle
The Times

The Town Planning Review
Transactions of the National Association for the Promotion of Social Science
The Wesleyan Methodist Magazine
The Westminster Review
The World To-Day
The World's Work
The Yorkshire Musical Record

(D) books, pamphlets and published reports

Aberdeen Branch, Socialist League, comp. *Socialist Songs*. Aberdeen: Socialist League, 1889.

Alden, Percy. *Democratic England*. New York: Macmillan, 1912.

Ancoats Recreation Committee. *Programmes of the Autumn and Winter Work of the ARC*. Manchester, 1893.

Another Standard. *Culture and Democracy. The Manifesto*. London: Comedia, 1986.

Bainton, Edgar L. *Music and Socialism*. Manchester: Fellowship Press, 1910(?).

Barnett, Henrietta. *Canon Barnett: His Life, Work and Friends*. London: John Murray, 1918.

Barnett, Samuel. *The Ideal City*. Bristol: Arrowsmith, 1894.

— —. *Worship and Work*. Letchworth: Garden City Press, 1913.

Barnett, Samuel and Henrietta. *Practicable Socialism: Essays on Social Reform*. London: Longmans, Green, 1888.

— —. *Towards Social Reform*. London: T. Fisher Unwin, 1909.

Baron, Barclay. *The Growing Generation: A Study of Working Boys and Girls in Our Cities*. London: Student Christian Movements, 1911.

Bax, Ernest Belfort. *The Ethics of Socialism*. London: Swan Sonnenschein, 1889.

— —. *Outlooks from the New Standpoint*. London: Swan Sonnenschein, 1891.

— —. *Outspoken Essays on Social Subjects*. London: William Reeves, 1897.

— —. *The Religion of Socialism*. London: Swan Sonnenschein, 1887.

Bellamy, Edward. *Looking Backward 2000–1887*. New York: Signet Classics, 1960 [1888].

Besant, Walter. *All Sorts and Conditions of Men*. London: Chatto & Windus, 1882.

— —. *Autobiography of Sir Walter Besant*. London: Hutchinson, 1902.

Binns, Henry Bryan. *A Modern Humanist: Miscellaneous Papers of B. Kirkman Gray*. London: A. C. Fifield, 1910.

Blatchford, Robert. *Britain for the British*. London: Clarion Press, 1902.

— —. *Dismal England*. London: Walter Scott, 1899.

— —. *Julie. A Study of a Girl by a Man*. London: Walter Scott, 1900(?).

— —. *Merrie England*. London: Journeyman Press, 1976 [1893].

— —. *My Eighty Years*. London: Cassell, 1931.

— —. *My Favourite Books*. London: Clarion Press, 1901.

— —. *The New Religion*. Clarion Pamphlet no. 20, 1897.

— —. *Real Socialism: What Socialism Is, and What Socialism Is Not*. Clarion Pamphlet no. 23, 1898.

— —. *Saki's Bowl*. London: Hodder & Stoughton, 1928.

— —. *A Son of the Forge*. London: A. D. Innes, 1894.

— —. *The Sorcery Shop: An Impossible Romance*. London: Clarion Press, 1907.

Booth, William. *In Darkest England and the Way Out*. London: International Head-Quarters of the Salvation Army, 1890.

Born, Helena. *Whitman's Ideal Democracy and Other Writings*. Boston: Everett Press, 1902.

Boughton, Rutland. *The Self-Advertisement of Rutland Boughton*. Privately printed, n.d.

Bourchier, Arthur. *Art and Culture in Relation to Socialism*. London: ILP Publications Department, 1926.

Bramah, Ernest. *The Secret of the League*. London: Thomas Nelson & Sons, 1909.

Bristol Socialists, comp. *The Labour Songbook*. London: William Reeves, 1888(?).

Brock, A. Clutton. *Socialism and the Arts of Use*. Fabian Tract no. 177, 1915.

Bulwer-Lytton, Edward. *The Coming Race*. Edinburgh: William Blackwood & Sons, 1871.

Burgess, Joseph. *John Burns: The Rise and Progress of A Right Honourable*. Glasgow: Reformers' Bookshelf, 1911.

Burnley, James. *Phases of Bradford Life*. London: Simpkin, Marshall, 1871.

Burns, John. *Address Given by the Rt Hon. John Burns, P.C. at the Opening of the Tudor Barn and Art Gallery*. 1936.

— —. *Brains Better than Bets or Beer*. Clarion Pamphlet no. 36, 1902.

— —. *Labour and Drink*. Fifth Lees and Raper Memorial Lecture, 1904.

— —. *Municipal Socialism*. Clarion Pamphlet no. 37, 1902.

— —. *Music and Musicians*. Manchester: William Peel, n.d.

Burrage, E. Harcourt. *J. Passmore Edwards, Philanthropist*. London: S. W. Partridge, 1902.

Carpenter, Edward. *Angel's Wings: A Series of Essays on Art and Its Relation to Life*. London: Swan Sonnenschein, 1898.

— —. *Chants of Labour*. London: Swan Sonnenschein, 1888.

— —. *England's Ideal, and Other Papers on Social Subjects*. London: Swan Sonnenschein, 1887.

— —. *My Days and Dreams*. London: George Allen & Unwin, 1916.

— —. *Towards Industrial Freedom*. London: George Allen & Unwin, 1917.

Chapman, Guy. *Culture and Survival*. London: Jonathan Cape, 1940.

The Cinderella Club. *Souvenir. 1913*. Manchester: E. Hulton, 1913.

Clapperton, Jane Hume. *A Vision of the Future*. London: Swan Sonnenschein, 1904.

Clayton, Joseph. *The Rise and Decline of Socialism in Great Britain 1884–1924*. London: Faber & Gwyer, 1926.

Coit, Stanton. *Ethical Democracy: Essays in Social Dynamics*. London: Grant Richards, 1900.

— —. *The Ethical Movement Defined*. London: Ethical World Publishing Co., 1898(?).

— —. *Neighbourhood Guilds: An Instrument of Social Reform*. London: Swan Sonnenschein, 1891.

Common, Jack. *Kiddar's Luck*. Glasgow: Blackie & Son, 1951.

Congregational Hymnary. London: Congregational Union, 1916.

Conway, Katharine St John, and J. Bruce Glasier. *The Religion of Socialism: Two Aspects*. Manchester: Labour Press Society, 1894.

Cooper, Thomas. *The Life of Thomas Cooper*. London: Hodder & Stoughton, 1886.

Crompton, Louis, ed. *Bernard Shaw: The Road to Equality. Ten Unpublished Essays and Lectures, 1884–1918*. Boston: Beacon Press, 1971.

Crooks, Will. *Percy Alden M.A.: His Public and Civic Life*. London: W. Conquest, 1903.

Crosland, C. A. R. *The Future of Socialism*. London: Jonathan Cape, 1956.

Davies, C. Stella. *North Country Bred: A Working Class Family Chronicle*. London: Routledge & Kegan Paul, 1963.

Diack, W. *The Moral Effects of Socialism*. Aberdeen: A. Martin, 1893.

Dolman, Frederick. *Municipalities at Work*. London: Methuen, 1895.

Ensor, R. C. K., ed. *Modern Socialism*. London: Harper & Brothers, 1904.

Escott, T. H. S. *England: Its People, Polity and Pursuits*. Rev. ed. London: Chapman & Hall, 1885.

— —. *Social Transformations of the Victorian Age: A Survey of Court and Country*. London: Seeley, 1897.

Fabian Society. *Municipal Drink Traffic*. Fabian Tract no. 86, 1898.

— —, comp. *Songs for Socialists*. London: Fabian Society, 1912.

[Fairfield]. *The Socialist Revolution of 1888, by an Eye-Witness*. London: Harrison & Sons, 1884.

Faucher, Leon. *Manchester in 1844: Its Present Condition and Future Prospects*. Translated and annotated by J. P. Culverwell. London: Frank Cass, 1969.

Foley, Alice. *A Bolton Childhood*. Manchester: Manchester University Extra-Mural Department, 1973.

Ford, Isabella. *On the Threshold*. London: Edward Arnold, 1895.

— —, ed. *Tom Maguire, a Remembrance*. Manchester: Labour Press Society, 1895.

Forster, E. M. *Howards End*. London: Edward Arnold, 1973 [1910].

Freeman, Arnold. *Boy Life and Labour: The Manufacture of Inefficiency*. London: P. S. King & Son, 1914.

Glasier, J. Bruce. *The Meaning of Socialism*. Manchester: National Labour Press, 1919.

— —. *Socialism in Song: An Appreciation of William Morris's 'Chants for Socialists'*. Manchester: National Labour Press, 1919.

— —. *Socialist Songs*. Glasgow: Labour Literature Society, 1893.

— —. *William Morris and the Early Days of the Socialist Movement*. London: Longmans, Green, 1921.

Gray, B. Kirkman. *Philanthropy and the State, or Social Politics*. London: P. S. King & Son, 1908.

Great Britain. Parliament. *Parliamentary Papers* (Commons), XVIII, 1892, 'Report from the select committee on theatres and places of entertainment'.

Greater London Council, *Campaign for a Popular Culture*. London: GLC, 1986.

Greenwood, Thomas. *Museums and Art Galleries*. London: Simpkin, Marshall, 1884.

Gregory, John. *My Garden and Other Verses*. Bristol: J. W. Arrowsmith, 1907.

Groos, Karl M. *The Play of Animals: A Study of Animal Life and Instinct*. London: Chapman & Hall, 1898.

— —. *The Play of Man*. New York: D. Appleton, 1901.

Gutteridge, Joseph. *Lights and Shadows in the Life of an Artisan*. Coventry: Curtis & Beamish, 1893.

Hall, Leonard, J. M. McLachlan, J. H. Belcher and C. T. Douthwaite. *Let Us Reform the Labour Party*. Manchester: Fellowship Press, 1910.

Hardie, J. Keir. *From Serfdom to Socialism*. London: George Allen, 1907.

Haw, George. *From Workhouse to Westminster: The Life Story of Will Crooks, M.P.* London: Cassell, 1907.

— —. *Today's Work: Municipal Government, the Hope of Democracy*. London: Clarion Newspaper, 1901.

Haweis, H. R. *Music and Morals*. London: Strahan, 1871.

— —. *My Musical Life*. 2nd ed. London: W. H. Allen, 1886.

Headlam, Stewart D. *The Function of the Stage*. London: Frederick Verinder, 1889.

— —. *On the Danger of Municipal Puritanism*. London: Guild of St Matthew, 1905.

— —. *The Socialist's Church*. London: George Allen, 1907.

Herbert, Edward. *Newaera: A Socialist Romance*. London: P. S. King & Son, 1910.

Hobart, H. W. *Social-Democracy, or Democratic Socialism*. London: Twentieth Century Press, 1907.

Hobson, S. G. *Pilgrim to the Left*. London: Edward Arnold, 1938.

Howorth, Edward G. and Mona Wilson. *West Ham: A Study in Social and Industrial Problems*. London: J. M. Dent, 1907.

Hymns Ancient and Modern. London: William Clowes, 1885(?).

Hymns and Anthems for the Use of the South Place Ethical Society. London: South Place Chapel, 1889.

Hyndman, H. M. *A Commune for London*. London: Justice Printery, 1887.

— —. *Further Reminiscences*. London: Macmillan, 1912.

— —. *The Social Reconstruction of England*. London: William Reeves, 1884.

— — and William Morris. *A Summary of the Principles of Socialism*. London: Modern Press, 1884.

Innominatus [Edward Heneage Dering]. *In the Light of the Twentieth Century*. London: Hodges, 1886.

Irving, Dan. *The Municipality, from a Worker's Point of View*. London: Twentieth Century Press, 1906(?).

Jowett, F. W. *The Socialist and the City*. London: George Allen, 1907.

Joynes, J. L. *Socialist Rhymes*. London: Modern Press, 1885.

Kenney, Annie. *Memories of a Militant*. London: Edward Arnold, 1924.

Labour and the New Social Order. A Report on Reconstruction. London: Labour Party, 1918.

The Labour Church Hymnbook. Manchester: Labour Church Institute, 1892.

Labour's Song Book. London: ILP Publications Department, 1931.

Lafargue, Paul. *'The Right to be Lazy' and Other Studies*. Chicago: Charles H. Kerr, 1907.

Lansbury, George. *My Life*. London: Constable, 1928.

229

Laurence, Dan H., ed. *Shaw's Music. The Complete Music Criticism in Three Volumes*. London: The Bodley Head, 1981.

Leatham, James. *An Eight Hours' Day, with Ten Hours' Pay: How to Get It and How to Keep It*. Aberdeen: James Leatham, 1890.

— —. *Labour's Garland, Being Poems for Socialists*. 2nd ed. Huddersfield: 'Worker' Office, n.d.

— —. *Shows and Showfolk I Have Known*. Turriff: Deveron Press, 1936.

— —. *Socialism and Character*. London: Twentieth Century Press, 1897.

— —. *Songs for Socialists*. 3rd ed. Aberdeen: James Leatham, 1890.

Leisure for Living. London: Labour Party, 1959.

Lemire, Eugene D. *The Unpublished Lectures of William Morris*. Detroit: Wayne State University Press, 1969.

Leonard, T. A. *Adventures in Holiday Making*. London: Holiday Fellowship, 1935.

Lowe, David. *John Barlas, Sweet Singer and Socialist*. Cupar, Fife: Craigwood House Publishing, 1915.

Lubbock, John. *The Uses of Life*. London: Macmillan, 1894.

Lyons, A. Neil. *Robert Blatchford: The Sketch of a Personality: An Estimate of Some Achievements*. London: Clarion Press, 1910.

MacDonald, J. Ramsay. *The Socialist Movement*. New York: Henry Holt, 1911.

Macmillan, Michael. *The Promotion of General Happiness*. London: Swan Sonnenschein, 1890.

Malleson, Miles. *The ILP Arts Guild. The ILP and its Dramatic Societies: What They Are and Might Become*. London: ILP Publications Department, 1925.

Mann, Tom. *The Regulation of Working Hours: As Submitted to the Royal Commission on Labour*. London: George Reynolds, 1891.

— —. *What a Compulsory Eight Hour Working Day Means to the Workers*. London: Modern Press, n.d.

Mansfield House Song-Book. London: Mansfield House, 1906.

Marx, Karl. *Capital, Volume III, The Process of Capitalist Production as a Whole*. Edited by Frederick Engels. New York: International Publishers, 1967 [1894].

Masterman, C. F. G. *The Condition of England*. London: Methuen, 1909.

Meek, George. *George Meek, Bath Chair-Man*. London: Constable, 1910.

Meier, Paul. 'An unpublished lecture of William Morris'. *International Review of Social History*, XVI, 1971, pp. 217–40.

Merrie England Fayre, City Hall, Liverpool, May 1895. Programme.

Methodist Free Church Hymns. London: Andrew Crombie, 1887.

Michaelis, Richard. *A Sequel to Looking Backward, or Looking Further Forward*. London: William Reeves, n.d.

Midgley, Samuel. *Music and the Municipality*. Bradford: G. F. Sewell, 1912.

— —. *My 70 Years' Musical Memories (1860–1930)*. London: Novello, 1934.

Mill, John Stuart. *Utilitarianism*. Indianapolis: Bobbs-Merrill, 1957.

Miller, William Haig. *The Culture of Pleasure; or, the Enjoyment of Life in Its Social and Religious Aspects*. London: James Nisbet, 1872.

Mitchell, Hannah. *The Hard Way Up*. London: Faber & Faber, 1968.

Morley, John. *Critical Miscellanies*. London: Macmillan, 1886.

Morris, May. *William Morris: Artist, Writer, Socialist*. Oxford: Basil Blackwell,

1936.

Morris, William. *Chants for Socialists*. London: Socialist League, 1885.

——. *The Collected Works of William Morris*. London: Longmans, Green, various dates.

——. *News From Nowhere: or, an Epoch of Rest*. London: Routledge & Kegan Paul, 1970 [1890].

—— and E. Belfort Bax. *Socialism: Its Growth and Outcome*. London: Swan Sonnenschein, 1893.

Mudie-Smith, Richard, ed. *The Religious Life of London*. London: Hodder & Stoughton, 1904.

Muse, Charles E. *Poverty and Drunkenness (A Socialist's View)*. Manchester: Labour Press Society, 1895.

Nesbit, Edith. *Ballads and Lyrics of Socialism 1883–1908*. London: Fabian Society, 1908.

Noel, Conrad. *Conrad Noel: An Autobiography*. Edited by Sidney Dark. London: J. M. Dent & Sons, 1945.

——. *The Day of the Sun*. London: David Nutt, 1901.

Norris, James, John Priest and John Teare. *Artisans' Prize Essays. 'On the Influence of Rational and Elevating Amusements Upon the Working Classes'*. Liverpool: Smith, Rogerson, 1849.

Oyston, H. Gifford. *Socialism and the Drink Evil*. London: Robert Culley, 1909.

Palace Theatre. *Souvenir 1913*. Manchester: Palace of Varieties, 1913.

Pearce, Georgia, ed. *The Clarion Song Book*. London: Clarion Press, 1906.

Pease, E. R. *The Case for Municipal Drink Trade*. London: P. S. King & Son, 1904.

Peppin, Talbot S. *Club-Land of the Toiler*. London: J. M. Dent, 1895.

Pethick-Lawrence, Emmeline. *My Part in a Changing World*. London: Victor Gollancz, 1938.

Pethick-Lawrence, F. W. *Fate Has Been Kind*. London: Hutchinson, 1942.

The Primitive Methodist Mission Hymnal. London: Thomas Mitchell, 1895.

Programmes of the Autumn and Winter Work of the ARC. Manchester: Ancoats Recreation Committee, 1893.

Quin, Malcolm. *Memoirs of a Positivist*. London: George Allen & Unwin, 1924.

Reason, Will, ed. *University and Social Settlements*. London: Methuen, 1898.

Report of the Committee to Inquire into the Condition of the Bristol Poor. Bristol: W. Lewis & Sons, 1885.

Richter, Eugene. *Pictures of the Socialist Future*. 3rd ed. London: Swan Sonnenschein, 1907.

Roberts, Robert. *The Classic Slum: Salford Life in the First Quarter of the Century*. Harmondsworth: Penguin, 1971.

Rowley, Charles. *Fifty Years of Ancoats, Loss and Gain*. Paper read before the Toynbee Debating Society, 1899.

——. *Fifty Years of Work Without Wages*. London: Hodder & Stoughton, 1912.

——. *Social Politics*. Manchester: John Heywood, 1885.

——. *A Workshop Paradise and Other Papers*. London: Sheratt & Hughes, 1905.

Rowntree, B. Seebohm, ed. *Betting and Gambling: A National Evil*. London: Macmillan, 1905.

Russell, Charles E. B. and Lilian M. Rigby. *Working Lads' Clubs*. London:

Macmillan, 1908.

Salt, H. S., ed. *Songs of Freedom*. London: Walter Scott, 1893.

Samuel, Herbert. *Leisure in a Democracy*. London: National Book League, 1949.

The SDF Songbook. London: Twentieth Century Press, 1910(?).

Shaw, George Bernard, ed. *Fabian Essays in Socialism*. London: Walter Scott Publishing, 1891.

Shimmin, Hugh. *Liverpool Life: Its Pleasures, Practices, and Pastimes*. Liverpool: Egerton, Smith, 1857.

Smart, H. Russell. *Socialism and Drink*. Manchester: Labour Press Society, 1890.

Snowden, Philip. *The Living Wage*. London: Hodder & Stoughton, 1912.

— —. *Socialism and the Drink Question*. London: ILP Press, 1908.

Squire, Jack C. *Socialism and Art*. London: Twentieth Century Press, 1907.

The Sunday Afternoon Songbook for 'Pleasant Sunday Afternoons' and Other Gatherings. London: James Clarke, 1892.

Suthers, R. B. *Mind Your Own Business: The Case for Municipal Management*. London: Clarion Press, 1905.

Terrett, J. J. *Municipal Socialism in West Ham*. London: Twentieth Century Press, 1902.

Thompson, William. *A Prospectus of Socialism, or, a Glimpse of the Millennium*. London: W. Reeves, n.d.

Thorne, Will. *My Life's Battles*. London: George Newnes, 1925.

Tillett, Ben. *An Address on Character and Environment*. Manchester: Labour Press Society, n.d.

Tressell, Robert. *The Ragged Trousered Philanthropists*. New York: Monthly Review Press, l962.

Trevor, John. *From Ethics to Religion*. Labour Prophet Tract no. 2, n.d.

— —. *The Labour Church in England*. Labour Prophet Tract no. 4, 1896.

— —. *My Quest for God*. London: Labour Prophet, 1897.

— —. *Our First Principle*. Labour Prophet Tract no. 3, n.d.

Tuckwell, William, Charles Leland and Walter Besant. *Art and Hand Work for the People*. Manchester: J. E. Cornish, 1885.

Urwick, E. J. *Luxury and Waste of Life*. London: J. M. Dent, 1908.

Veblen, Thorstein. *The Theory of the Leisure Class*. New York: Mentor Books, 1953 [1899].

'W'. *The Anti-Puritan; or, an Effort to Drive the Puritans From Paradise*. Lichfield, 1828.

Webb, Beatrice. *My Apprenticeship*. London: Longmans, Green, 1926.

Webb, Sidney. *The London Programme*. London: Swan Sonnenschein, 1891.

— —. *A Plea for an Eight Hours Bill*. Fabian Tract no. 16, 1892.

— — and Beatrice Webb. *A Constitution for the Socialist Commonwealth of Great Britain*. Introduction by Samuel H. Beer. Cambridge: Cambridge University Press, 1975.

— — and Harold Cox. *The Eight Hours Day*. London: Walter Scott, 1891.

Wicksteed, Philip H. *What Does the Labour Church Stand For?* London: Labour Prophet, n.d.

Wright, Thomas. *Some Habits and Customs of the Working Class*. London: Tinsley Brothers, 1867.

Wylie, Alex. *Labour, Leisure and Luxury: A Contribution to Present Political Economy*. London: Longmans, Green, 1884.

Yates, Edmund. *The Business of Pleasure*. London: Chapman & Hall, 1865.

Zimmern, Alice. *Unpaid Professions for Women*. London: The Guardian Office, 1906.

II. Secondary works

(A) books, pamphlets and articles

Ainsworth, A. J. 'Aspects of socialism at the branch level, 1890–1900: some notes towards analysis'. *North West Labour History Society Bulletin*, IV, 1977, pp. 6–35.

— —. 'Religion in the working class community, and the evolution of socialism in late nineteenth century Lancashire: a case of working class consciousness'. *Histoire sociale/Social History*, X, 1977, pp. 354–80.

Anderson, G. L. 'Victorian clerks and voluntary associations in Liverpool and Manchester'. *Northern History*, XII, 1976, pp. 202–19.

Anderson, Perry. *Arguments within English Marxism*. London: Verso, 1980.

Appleton, Ian, ed. *Leisure Research and Policy*. Edinburgh: Scottish Academic Press, 1974.

Bailey, Peter. *Leisure and Class in Victorian England: Rational Recreation and the Contest for Control, 1830–1885*. London: Routledge & Kegan Paul, 1978 [Rev. ed. 1987].

— —, ed. *Music Hall: The Business of Pleasure*. Milton Keynes: Open University Press, 1986.

— —. ' "Will the real Bill Banks please stand up?" Towards a role analysis of mid-Victorian working-class respectability'. *Journal of Social History*, XII, 1979, pp. 336–53.

Bainton, Helen. *Remembered On Waking*. Sydney: Currawong Publishing, 1960.

Baker, William J. 'The making of a working-class football culture in Victorian England'. *Journal of Social History*, XIII, 1979, pp. 241–51.

Barker, Kathleen. *Entertainment in the Nineties*. Bristol Branch of the Historical Association. Local Pamphlet no. 33, 1973.

Barker, Rodney. 'The Labour Party and education for socialism'. *International Review of Social History*, XIV, 1969, pp. 22–53.

Bauman, Zygmunt. *Socialism: The Active Utopia*. London: George Allen & Unwin, 1976.

Beith, Gilbert, ed. *Edward Carpenter: An Appreciation*. London: George Allen & Unwin, 1931.

Bellamy, Joyce and John Saville, eds. *Dictionary of Labour Biography*. London: Macmillan, 1972–date.

Bennett, Tony, Colin Mercer and Janet Woollacott, eds. *Popular Culture and Social Relations*. Milton Keynes: Open University Press, 1986.

Benson, John, ed. *The Working Class in England 1875–1914*. London: Croom Helm, 1985.

Benz, Ernst. *Das Recht auf Faulheit, oder die friedliche Beendigung des Klassen-kampfes.* Stuttgart: Ernst Klett Verlag, 1974.

Best, Geoffrey. *Mid-Victorian Britain 1851–75.* New York: Schocken Books, 1972.

Bettany, F. G. *Stewart Headlam: A Biography.* London: John Murray, 1926.

Beynon, Huw. 'Jeremy Seabrook and the British working class'. *The Socialist Register*, 1982, pp. 285–301.

Bianchini, Franco. 'GLC R. I. P. Cultural policies in London 1981–1986'. *New Formations*, I, 1987, pp. 103–17.

Bienefeld, M. A. *Working Hours in British Industry: An Economic History.* London: Weidenfeld & Nicolson, 1972.

Boos, Florence and Carole Silver. *Socialism and the Literary Artistry of William Morris.* Columbia, Mo.: University of Missouri Press, 1989.

Boyce, George, James Curran and Pauline Wingate, eds. *Newspaper History From the Seventeenth Century to the Present Day.* London: Constable, 1978.

Brantlinger, Patrick. ' "News from Nowhere": Morris's socialist anti-novel'. *Victorian Studies*, XIX, 1975, pp. 35–49.

Bratton, J. S., ed. *Music Hall: Performance and Style.* Milton Keynes: Open University Press, 1986.

Briggs, Asa. *Mass Entertainment: The Origins of a Modern Industry.* Adelaide: The Griffin Press, 1960.

– – and John Saville, eds. *Essays in Labour History in Memory of G. D. H. Cole.* London: Macmillan, 1967 [1960].

Britain, Ian. *Fabianism and Culture: A Study in British Socialism and the Arts, c. 1884–1918.* Cambridge: Cambridge University Press, 1982.

Brockway, Fenner. *Socialism Over Sixty Years: The Life of Jowett of Bradford.* London: George Allen & Unwin, 1946.

Brom, Eric. *Grove's Dictionary of Music and Musicians.* 5th ed. London: Macmillan, 1954.

Brown, Kenneth D., ed. *Essays in Anti-Labour History: Responses to the Rise of Labour in Britain.* London: Macmillan, 1974.

– –. *John Burns.* London: Royal Historical Society, 1977.

Bryher, Samson. *An Account of the Labour and Socialist Movement in Bristol.* Bristol: Bristol Labour Weekly, 1931.

Cage, R. A., ed. *The Working Class in Glasgow 1750–1914.* London: Croom Helm, 1987.

Cahill, Michael and Tony Jowitt. 'The new philanthropy: the emergence of the Bradford City Guild of Help'. *Journal of Social Policy*, IX, 1980, pp. 359–82.

Clarke, David. *Colne Valley: Radicalism to Socialism.* London: Longman, 1981.

Clarke, John, Chas Critcher and Richard Johnson, eds. *Working Class Culture: Studies in History and Theory.* London: Hutchinson, 1979.

– – and Chas Critcher. *The Devil Makes Work: Leisure in Capitalist Britain.* London: Macmillan, 1985.

Clarke, Peter. 'The Progressive movement in England'. *Transactions of the Royal Historical Society*, XXIV, 1974, pp. 159–81.

Claudin-Urondo, Carmen. *Lenin and the Cultural Revolution.* Hassocks: Harvester Press, 1979.

Clayre, Alasdair. *Work and Play: Ideas and Experience of Work and Leisure.*

London: Weidenfeld & Nicolson, 1974.

Colls, Robert and Philip Dodd. *Englishness. Politics and Culture 1880–1920*. London: Croom Helm, 1986.

Cox, David. 'The Labour Party in Leicester: a study of branch development'. *International Review of Social History*, VI, 1961, pp. 197–211.

Crossick, Geoffrey. *An Artisan Elite in Victorian Society: Kentish London 1840–1880*. London: Croom Helm, 1978.

— —, ed. *The Lower Middle Class in Britain 1870–1914*. London: Croom Helm, 1977.

Cunningham, Hugh. *Leisure in the Industrial Revolution c. 1780–c. 1880*. London: Croom Helm, 1980.

Currie, Robert. *Methodism Divided: A Study in the Sociology of Ecumenicalism*. London: Faber & Faber, 1968.

Donajgrodzki, A. P., ed. *Social Control in Nineteenth Century Britain*. London: Croom Helm, 1977.

Dowe, Dieter. 'The workingmen's choral movement in Germany before the First World War'. *Journal of Contemporary History*, XIII, 1978, pp. 269–96.

Duncan, Bob. *James Leatham, 1865–1945: Portrait of a Socialist Pioneer*. Aberdeen: Aberdeen People's Press, 1978.

Dupont, V. *L'utopie et le roman utopique dans la littérature anglaise*. Cahors: Imprimene typographique a. Coueslant, 1941.

Fahey, David M. 'Brewers, publicans, and working-class drinkers: pressure group politics in late Victorian and Edwardian England'. *Histoire sociale/ Social History*, XIII, 1980, pp. 85–103.

— —. 'Drink and the meaning of reform in late Victorian and Edwardian England'. *Cithara*, XIII, 1974, pp. 46–56.

Formations Collective, ed. *Formations of Pleasure*. London: Routledge & Kegan Paul, 1983.

Frayling, Christopher and Helen Snowdon. 'Perspectives on craft'. *Craft*, LIV to LIX, 1982.

Fullerton, Ronald A. 'Toward a commercial popular culture in Germany: the development of pamphlet fiction, 1871–1914'. *Journal of Social History*, XII, 1979, pp. 489–511.

Gaskell, S. Martin. 'Gardens for the working class: Victorian practical pleasure'. *Victorian Studies*, XXIII, 1980, pp. 479–501.

Giddens, Anthony. 'Notes on the concept of play and leisure'. *Sociological Review*, XII, 1964, pp. 73–89.

Gillis, John. *Youth and History: Tradition and Change in European Age Relations, 1770–Present*. Rev. ed. New York: Academic Press, 1981.

Golby, J. M. and A. W. Purdue. *The Civilisation of the Crowd: Popular Culture in England 1750–1900*. New York: Schocken Books, 1985.

Goldman, Robert and John Wilson. 'The rationalization of leisure'. *Politics and Society*, VII, 1977, pp. 157–87.

Gow, A. H. M. 'Robert Blatchford as a man of letters'. *The Manchester Quarterly*, XXXII, 1913, pp. 200–12.

Gray, Robert Q. *The Labour Aristocracy in Victorian Edinburgh*. Oxford: Clarendon Press, 1976.

Green, Nicholas and Frank Mort. 'Metropolitan culture policies, politics and the GLC'. *Another Standard*, Summer 1984, pp. 12–13.

Groves, Reginald. *Conrad Noel and the Thaxted Movement*. London: Merlin Press, 1967.

— —. *The Mystery of Victor Grayson*. London: Pendulum Publications, 1946.

Haley, Bruce. *The Healthy Body and Victorian Culture*. Cambridge, Mass.: Harvard University Press, 1978.

Hall, Stuart. 'The culture gap'. *Marxism Today*, XXVIII, 1984, pp. 18–22.

Hammond, J. L. and Barbara Hammond. *The Age of the Chartists*. Hamden, Conn.: Archon Books, 1962.

Harker, Dave. *Fakesong: The Manufacture of British 'Folksong' 1700 to the Present Day*. Milton Keynes: Open University Press, 1985.

— —. 'May Cecil Sharp be praised?' *History Workshop Journal*, XIV, 1982, pp. 45–62.

Harrison, Brian. *Drink and the Victorians: The Temperance Question in England 1815–72*. London: Faber & Faber, 1971.

— —. 'For church, queen, and family: the Girls' Friendly Society 1874–1920'. *Past and Present*, LXI, 1973, pp. 107–38.

— —. *Peaceable Kingdom: Stability and Change in Modern Britain*. Oxford: Clarendon Press, 1982.

— —. 'Teetotal Chartism'. *History*, LVIII, 1973, pp. 193–217.

Harrison, Royden, Gillian B. Woolven and Robert Duncan. *The Warwick Guide to British Labour Periodicals 1790–1970*. Hassocks: Harvester Press, 1977.

Hartman, Mary S. and Lois Banner, eds. *Clio's Consciousness Raised: New Perspectives on the History of Women*. New York: Harper & Row, 1974.

Hawthorn, Jeremy, ed. *The British Working-Class Novel in the Twentieth Century*. London: Edward Arnold, 1984.

Hayler, Guy. 'Labour and temperance: a brief historical survey of Labour's attitude to the drink problem'. *Alliance Year Book and Temperance Reformers' Handbook*, 1928, pp. 65–81.

Hinton, James. *The First Shop Stewards' Movement*. London: George Allen & Unwin, 1973.

Hobsbawm, E. J. *Labouring Men: Studies in the History of Labour*. London: Weidenfeld & Nicolson, 1964.

— —. *Primitive Rebels: Studies in Archaic Forms of Social Movements in the 19th and 20th Centuries*. New York: W. W. Norton, 1965.

— —. *Worlds of Labour: Further Studies in the History of Labour*. London: Weidenfeld & Nicolson, 1984.

Hollis, Patricia, ed. *Pressure from Without in Early Victorian England*. London: Edward Arnold, 1974.

Holton, R. J. 'Daily Herald v. Daily Citizen, 1912–15: the struggle for a labour daily in relation to "the labour unrest" '. *International Review of Social History*, XIX, 1974, pp. 347–76.

Hopkin, Deian. 'Local newspapers of the Independent Labour Party, 1893–1906'. *Bulletin of the Society for the Study of Labour History*, XXVIII, 1974, pp. 28–37.

— —. 'The membership of the Independent Labour Party, 1904–10: a spatial and occupational analysis'. *International Review of Social History*, XX, 1975, pp. 175–97.

Howell, David. *British Workers and the Independent Labour Party 1888–1906*. Manchester: Manchester University Press, 1983.

Howes, Frank. *The English Musical Renaissance*. London: Secker & Warburg, 1966.

Hunt, E. H. *Regional Wage Variations in Britain, 1850–1914*. Oxford: Clarendon Press, 1973.

Hunt, Karen. 'Women and the Social Democratic Federation: some notes on Lancashire'. *North West Labour History Society Bulletin*, VII, 1980–1, pp. 49–64.

Hurd, Michael. *Immortal Hour: The Life and Period of Rutland Boughton*. London: Routledge & Kegan Paul, 1962.

Ingle, S. J. 'Socialism and literature: the contribution of imaginative writers to the development of the British Labour Party'. *Political Studies*, XXII, 1974, pp. 158–67.

Inglis, K. S. 'The Labour Church movement'. *International Review of Social History*, III, 1958, pp. 445–60.

Jones, Stephen G. *The British Labour Movement and Film, 1918–1939*. London: Routledge & Kegan Paul, 1987.

— —. 'Labour, society and the drink question in Britain, 1918–1939'. *The Historical Journal*, XXX, 1987, pp. 105–22.

— —. *Workers at Play: A Social and Economic History of Leisure 1918–1939*. London: Routledge & Kegan Paul, 1986.

Jowitt, J. A. and R. K. S. Taylor, eds. *Bradford 1890–1914: The Cradle of the Independent Labour Party*. Bradford Centre Occasional Papers no. 2, October 1980.

Joyce, Patrick. *Work, Society and Politics: The Culture of the Factory in Later Victorian England*. New Brunswick, NJ: Rutgers University Press, 1980.

Kapp, Yvonne. *Eleanor Marx*. New York: Pantheon Books, 1972–6.

Keating, P. J. *The Working Classes in Victorian Fiction*. New York: Barnes & Noble, 1971.

Kellett, J. R. 'Municipal socialism, enterprise and trading in the Victorian city'. *Urban History Yearbook*, 1978, pp. 36–45.

Kent, J. H. S. 'The role of religion in the cultural structure of the later Victorian city'. *Transactions of the Royal Historical Society*, XXIII, 1973, pp. 153–73.

Kidd, Alan J. and K. W. Roberts, eds. *City, Class and Culture: Studies of Social Policy and Cultural Production in Victorian Manchester*. Manchester: Manchester University Press, 1985.

Kolakowski, Leszek. *Main Currents of Marxism*. Oxford: Clarendon Press, 1978.

Langan, Mary and Bill Schwarz, eds. *Crises in the British State 1880–1930*. London: Hutchinson, 1985.

Langewiesche, Dieter. 'The impact of the German labor movement on workers' culture'. *Journal of Modern History*, LIX, 1987, pp. 506–23.

LeMire, Eugene D. 'The Socialist League leaflets and manifestos: an annotated checklist'. *International Review of Social History*, XXII, 1977, pp. 21–9.

Levy, Carl, ed. *Socialism and the Intelligentsia 1880–1914*. London: Routledge & Kegan Paul., 1987.

Liddington, Jill. *The Life and Times of a Respectable Radical: Selina Cooper*

237

(1864–1946). London: Virago, 1984.

— — and Jill Norris. *One Hand Tied Behind Us: The Rise of the Women's Suffrage Movement*. London: Virago, 1978.

Lidtke, Vernon L. *The Alternative Culture*. New York: Oxford University Press, 1985.

— —. 'Songs and politics: an exploratory essay on *Arbeiterlieder* in the Weimar Republic'. *Archiv für Sozialgeschichte*, XIV, 1974, pp. 253–73.

Lloyd, A. L. *Folk Song in England*. London: Lawrence & Wishart, 1967.

Lowenthal, Leo. *Literature, Popular Culture and Society*. Palo Alto: Pacific Books, 1961.

Lowerson, John and John Myerscough. *Time to Spare in Victorian England*. Brighton: Harvester Press, 1977.

MacIntyre, Stuart. 'British labour, marxism and working-class apathy in the nineteen twenties'. *The Historical Journal*, XX, 1977, pp. 479–96.

Mackerness, E. D. *A Social History of English Music*. London: Routledge & Kegan Paul, 1964.

Mackillop, I. D. *The British Ethical Societies*. Cambridge: Cambridge University Press, 1986.

Manuel, Frank E., ed. *Utopias and Utopian Thought*. Boston: Houghton Mifflin, 1966.

Marshall, T. H. *Class, Citizenship and Social Development*. Chicago: University of Chicago Press, 1963.

Mason, Tony. *Association Football and English Society 1863–1915*. Hassocks: Harvester Press, 1980.

Mayall, David. 'Places for entertainment and instruction: a study of early cinema in Birmingham, 1908–1918', *Midland History*, X, 1985, pp. 94–109.

McBriar, A. M. *Fabian Socialism and English Politics 1884–1918*. Cambridge: Cambridge University Press, 1962.

McKibbin, Ross. *The Evolution of the Labour Party 1910–1924*. London: Oxford University Press, 1974.

— —. 'Why was there no marxism in Great Britain?'. *English Historical Review*, XCIX, 1984, pp. 297–331.

— —. 'Working-class gambling in Britain 1880–1939'. *Past and Present*, XLIX, 1979, pp. 147–78.

Meacham, Standish. *A Life Apart: The English Working Class, 1890–1914*. Cambridge, Mass.: Harvard University Press, 1977.

Meier, Paul. *William Morris: The Marxist Dreamer*. Hassocks: Harvester Press, 1978.

Meller, H. E. *Leisure and the Changing City, 1870–1914*. London: Routledge & Kegan Paul, 1976.

Merriman, John M., ed. *Consciousness and Class Experience in Nineteenth Century Europe*. New York: Holmes & Meier, 1979.

Miliband, Ralph. *Parliamentary Socialism: A Study in the Politics of Labour*. New York: Monthly Review Press, 1972.

Miller, John. 'Songs of the British radical and labour movement'. *Marxism Today*, VII, 1963, pp. 180–6.

Minihan, Janet. *The Nationalisation of Culture: The Development of State Subsidies to the Arts in Great Britain*. New York: New York University Press, 1977.

238

More, Charles. *Skill and the English Working Class, 1870–1914*. London: Croom Helm, 1980.

Morgan, Kenneth O. *Keir Hardie: Radical and Socialist*. London: Weidenfeld & Nicolson, 1975.

Morris, A. J. A., ed. *Edwardian Radicalism 1900–1914: Some Aspects of British Radicalism*. London: Routledge & Kegan Paul, 1974.

Morton, A. L. *The English Utopia*. London: Lawrence & Wishart, 1952.

Mulgan, Geoff and Ken Worpole, *Saturday Night or Sunday Morning? From Arts to Industry – New Forms of Cultural Policy*. London: Comedia, 1986.

Munby, Lionel. *The Luddites and Other Essays*. London: Michael Katanka, 1971.

O'Brien, Margaret and Lorna McKee, eds. *The Father Figure*. London: Tavistock, 1982.

Odom, W. *Two Sheffield Poets: James Montgomery and Ebenezer Elliot*. Sheffield: W. C. Leng, 1929.

Open University. *Popular Culture* (U203). Milton Keynes: Open University Press, 1981–2.

Orens, John R. 'The mass, the masses, and the music hall: Stewart Headlam's radical Anglicanism'. *A Jubilee Paper*. London: Jubilee Group, 1979.

Owen, David. *English Philanthropy 1660–1960*. Cambridge, Mass.: Harvard University Press, 1964.

Pearson, Nicholas. 'Art, socialism, and the division of labour'. *Journal of the William Morris Society*, IV, 1981, pp. 7–25.

Pelling, Henry. *The Origins of the Labour Party*. London: Oxford University Press, 1965 [1954].

Pierson, Stanley. *British Socialists: The Journey from Fantasy to Politics*. Cambridge, Mass.: Harvard University Press, 1979.

— —. *Marxism and the Origins of British Socialism: The Struggle for a New Class Consciousness*. Ithaca, NY: Cornell University Press, 1973.

— —. 'John Trevor and the Labour Church movement in England, 1891–1900'. *Church History*, XXIX, 1960, pp. 463–78.

Pimlot, J. A. R. *Toynbee Hall: Fifty Years of Social Progress, 1884–1934*. London: J. M. Dent & Sons, 1935.

Pinchbeck, Ivy. *Women Workers and the Industrial Revolution 1750–1850*. London: George Routledge & Sons, 1930.

Pirie, Peter J. *The English Musical Renaissance*. London: Victor Gollancz, 1979.

Plumb, J. H. *The Commercialisation of Leisure in Eighteenth Century England*. Reading: University of Reading, 1974.

Poirier, Philip. *The Advent of the British Labour Party*. New York: Columbia University Press, 1958.

Polak, Fred L. *The Image of the Future*. Leyden: A. W. Sythoff, 1961.

Pollard, Sydney and John Salt, eds., *Robert Owen: Prophet of the Poor*. London: Macmillan, 1971.

Prochaska, F. K. *Women and Philanthropy in Nineteenth-Century England*. Oxford: Clarendon Press, 1980.

Prynn, David. 'The Clarion clubs, rambling and the holiday associations in Britain since the 1890s'. *Journal of Contemporary History*, XI, 1976, pp. 65–77.

Pugh, Martin. *The Tories and the People 1880–1935*. Oxford: Basil Blackwell,

1985.

Rainbow, Bernarr. *The Land Without Music: Music Education in England 1800–1860 and its Continental Antecedents*. London: Novello, 1967.

Reckitt, Maurice B., ed. *For Christ and the People. Studies of Four Socialist Priests and Prophets of the Church of England Between 1870 and 1930*. London: SPCK, 1968.

Reé, Jonathan. *Proletarian Philosophers: Problems in Socialist Culture in Britain 1900–1940*. Oxford: Oxford University Press, 1984.

Reid, Alastair. 'Politics and economics in the formation of the British working class: a response to H. F. Moorhouse'. *Social History*, III, 1978, pp. 347–61.

Reid, Douglas. 'The decline of Saint Monday 1766–1876'. *Past and Present*, LXXI, 1976, pp. 76–101.

Reid, Fred. *Keir Hardie: The Making of a Socialist*. London: Croom Helm, 1978.

— —. 'Socialist Sunday schools in Great Britain 1892–1939'. *International Review of Social History*, XI, 1966, pp. 18–47.

Rendall, Jane, ed. *Equal or Different: Women's Politics 1800–1914*. Oxford: Basil Blackwell, 1987.

Ritter, Gerhard A. 'Workers' culture in imperial Germany: problems and points of departure for research'. *Journal of Contemporary History*, XIII, 1978, pp. 165–89.

Rössler, Horst and Ian Watson. 'In defence of Ernest Jones'. *Gulliver: Deutsch-Englische Jahrbücher*, XII, 1983, pp. 134–9.

Rogers, Pat. *Literature and Popular Culture in Eighteenth-Century England*. Brighton: Harvester Press, 1985.

Ross, Ellen. ' "Not the sort that would sit on the doorstep": respectability in pre-World War I London neighbourhoods'. *International Labor and Working Class History*, XXVII, 1985, pp. 39–59.

Roth, Günther. *The Social Democrats in Imperial Germany: A Study in Working Class Isolation and National Integration*. Totowa, NJ: Bedminster Press, 1963.

Rowbotham, Sheila and Jeffrey Weeks. *Socialism and the New Life: The Personal and Sexual Politics of Edward Carpenter and Havelock Ellis*. London: Pluto Press, 1977.

Rubinstein, David. *Before the Suffragettes: Women's Emancipation in the 1890s*. Brighton: Harvester Press, 1986.

— —. 'Cycling in the 1890s'. *Victorian Studies*, XXI, 1977, pp. 47–71.

Russell, Dave. *Popular Music in England, 1840–1914: A Social History*. Manchester: Manchester University Press, 1987.

Sadie, Stanley, ed. *The New Grove Dictionary of Music and Musicians*. London: Macmillan, 1981.

Saint, Andrew, ed., *Politics and the People of London: The London County Council, 1889–1965*. London: Hambledon Press, 1989.

Samuel, Raphael. 'British marxist historians, 1880–1980. Part one'. *New Left Review*, CXX, 1980, pp. 21–96.

— —, ed. *People's History and Socialist Theory*. London: Routledge & Kegan Paul, 1981.

— — and Gareth Stedman Jones, eds. *Culture, Ideology, and Politics: Essays for Eric Hobsbawm*. London: Routlege & Kegan Paul, 1982.

Schneer, Jonathan. *Ben Tillett: Portrait of a Labour Leader*. Urbana: University of

Illinois Press, 1982.

Sewell, William H. *Work and Revolution in France: The Language of Labor From the Old Regime to 1848*. Cambridge: Cambridge University Press, 1980.

Shiman, Lilian Lewis. 'The Band of Hope movement: respectable recreation for working-class children'. *Victorian Studies*, XVII, 1973, pp. 49–74.

Smith, David. *Socialist Propaganda in the Twentieth-Century British Novel*. London: Macmillan, 1978.

Smith, Joan. 'Labour tradition in Glasgow and Liverpool'. *History Workshop Journal*, XVII, 1984, pp. 32–56.

Stansky, Peter. *Redesigning the World: William Morris, the 1880s and the Arts and Crafts*. Princeton: Princeton University Press, 1984.

Stearns, Peter. 'The effort at continuity in working-class culture'. *Journal of Modern History*, LII, 1980, pp. 626–55.

Stedman Jones, Gareth. *Languages of Class: Studies in English Working-Class History 1832–1982*. Cambridge: Cambridge University Press, 1983.

— —. *Outcast London: A Study in the Relationship Between Classes in Victorian Society*. Harmondsworth: Penguin, 1976 [1971].

Storch, Robert, ed. *Change and Continuity in Victorian Popular Culture*. London: Croom Helm, 1981.

Temperley, Nicholas, ed. *Music in Britain: The Romantic Age 1800–1914*. London: Athlone Press, 1981.

Thompson, E. P. 'Time, work-discipline, and industrial capitalism'. *Past and Present*, XXXVIII, 1967, pp. 56–97.

— —. *William Morris: Romantic to Revolutionary*. 2nd ed. New York: Pantheon Books, 1976.

Thompson, Laurence. *The Enthusiasts. A Biography of John and Katharine Bruce Glasier*. London: Victor Gollancz, 1971.

— —. *Robert Blatchford: Portrait of an Englishman*. London: Victor Gollancz, 1951.

Thompson, Paul. *Socialists, Liberals and Labour: The Struggle for London, 1885–1914*. London: Routledge & Kegan Paul, 1967.

Tomkins, Alan. 'The state and public cultural policies'. *Another Standard*, spring 1984, pp. 20–3.

Trommler, Frank. 'Working-class culture and modern mass culture before World War I'. *New German Critique*, XXIX, 1983, pp. 57–70.

Tsuzuki, Chushichi. *Edward Carpenter 1844–1929: Prophet of Human Fellowship*. Cambridge: Cambridge University Press, 1980.

— —. *H. M. Hyndman and British Socialism*. London: Oxford University Press, 1961.

Vicinus, Martha. *The Industrial Muse: A Study of Nineteenth Century British Working-Class Literature*. New York: Barnes & Noble, 1974.

— —. 'The study of Victorian popular culture'. *Victorian Studies*, XVIII, 1975, pp. 473–83.

— —, ed. *Suffer and Be Still: Women in the Victorian Age*. Bloomington: Indiana University Press, 1972.

Walton, John K. *The Blackpool Landlady: A Social History*. Manchester: Manchester University Press, 1978.

— —. 'The demand for working-class seaside holidays in Victorian England'.

Economic History Review, XXXIV, 1981, pp. 249–65.

— — and James Walvin, eds. *Leisure in Britain 1780–1939*. Manchester: Manchester University Press, 1983.

Walvin, James. *Leisure and Society 1830–1978*. London: Longman, 1978.

Walzer, Michael. 'Socialism and the gift relationship'. *Dissent*, XXIX, 1982, pp. 431–41.

Waters, Chris. ' "All sorts and any quantity of outlandish recreations": history, sociology, and the study of leisure in England, 1820–1870'. *Historical Papers/ Communications Historiques*, 1981, pp. 8–33.

— —. 'William Morris and the socialism of Robert Blatchford'. *Journal of the William Morris Society*, V, 1982, pp. 20–31.

Watson, Ian. *Song and Democratic Culture in Britain: An Approach to Popular Culture in Social Movements*. London: Croom Helm, 1983.

Watt, Ian. *The Rise of the Novel*. Berkeley: University of California Press, 1957.

Wigley, John. *The Rise and Fall of the Victorian Sunday*. Manchester: Manchester University Press, 1980.

Williams, Raymond. *Communications*. 3rd ed. Harmondsworth: Penguin, 1976.

— —. *Culture and Society, 1780–1950*. 2nd ed. New York: Harper & Row, 1966.

— —. *Keywords: A Vocabulary of Culture and Society*. New York: Oxford University Press, 1976.

— —. *Problems in Materialism and Culture: Selected Essays*. London: Verso, 1980.

Winter, Jay, ed. *The Working Class in Modern British History: Essays in Honour of Henry Pelling*. Cambridge: Cambridge University Press, 1983.

Wright, D. G. and J. A. Jowitt, eds. *Victorian Bradford*. Bradford: Metropolitan Council, 1981.

Yeo, Eileen & Stephen Yeo, eds. *Popular Culture and Class Conflict 1590–1914: Explorations in the History of Labour and Leisure*. Hassocks: Harvester Press, 1981.

Yeo, Stephen. 'A new life: the religion of socialism in Britain, 1883–1896'. *History Workshop Journal*, IV, 1977, pp. 5–56.

— —. *Religion and Voluntary Organizations in Crisis*. London: Croom Helm, 1976.

Young, James D. 'Militancy, English socialism and the ragged trousered philanthropists'. *Journal of Contemporary History*, XX, 1985, pp. 283–303.

(B) unpublished material

Ashplant, T. G. 'The Working Men's Club and Institute Union and the Independent Labour Party: working-class organisation, politics and culture *c.* 1880–1914'. D.Phil. thesis. University of Sussex, 1983.

Barrow, Logie. 'The socialism of Robert Blatchford and the Clarion newspaper 1889–1918'. Ph.D. thesis. University of London, 1975.

Chapman, Andrew. 'The People's Palace for East London: a study of Victorian philanthropy'. M.Phil. thesis. University of Hull, 1979.

Drake, Hugh J. O'H. 'John Lister of Shibden Hall (1847–1933): a portrait of an individual in late Victorian provincial society'. Ph.D. thesis. University of Bradford, 1973.

Fincher, Judith A. 'The Clarion movement: a study of a socialist attempt to implement the co-operative commonwealth in England, 1891–1914'. MA thesis. University of Manchester, 1971.

Harris, Michael. 'The decline of the Labour Church movement: a study of the Labour Church at Bradford, 1892–1900'. Unpublished dissertation in the Bradford Central Library.

Hopkin, D. R. 'The newspapers of the Independent Labour Party, 1893–1906'. Ph.D. thesis. University College of Wales, 1981.

Koven, Seth David. 'Culture and poverty: the London settlement house movement 1870 to 1914'. Ph.D. thesis. Harvard University, 1987.

Lohman, Judith S. 'Sex or Class? English socialists and the woman question, 1884–1914'. Ph.D. thesis. Syracuse University, 1979.

Rushton, J. I. 'Charles Rowley and the Ancoats recreation movement'. M.Ed. thesis. University of Manchester, 1959.

Russell, David. 'The popular musical societies of the Yorkshire textile district, 1850–1914: a study of the relationship between music and society'. Ph.D. thesis. University of York, 1979.

Scherr, Abraham. 'Robert Blatchford and Clarion socialism 1891–1914'. Ph.D. thesis. University of Iowa, 1974.

Summers, David Fowler. 'The Labour Church and allied movements of the late 19th and early 20th centuries'. Ph.D. thesis. University of Edinburgh, 1958.

Trodd, Geoffrey. 'Political change and the working class in Blackburn and Burnley, 1880–1914'. Ph.D. thesis. University of Lancaster, 1978.

Vamplew, Wray, ed. 'The economic history of leisure'. Papers presented at the Eighth International Economic History Congress, Budapest, August 1982.

Whelan, John F. 'The working class in British socialist thought, 1880–1914'. M.Phil. thesis. University of Leeds, 1974.

Wilson, D. D. 'The search for fellowship and sentiment in British socialism, 1880–1914'. M.A. thesis. University of Warwick, 1971.

INDEX

Abensour, Miguel, 45
Aberdeen, 8, 29, 54, 107, 109, 117
Aberdeen Socialist Society, 14
Accrington, 24
Adams, Francis, 120
Alden, Percy, 83–5, 92, 95, 134, 142–3, 179
alternative culture, 1, 2, 15, 36, 41, 65, 107, 116, 126–7, 154–5, 163, 174, 185, 192
   see also socialist culture
Ancoats, 7, 78–9, 134
Ancoats Brotherhood, 78–9
Anderson, Perry, 45
Anti-Puritan League, 151
anti-utopian fiction, 44, 62–4, 136
Archer, William, 150
Arnold, Matthew, 103, 153, 194
art, 58, 60, 66, 68, 72, 79–80, 82
art galleries and exhibitions, 48, 53, 60, 81, 84, 89, 132, 140, 143, 148
artisans, 3, 11, 22–3, 76, 102, 157, 164, 166
arts and crafts movement, 90, 157, 170, 173–4
   see also Clarion Handicraft Guild
Arts Council, 144
autodidacts, 11, 22–3, 103, 143, 158, 160, 165, 177–8, 190

Bainton, Edgar, 103–4, 118
Band of Hope, 12, 86, 99, 157
Bank Holiday Act (1871), 20, 37
bank holiday excursions, 27–8, 30, 37–8, 41
Barnett, Henrietta, 68, 73
Barnett, Samuel, 12, 20, 53, 65–6, 68, 73, 99–100, 134, 143, 149
Barrett, T. A., 124
Barrow, Logie, 176–7
Battersea, 31, 139–41, 143
Bax, Ernest Belfort, 28, 61–2, 146, 149, 183
bazaars, 89–94, 121, 169
Beaumont Institute, 81
Bellamy, Edward, 51, 55–6, 59, 61, 63, 154
Bennett, William Sterndale, 123–4
Besant, Annie, 44–5, 51
Bessant, Walter, 10, 80–4, 95, 102, 166
Bethnal Green, 98
betting, *see* gambling
Bevin, Ernest, 47, 61
Birmingham, 31, 69, 133, 135
Blackburn, 178

Blackburn Labour Journal, 178
Blackpool, 17, 37–8, 41, 75–6
Blackwell, James, 5–6
Blackwood's Edinburgh Magazine, 53
Blatchford, Montague, 2, 50, 93, 97–8, 103, 105, 121–6, 129, 161–2, 173
Blatchford, Robert, 1–2, 4–5, 7–8, 14, 39, 47, 60, 70, 101, 158–9, 161, 166, 171, 175, 180–1
   and Cinderella clubs, 87–8
   critique of leisure industry, 32–3, 36–7, 179–80, 182, 185, 191
   Julie, 102–4
   Merrie England, 4, 131, 154
   and philanthropy, 74–6, 78–9, 82–3
   and puritanism, 147–50, 154
   A Son of the Forge, 158–9
   The Sorcery Shop, 44, 50–1, 57–9, 61, 63, 65, 148
   and women, 168
blood sports, 3, 18
Blount, Godfrey, 173
Bolton, 2
Bonar, Horatio, 115
Booth, William, 75
Born, Helena, 85–6
Boughton, Rutland, 103–5, 118, 125–6, 188
Bourchier, Arthur, 192
Bournemouth, 137
Bradford, 31–2, 38, 70–1, 84, 99–100, 105, 122–5, 132, 144–5, 162, 178
Bradford Labour Echo, 32, 84, 180
Bradford Pioneer, 106, 181
Bradford Trades Council, 34
Bramah, Ernest, 44, 63
Briggs, Asa, 20
Bristol, 11, 20, 68, 85, 118
Bristol Socialist Choir, 121
Bristol Socialist Society, 85, 107, 109, 136, 189
Bristol Trades Council, 119
British Communist Party, 103
British Socialist Party, 149, 176–7
British Workman, 69
Brixton, 150
Broadhurst, Henry, 148
Brocklehurst, Fred, 89, 133, 141
Brockway, Fenner, 184–5
Browning Settlement, 73

INDEX

Pleasant Sunday Afternoon movement, 84, 87, 115

pleasure, 6, 13, 43–4, 50–64
  taxonomies of, 11–12, 23, 33
  higher, 43, 46–7, 52, 60, 63

Plebs League, 193

Plumb, J. H., 19

Poplar, 139

press
  mass circulation, 17, 39, 41, 68, 177, 181, 183, 191, 193
  radical, socialist and labour, 85, 89, 131, 137, 157, 161, 168, 180–3, 191, 193

Primitive Methodism, 115

Primrose League, 2, 172

Progressive Alliance, 139, 142, 151

Progressive movement, 40, 139–44, 150–1, 154

Progressive Review, 53

Proprietors of Entertainments Association, 20

public halls, 64, 73, 80, 91–2, 137
  see also socialist halls

Public Health Act (1848), 133

Public Health Amendment Act (1907), 133

public houses, 7, 9, 20, 34, 39, 58, 138, 140, 150–1, 159, 162, 166, 177, 193
  see also drink trade

publicans, 20, 100, 132

Pugh, Martin, 2

puritanism, 33, 146–52, 178, 180–1, 191, 194
  see also municipal puritanism

Quelch, Harry, 154, 183

Quin, Malcolm, 115

Rainbow Circle, 40

Ransom, Arthur, 73, 182

rational recreation, 3–4, 6, 11, 13, 18, 21–32, 36–44, 53, 57–62, 66, 75–6, 78, 80–1, 83, 97–9, 135, 137–8, 140, 144–6, 149–50, 152, 165, 179, 182–3, 190, 193

reading, 9, 37, 53, 172

Reason, Will, 84, 142

recreation grounds, *see* parks

Reform Act (1867), 3

religion, 28, 78, 83, 86–7, 98, 114–15, 146, 149, 160
  see also Church of England; Labour Church; Methodism; nonconformity; 'religion of socialism'

'religion of socialism', 13–14, 73, 87, 108, 113, 132, 161, 174, 176, 184–5

Religious Tract Society, 12, 69

respectability, 3, 23–5, 31–2, 96, 162–6

Richter, Eugene, 62–3

Rigby, Lilian, 30–1

Roberts, Robert, 37

Rochdale, 20, 121, 138

Rochdale Labour News, 76

Rogers, Frederick, 138

Rotherham, 88

Rowley, Charles, 78–80, 134

Russell, Charles, 30–1

Rutland, Philip, 20

Sabbatarianism, 73, 145, 148–9, 151, 175, 180
  see also municipal puritanism; puritanism; Sunday openings

'Saint Monday', 166

Salford, 7, 87–8, 121

Salt, H. S., 109–12

Saturday half-holiday, 6, 167

Scheu, Andreas, 110

Scott, Clement, 133

SDF, *see* Social Democratic Federation

Seabrook, Jeremy, 194

Select Committee (Commons) on Theatres and Places of Entertainment, 30

self-help, self-culture and self-improvement, 8, 71, 74–7, 81–2, 84, 87, 95–6, 100, 115, 138, 165, 179, 182–3, 187, 190, 192

settlement house movement, 9, 12, 68, 75, 78, 83–5, 95, 99, 115, 134, 142, 149, 157, 167, 179, 184
  see also Browning Settlement; Mansfield House; Toynbee Hall

Sewell, William, 22

Sharland, Robert, 118, 121

Sharp, Cecil, 104–6, 119

Sharpe, Joseph, 27

Shaw, George Bernard, 79, 85, 102, 124, 148, 185

Sheffield, 73, 121, 124, 145–6

Sheffield Guardian, 36, 59, 73, 124, 145–6, 191

Sheffield Secular Society, 98

Shelley, Percy B., 109–11, 116

Shimmin, Hugh, 25

showmen, *see* fairs; travelling showmen

Simm, Matt, 35

INDEX

West Ham Municipal Alliance, 143
West Riding, 170
Whitechapel Gallery, 143
Whitman, Walt, 109
Whittier, John G., 115
Wicksteed, Philip, 13
Wilkinson, William Scott, 124
Willesden Call, 41
Williams, Ernest E., 171–2, 174, 183
Williams, Raymond, 9, 45, 192
Wilson, William, 119
Woman Worker, 51
women, 11, 24
  and leisure, 166–70, 181
  middle-class, 167, 169
  and philanthropy, 89–90, 94, 102, 167,
    169
  in the socialist movement, 165–70
  and utopian thought, 51
  working-class, 6–7, 166–7
Women Folk, 13
Wood, Joseph, 135
work and leisure, 38–9, 44, 48, 52–7, 59,

159, 164–5, 171, 190
Worker (Huddersfield), 51, 59, 73
working-class culture, 3–4, 9–10, 33, 43,
  68–9, 80, 83, 126, 138, 141, 145, 158,
  160, 165, 167, 174, 176–8, 184, 187,
  191, 193
working hours, 1, 4, 6–9, 43–4, 46, 55, 63,
  77, 140, 164, 193
working lads' clubs, *see* clubs
working men's clubs, *see* clubs
Worpole, Ken, 2
Wright, Thomas, 9–10, 20, 52–3, 168, 191

Yarmouth, 21
Yates, Edmund, 20
Yeo, Stephen, 13, 20, 161, 189
Yorkshire, 37
Yorkshire Musical Record, 123
youth, 69, 81, 157, 172
  see also children

Zimmern, Alice, 167